# RE-ENCHANTING EDUCATION AND SPIRITUAL WELLBEING

Education is in a constant state of renewal internationally where it responds to a number of pressing social, political and cultural issues. Processes of globalisation, a number of conflicts and acts of terror and economic and environmental crises have led to large waves of migration and asylum seekers arriving in countries with the hope of finding safer and more stable places to settle. This, in turn, has led to cultural and religious pluralism being a key characteristic of many societies with corresponding issues of belonging and identity.

As well, for many people, there has been a shifting influence of and allegiance away from traditional religious frameworks with the emergence of new religious movements, both peaceful and violent, and a rise in popularity of spirituality and non-religious worldviews which provide alternate frameworks for living healthy and ethical lives. In order to prepare today's student for tomorrow's world, one which is confronted by a range of risks and crises and which is being shaped by rapidly changing technologies, educators and researchers are investigating new ways of equipping students to deal with these challenges and opportunities, including the nurturing of spiritual wellbeing.

This book brings together the voices of many experienced educators to discuss ways to re-enchant education and re-enliven learning programs in response to these twenty-first century issues in an increasingly global and interconnected world. It examines a range of international contexts, including secular and religious educational settings, and provides an avenue for visionary voices that identify problems and offer solutions to help shape a more promising education system that will prepare children more constructively and beneficially to flourish in their future worlds.

**Dr Marian de Souza** has spent more than twenty years researching contemporary understandings of spirituality and the implications for education and wellbeing of children and young people. Her recent publications include *Spirituality in Education in a Global, Pluralised World* (Routledge).

**Dr Anna Halafoff** is a Senior Lecturer in Sociology of Religion at Deakin University and a Research Associate of the UNESCO Chair in Interreligious and Intercultural Relations – Asia Pacific at Monash University. Her most recent publications with Routledge are a co-edited book, *Education about Religions and Worldviews: Promoting Intercultural and Interreligious Understanding in Secular Societies* (with Elisabeth Arweck and Donald Boisvert), and a co-authored book, *Religion and Development in the Asia-Pacific: Sacred Places as Development Spaces* (with Matthew Clarke).

# RE-ENCHANTING EDUCATION AND SPIRITUAL WELLBEING

## Fostering Belonging and Meaning-Making for Global Citizens

*Edited by*
*Marian de Souza and Anna Halafoff*

Routledge
Taylor & Francis Group

LONDON AND NEW YORK

First published 2018
by Routledge
2 Park Square, Milton Park, Abingdon, Oxon OX14 4RN

and by Routledge
711 Third Avenue, New York, NY 10017

*Routledge is an imprint of the Taylor & Francis Group, an informa business*

© 2018 selection and editorial matter, Marian de Souza and Anna Halafoff;
individual chapters, the contributors

*British Library Cataloguing in Publication Data*
A catalogue record for this book is available from the British Library

*Library of Congress Cataloging in Publication Data*
A catalog record for this book has been requested

ISBN: 978-1-138-09567-0 (hbk)
ISBN: 978-1-138-09568-7 (pbk)
ISBN: 978-1-315-10561-1 (ebk)

Typeset in Bembo and Stone Sans
by Florence Production Ltd, Stoodleigh, Devon, UK
Printed and bound by CPI Group (UK) Ltd, Croydon, CR0 4YY

# CONTENTS

# 1

# INTRODUCTION

*Marian de Souza and Anna Halafoff*

Our planet and societies are currently facing numerous pressures and tensions linked to globalisation, neo-liberal capitalism and environmental crises. In these times of insecurity and significant social change, a disturbing and growing number of young people and children are suffering from depression and other mental health conditions, including anxiety, self-harm and suicidal behaviour. Another, and related, area of concern is the rise in incidents of discrimination, racism and xenophobia internationally. The use of social media and proliferation of fake news has intensified all of these issues. A new generation has grown up in a climate of fear, and against this backdrop of divisiveness and hostility to the so-called Other. This context places particular stresses on children and young people from minority groups, and on the broader community. These concerns have led many to question how best to address these issues, and to foster inclusive and compassionate communities, where young people feel a sense of belonging, meaning and purpose, in our increasingly globalised and interconnected world.[1] They have also stimulated the need to address the wellbeing of children and young people, in educational as well as other settings. One dimension of wellbeing is spiritual wellbeing, although this term is little understood, and viewed with some trepidation, especially in secular contexts.

The concept of spirituality in education is treated and received very differently in diverse cultural and school contexts (Watson et al., 2014). In many societies and education systems, particularly those that identify as non-religious or secular, it is sometimes rejected entirely or at best little understood, and therefore is not often adequately addressed or reflected in educational curricula or practices. Nevertheless, there is some evidence that there has recently been more emphasis on spiritual development and wellbeing in many states and nations, as these and similar terms are being included in recent educational policies and documents aimed at educating and considering the whole child in response to life's big questions and issues, and also in part to build resilience and address issues of social inclusion.

The real problem with speaking of spirituality in education lies in the fact that for centuries, it has been closely associated with organised religion. This is particularly the case with Western understandings and expressions of Christianity, where spirituality appeared to dissolve into religiosity and became synonymous with religion and religious practice. In secular societies, which may paradoxically derive their mainstream culture at least in part from their dominant religious culture or cultures, religion is usually separated from state education and when the word 'spirituality' is combined with education, it is often viewed with suspicion, possibly because of the practice among some of using spirituality interchangeably with religion.[2] Similar concerns have been raised about mindfulness, meditation and yoga programs, conceived by some as spiritual and religious in nature, given their association with so-called Eastern religions of Buddhism, Hinduism and Jainism (Jain, 2015). Hence, for many, this becomes problematic, precisely because the education system is perceived as a hard secular, non-religious enterprise, that caters for all students who come from various religious and non-religious backgrounds, yet in which religion is regarded as a private matter for the individual and is therefore largely excluded. Generally speaking, addressing the spirituality of students has remained an elusive element in educational practice in many secular state schools internationally.

Instead, learning programs, drawn from a philosophical approach, which generate values-based and/or quality of life education, are examined. In some instances, there may be influences from religious, spiritual and indigenous wisdom literature, however, the main focus of such programs is on developing the students' ability to examine the big questions and deeper meanings in life within a distinctly secular context. In all such approaches, be they spiritual or secular, there is an expectation that teachers be knowledgeable and will provide a safe space where students are encouraged to be curious, creative, critical, reflexive and to grow in self-knowledge and knowledge of the Other, in order to live a good life in harmony with all beings.

With reference to living a good life, the use of the term 'wellbeing' has simultaneously crept into regular usage in the media and has also increasingly been the subject for academic and professional research studies and debates from the 1990s. Not surprisingly, since educational systems reflect the wider society within which they function, 'wellbeing' has been identified as an important element that should be addressed in schools. Wellbeing in and of itself is a less controversial term, although when coupled with spirituality as spiritual wellbeing it presents similar challenges, particularly in secular education settings. Nevertheless, in this book we have chosen to use the concept of spiritual wellbeing to describe educational settings where the individual is provided with nurturing that allows him/her to develop understanding and awareness of self and the Other, and to grow their potential to be aware and active global citizens.

As an active response to the lack of understanding of how to nurture spiritual development and wellbeing in education, particularly in secular settings, we facilitated a Workshop on Spirituality, Wellbeing and Education at Deakin University, in Melbourne, on 20 November, 2015, for scholars, educators, policy makers and curriculum writers, to develop a greater knowledge of best practices and debates in this field. Dr Kate Adams delivered the keynote address via Skype from the Bishop Grosseteste University, Lincoln, UK, and many of the contributors to this volume presented their papers on the day. We subsequently invited chapters from global experts in and beyond Australia, to internationalise the discussion. The result is this edited collection of 15 chapters, covering the following themes:

## Globalisation and (post-)secular societies

Andrew Singleton sets the scene with his chapter on demographic changes and religious transformations that are shaping how young people find meaning in contemporary societies. He draws on data generated in major studies on religion, spirituality and youth, conducted in Australia, the UK, Canada and the United States, to open the dialogue on what implications this might have for education.

Following this, Terence Lovat provides a concise overview of the secular nature of the public education system in Australia and identifies anti-religious scholarship and civic institutionalism as factors which have resulted in religion and spirituality education having little or no role in public school curricula for most of the past two centuries.

Moving further afield, Tony Eaude examines the foundations of global citizenship. This is an important area of study today since globalisation has impacted on most people's lives, especially in relation to identity and belonging which are important elements in the spiritual wellbeing of children. Eaude argues that we need to address this situation by emphasising an education for care where attention is given to children's agency and voice in inclusive learning environments.

The final chapter in this section comes from Dzintra Iliško who uses Latvian society as a case study to explore the impact of migration, which has resulted in student populations marked by diversity. She investigates worldview education as an efficient alternative to mainstream education which, she contends, will meet the different needs of such students, particularly in issues related to identity, belonging and wellbeing, so that they will learn to live together as global citizens.

## Theoretical, psychological and philosophical approaches

R. Scott Webster discusses two primary modes of human existence – *having* and *being* – arguing that education, and spiritual education in particular, should focus more on the *being* mode rather than on the *having* mode's acquisition of knowledge and skills. He proposes an existential approach, centred on enabling students *becoming* or *being* spiritually educated in order to tackle life's many challenges and global threats.

Fumiaki Iwata's paper presents an analysis of Japan's treatment of religion and spirituality in its secular schools. In particular he discusses debates around the cultivations of religious sentiment in education, and the capacity of Life-Education to contribute to students' spiritual development and wellbeing.

Ruth Wills explores spirituality as something intrinsic in all aspects of the lived experience of children and young people, which instils in them a sense of identity, belonging and meaning-making. She then proposes a program in music education that is based on Heideggerian themes which, through listening exercises, may inspire in students an awareness of *something other* as well as critical questioning and meaning-making on the wider themes of existence. Wills argues that such a program can play a valuable role in contributing to critical reflection that encourages a wider sense of identity and responsibility, thereby leading to growth and change.

Drawing on an extensive repertoire of religious and philosophical sources, Rev. Dr John Dupuche proposes a new framework founded on 'seeing what is true and holy in others' which can be used as a framework for interreligious education. He presents a portrait of students receiving such an education, outlining its benefits for students' spiritual wellbeing and also for their broader communities.

## Reflections on policy, pedagogy and programs

Kate Adams' chapter focuses on the UK context, where spiritual development has been included in education since the 1940s. Despite the UK's advances in this field, Adams notes that as education systems in many Western countries are increasingly performativity-oriented; the whole child, and indeed childhood is being neglected. She applies a reflexive approach to understanding researchers and teachers' diverse views on children's spiritual wellbeing and how it can be nurtured through education.

In the next chapter, Dorothea Filus presents some disturbing findings of the negative impact that the high pressure to achieve outstanding educational outcomes and to conform to societal norms is having on Japanese young people. She also examines how well the Japanese education system is preparing students to live and work in a globalised world.

Mualla Yildiz's chapter identifies gender discrimination as a serious social problem in Turkey. She then analyses the visual images in religious education textbooks over a few year levels to show how they present a particular view of women as individuals with limited education and/or career prospects outside the home. She contends that such discriminatory material contributes to identity formation among young female students and has a negative impact on their expectations and aspirations, as they grow into adulthood, to achieving important, decision-making and influential positions in society.

The importance of nurturing children's spirituality is the primary focus of Olga Buttigieg's writings after which she turns her attention to an Australian Indigenous program, the Yingadi program. Buttigieg states that the aim of the program is to promote students' understanding and awareness of the issues linked to cultural and religious diversity where prejudicial attitudes towards the different Other often surface. She discusses how an experience of Yingadi may help young people to overcome their fear of the otherness of Other and become more accepting and inclusive of others. Such learning, she maintains, will prepare and empower students to confront the challenges of diversity that they encounter.

Avril Howard's argument, based on the findings of several recent academic studies, is that Australia's National School Chaplaincy Program (NSCP) has contributed substantively to students' spiritual wellbeing and development, particularly in light of there being an inadequate focus on spirituality and spiritual wellbeing in the Australian Curriculum. Howard analyses the NSCP through a conceptual framework of existential spirituality, drawing on Søren Kierkegaard and other scholars' interpretation of his work.

The contribution music can make to influencing and shaping people's identity and sense of belonging is the subject of Dawn Joseph's chapter. Her findings show that music in a Christian community setting can positively engender wellbeing and people's sense of belonging where spiritual connections can be made between God and man.

Finally, Brendan Hyde examines the 'habits of mind' that young Australians bring to learning about religion and spirituality, through an analysis of teacher's learning stories. Hyde expands his original dispositional framework (Hyde, 2010), adding a sixth dimension of 'connecting to life', and making several recommendations as to how teachers might nurture the spiritual development and wellbeing of their students.

As can be seen from this brief overview, the chapters in this collection demonstrate that diverse approaches to education for spiritual wellbeing, including non-spiritual life-education, are currently being implemented in diverse contexts. However, they also indicate that there needs to be further critical thinking, research and pedagogical development to address this area in local and international curricula and policy, and to ensure that creative, effective and resourceful teaching materials are developed which will enhance the classroom programs and students' learning and wellbeing. This re-enchanted education thereby aims to have the capacity to foster a sense of belonging, meaning-making and peaceful and sustainable relations among students, and with the natural world, for themselves and future generations.

## Notes

1   Empirical evidence and further in-depth discussion of these issues, particularly in the Australian context, is presented in our, deSouza and Halafoff's, first chapter in this volume. Following chapters examine them from a variety of theoretical perspectives and geographical contexts.

2   For instance, Neil Hawkes who was a British consultant to the Values Education Good Practice Schools Project funded by the Australian Government's Department of Education, Science and Training (DEST) stated at the National Forum on Values Education in 2005 that he had been warned not to use the word 'spirituality' when talking about values education despite the fact that it had been part of the Education policy in Britain for some years. The Values Education Good Schools Practice Project was managed by the Curriculum Corporation and more information may be found on the website: http://curriculum.edu.au/values/val_vegps_1_and_2,8877.html

## References

Hyde, B. (2010). A dispositional framework in religious education: Learning dispositions and early years' religious education in Catholic schools. *Journal of Beliefs and Values, 31*(3), 261–269.

Jain, R. A. (2015). *Selling yoga: From counterculture to pop culture.* New York: Oxford University Press.

Watson, J., de Souza, M., & Trousdale, A. (eds). (2014). *Global perspectives on spirituality and education.* Abingdon, Oxon: Routledge.

# 2

# SPIRITUAL WELLBEING IN EDUCATION

*Marian de Souza and Anna Halafoff*

## Introduction

This book is composed of a collection of chapters which examine different perspectives and understandings of the role of spirituality and wellbeing in education. Our first chapter intends to provide a scholarly overview of contemporary spirituality, wellbeing and spirituality in education, to enable a greater understanding of how spiritual wellbeing may or may not be nurtured in both religious and secular school contexts. We draw on both international and local, in our case Australian examples, to illustrate our arguments. This chapter develops and presents one argument of the concept of spiritual wellbeing as an important, and indeed, integral element in human life, that should not be ignored or divorced from educational practices if educators aim to teach and nurture students in their wholeness. Nonetheless, it also acknowledges that there are alternate views and secular contexts where the language and concept of spiritual wellbeing is not seen as appropriate and therefore, alternative approaches and terminology are also explored.

## Contemporary spirituality

Our research into spirituality, religion and education stretches back over 20 years (see for instance, de Souza, 2001, 2003, 2004, 2005, 2016; Bouma & Halafoff, 2009; Ezzy & Halafoff, 2015; Halafoff, 2013a, 2015). In that time, we have noted the increasing number of professionals from different disciplines who have turned their attention to the role of spirituality in human endeavour.[1] Accompanying such discourse is a significant question: What do we mean by spirituality? It has been a source of frustration for us that discussions continue to both emphasise and accept the notion that spirituality creates ambiguity. This is despite the fact that such notions tend to reduce the credibility of spirituality as an area for serious research as well as the fact that there appears to be some agreement in the way spirituality is described across many disciplines. For instance, many scholars begin with a clear statement that they are not defining spirituality but proceed to cite qualities which have traditionally been applied to spiritual experiences, such as wonder, awe, freedom and transcendence, meaning and purpose, and so on (Ammerman, 2013; de Souza, 2012, 2016). We may observe that, in general, these words reflect the individual's response to a perception of an inner or deeper sense of self or to something outside the self, be it nature, other humans or supernatural beings, so that they are expressions of relationality (see de Souza, 2012, 2016). Therefore, we may conclude that, from these observations, an overarching theme emerges that points to spirituality being about human relationality and connectedness (see de Souza & Watson, 2016).

For educators, there is a further relevant question: Does spirituality have a role in education? This interest has generated several research publications examining the role of spirituality in education.[2] Nonetheless, for the most part, this interest has been confined to only a few academics and practitioners in education other than in Britain where legislation in the 1990s introduced the concept of spiritual education to be applied in all schools (Ofsted, 1994; SCAA). And while this scholarship has been growing, the situation has not achieved significant clarity because many of the ensuing discussions have been coloured by some tensions emanating from the existing diversity linked to religious, secular and cultural difference (de Souza, 2016; Watson et al., 2013). As well, the lack of effective language in the Western world to capture this particular dimension of human experience and expression, more often than not, can lead to further obscurity rather than transparency.

Because of the uncertainty aligned with the concept of spirituality any discussion or research on the subject first requires an identification of how the concept is being used and applied. For this chapter, we would like to draw on the findings from a recent project where different researchers were invited to explain how the concept of spirituality was interpreted in their specific fields of research, with implications for application and practice (de Souza et al., 2016). One important point that emerged from this analysis was that two distinct perspectives on spirituality could be identified: Traditional and Contemporary. The former was clearly generated by religious beliefs and practices which related to the search for and a relationship with God. As such, spirituality was perceived and expressed in the affective dimension of religious activity – such as rites and rituals. In other words, it formed the experiential dimension of religiously active lives. Additionally, there was much emphasis on interiority so that the inner journey was given greater emphasis than the individual's outer, existential life. From this vantage point, transcendence and mysticism was God-centred (de Souza & Watson, 2016).

From a contemporary perspective, one distinct difference is that spirituality is not necessarily God-related. Transcendence, here, is not focused on a divine mystery or divine person but is extended to include 'an awareness that one is connected to something more, beyond the individual self, but which can be grounded in an existential reality' (de Souza & Watson, 2016, p. 345). Thus, while an individual may experience transcendence in traditional terms so that it is God-related, they may also have experiences of transcendence which include emotions and experiences that are inspired by their relationship or response to another person, to truth and beauty in creation and the arts, to social and community action and/or connections to the earth and universe, all of which may arouse a sense of unity and oneness.

In the end, contemporary understandings indicate that spirituality is not reserved for the few who belong to religious traditions. Instead, it is recognised by some as a shared, innate human trait (Hay, 2006, O'Múrchú, 1997) which is as essential to the wholeness of being as intellectual, physical and emotional attributes. In this sense it can be argued to apply equally to all people, religious and non-religious (de Souza & Watson, 2016). Further, while history has shown that organised religion is one avenue through which the human world has tried to express its spiritual nature (see Ammerman, 2013; Armstrong, 2009; Hay, 2006; O'Múrchú, 1997 among others), thereby leading to religious expressions of spirituality, in today's world many seekers are finding more holistic ways and means to engage and practise their spirituality, expressed in everyday, lived connections with nature, community, activism and creativity (Ezzy & Halafoff, 2015; McGuire, 2008).

An additional important factor pertinent to this discussion is that, generally, there is little or no ambiguity attached to the traditional concept of spirituality. Rather, there is a distinct understanding of a transcendent dimension that is God-related which influences the way one lives one's life (de Souza & Watson, 2016). Consequently, it is important to recognise that while human spirituality, in some form or other, may have been recognised from the earliest years of known human existence, the ambiguity that now envelopes the concept is a relatively new phenomenon. From the latter half of the twentieth century, as the influence of organised religion dwindled in the Western world so that spirituality began to emerge as something distinct from religion, it appears to have moved into a state of transition. This has involved finding new ways and language to discuss, study and understand human spirituality as something holistic and essential to the flourishing and wellbeing of the human person.

Finally, Marian de Souza, Jane Bone and Jaqueline Watson's (2016) research suggests that we now appear to have reached a more settled stage in the transitional process of this emerging discipline where spirituality is being recognised by many as an implicit element in human relationality, reflected in experiences and expressions of connectedness that the individual has with the human and, sometimes, the more than human world. Thus, expressions and felt emotions pertaining to human relationality, such as connectedness, experiences of joy, wonder and awe, compassion, search for the sacred, silence and solitude, ecological concerns for Planet Earth, freedom and self-transcendence, relationship with God, prayer and ritual, responses to nature and the arts, were among the key traits that were identified and were, unmistakeably, shared understandings of spirituality across the many and varied disciplinary voices (de Souza et al., 2016). These findings indicate that Studies in Spirituality have begun to emerge into a distinct discipline, which has both credibility and validity as a field of inquiry, which can inform and further our knowledge and understanding about the human condition. Ultimately, the implication of this analysis is that the role of spirituality in education should be further examined for its ability to enhance the learning and lives of our students and promote their wellbeing (de Souza, 2016).

An important further consideration is that in our increasingly globalised and plural world and societies, we find a wealth of expressions of contemporary spirituality which reflect the diversity associated with human beliefs, practices and endeavours, and each has its own integrity and credibility because spirituality comprises both collective and individual elements. This is occurring at the same time as our societies are becoming increasingly religiously diverse and also non-religious. Learning to live among this super-diversity presents many opportunities and challenges, for individuals, communities, state actors, and educators who need to adapt existing policies and pedagogies to this new reality. There is a need to affirm respect for diversity and maintain a commitment to respecting the rights of others, while at the same time counter cultures of direct and structural violence, such as gender and sexuality inequality linked with some traditional religious beliefs. In addition, navigating the superiority claims made by religious, spiritual and non-religious groups also presents a significant challenge to peacebuilding and education (Halafoff, 2015; Schmidt-Leukal, 2004). Given the diversity of spiritual, religious and non-religious orientations within many societies and schools, it is important to acknowledge that not everyone will share the view that people are inherently spiritual, nor wish to participate in activities aimed at nurturing spiritual development and wellbeing. These views must be respected, and alternatives sought, that still recognise relationality, connectedness, awe, and meaning-making as common human qualities, which should be nurtured in all young people, not just in religious and spiritual contexts but also in a non-religious and non-spiritual capacity.

## The concept of wellbeing

In a previous collection of essays (de Souza et al., 2009), spirituality, care and wellbeing in education was a major focus of a large group of academics and educators from across the globe. This was generated by the growing concern that emotional and mental health issues were having a serious impact on the wellbeing of children and young people. Seven years later, the situation seems to have worsened rather than improved.[3] The number of government and non-government agencies that are actively dealing with problems associated with children and young people's mental health is expanding. For instance, in the Australian context, Mindblank,[4] ReachOut,[5] headspace National Youth Mental Health Foundation,[6] and 'youth beyond blue'[7] have been set up in the past two decades to educate and address problems corresponding to mental health issues among our young and very young. Some disturbing findings from surveys in 2013 and 2015 which have been posted on the 'youth beyond blue' website[8] reveal that a disturbing number of adolescents and children have been suffering from depression and other mental health conditions over 2013 and 2015. For instance, one in sixteen young Australians were experiencing depression, one in six were experiencing an anxiety condition and suicide was the biggest killer of young Australians and accounts for the deaths of more young people than car accidents. Further, the findings from the most recent survey, The Youth Survey 2016, which is conducted annually by Mission Australia, found that for the record number of 21,846 15- to 19-year-olds who took part, alcohol and drugs and equity and discrimination were the top two issues facing Australia today, with mental health entering the top three for the first time in its 15-year history. Concerns about mental health have doubled since 2011.[9]

Another source indicating the size of the contemporary problem may be found in a 2015 report from the Australian Department of Health on children and adolescents' mental health.[10] A comparison was made between the findings from a 1998 survey and a more recent one from 2013–2014 and it found that there was an increase in the prevalence of major depressive disorder particularly among 12–17-year-olds.

Such statistics indicate that an investigation into the notion of wellbeing in education is, indeed, timely and it provides another focus for the chapters contained in this book. It is, therefore, important to examine the concept of wellbeing and what it may mean in an educational context.

As Bache and Reardon (2016, p. 1) note, debates on what 'the good life' might entail and the state's role in contributing to it, date back to ancient Greece. However, they argue that more contemporary policy discourse on wellbeing stems from post-World War II concerns with the inadequacy of Gross Domestic Product (GDP) as the primary indicator of a nation's welfare. As Senator Robert Kennedy (1960 cited in Bache & Reardon, 2016, p. 2) stated, GDP 'measures everything in short, except that which makes life worthwhile'. These concerns were compounded in the 1990s, with growing fears of an environmental crisis emerging following the Chernobyl nuclear disaster and the evidence of global warming gaining increased credibility, in what Ulrich Beck (1992, 1999) termed 'risk society'. This led to the development of the Millennium Development Goals, and many other indices that measured progress beyond economic development, thereby focusing on subjective wellbeing and 'quality of life'. The UK has been a leader in developing policies on wellbeing and introduced indicators for its measurement in the 1990s. Australia, Bhutan and France are also cited as being at the 'forefront of wellbeing developments' (Bache & Reardon, 2016).

In 2005, The Australian Institute launched the Wellbeing Manifesto.[11] One of the research studies which informed the project was conducted by Richard Eckersley (2007) who offered the following description of wellbeing:

> Scientific interest in happiness – or subjective wellbeing, as most scientists prefer to call it – has surged in the past couple of decades. Wellbeing is about more than experiencing positive emotions; it is about being satisfied with life, fulfilling our potential and feeling that our lives are worthwhile and have

meaning. I am not concerned here with the happiness of deep personal transformation or the bliss of enlightenment, but about everyday happiness: the things that make ordinary people happy – or unhappy – their personal lives.

(Eckersley, 2007, p. 6)

Eckersley's contention, then, is that fulfilling one's potential and feeling that one's life has meaning and is worthwhile are fundamental elements in human wellbeing. These elements are also found in the concepts of human wellbeing and flourishing as discussed among those working in the field of positive psychology. For instance, Martin Seligman (2011) advises that he uses *happiness* and *wellbeing* interchangeably as the overarching goals of the whole of the Positive Psychology enterprise. In addition, he cautions that it is important to recognise that these two terms can refer to, both, feelings or to activities in which no feelings occur. Seligman contends that, 'authentic happiness comes from identifying and cultivating your most fundamental strengths and using them every day in work, love, play, and parenting' (Seligman, 2011, p. xiii). Further, Seligman provides three groups of positive emotions. One group is past-oriented emotions which include satisfaction, contentment and serenity. The second group is future-oriented emotions such as optimism, hope, trust, faith and confidence. The third group consists of positive emotions in the present; Seligman determines two categories: pleasures and gratifications. The pleasures are momentary whether they are the result of physical pleasures achieved through the senses or whether they are higher pleasures which are the result of more complex feelings which generate rapture, ecstasy, delight, amusement, relaxation and so on. Gratifications, however, are generated by activities that the person enjoys such as reading, listening to or playing music, dancing, rock climbing and so on. Gratifications improve over time with the development of personal strengths or virtues and can, potentially, last longer than pleasurable emotions. According to Seligman (2011, p. 262):

> Gratifications absorb and engage us fully; they block self-consciousness; they block felt emotion, except in retrospect ('Wow, that was fun!'); and they create flow, the state in which time stops and one feels completely at home.

Two aspects of Seligman's discussion on wellbeing/happiness are pertinent to this chapter. First, if one examines the positive emotions he identifies, a clear link can be made to the elements that characterise the human response to something other than self, in other words, they are expressions of connectedness or relationality, and therefore, share similarities with spirituality as presented above. Second, Seligman refers to the concept of 'flow' which Mihaly Csikszentmihalyi first coined in 1990 (Csikszentmihalyi, 1992, 2002, p. ix) during his research into the positive aspects of human experience, that is, the process of total involvement with life. As Cskiszentmihalyi asserted, those optimal experiences when we feel we are 'in control of our own actions, masters of our own fate' (p. 3), generate feelings of exhilaration and a deep sense of enjoyment and contentment. Csikszentmihalyi also observed that such experiences are not passive. Rather they occur when we are deeply engrossed in trying to accomplish something that is intricate and challenging and, critically, something that we believe is worthwhile. Optimal experience is, therefore, something we can control and act upon, and that can be facilitated.

To sum up, 'Flow' is the way people describe their state of mind, or conscious-ness, when it is harmoniously ordered, and they want to pursue whatever they are doing for its own sake (p. 6). Since most people spend a significant part of their lives working and interacting with others it is important for them to learn how to *'transform jobs into flow-producing activities'* (p. 7, italics in original) and to think of ways of enhancing their relationships so that they enjoy them. And finally, if people can manage to *'join all experience into a meaningful pattern'* (p. 7, italics in original) they are more likely to feel that their lives make sense and that they are in control. If this is achieved, there is less likelihood that they will continue to strive for things beyond their reach because such things will become less significant in the totality of their existence.

Thus, if we ponder the ideas contained in this exposition on wellbeing, we can identify some aspects that have relevance for promoting wellbeing in education. To begin with, wellbeing is closely connected to states of happiness so that these terms are sometimes used interchangeably. Wellbeing and happiness are often cultivated and expressed in relationships, and a sense of connectedness to family, friends and community. As well, states of happiness can be fleeting but if we create opportunities for students to engage in optimal experiences where they are absorbed in deep reflections and meaningful actions, they can derive a sense of self-mastery, contentment and satisfaction. Finally, the more occasions that they are involved in such activities, the more likely that this may lead to a sense of harmony and balance in their everyday lives and relationships with others. This, in turn, positions them favourably to actualise their full potential and to derive some meaning from their lived experiences. For some, this nurturing of wellbeing and happiness may be equated with spirituality, yet it need not be.

## Spiritual wellbeing

For the past century, the research examining a causal association between religious involvement and better health status has found a positive effect at both the individual and group level (Nelson, 2009, p. 313). Nelson points out that much of the research, in fact, indicates that religious involvement does protect individuals from disease and improves their health (for instance, Ellison & Levin, 1998; Thorensen et al., 2001). However, he notes (p. 359), that some scholars, such as Craig Ellison (1983) have gone further to investigate mental health as spiritual wellbeing. Ellison's argument is that apart from other human needs such as the need for self-fulfilment, there is an additional need for transcendence: 'the sense of well-being that we experience when we find purposes to commit ourselves to which involve ultimate meaning for life' (Ellison, 1983, p. 330). Thus, Nelson concludes that spiritual wellbeing, for Ellison, is two-pronged. There is a vertical movement (with God or an Ultimate Being) which is religious wellbeing and there is a horizontal movement (to one's community and the world), an existential wellbeing. Finally, achieving a sense of spiritual wellbeing incorporates an act or acts of self-realisation (Nelson, 2009, p. 359), that is, the relationship to one's inner life or self.

These views are mirrored in a number of religious and spiritual frameworks that seek to assist individuals and communities to live good and meaningful lives, for the benefit of all. Religions and different expressions of spirituality, be they indigenous ways of knowing, traditional religions or much newer spiritual movements, have long sought to remedy the world's problems. And religious and spiritual peacebuilders have long called for a critical examination of one's own actions and of the teachings of many traditions to move away from self-centredness and vice, to a greater sense of interconnectedness, collective responsibility and virtue for personal and collective peace realisation (Halafoff, 2013b; Knitter, 1995; Vendley & Little, 1994). However, not everyone shares these views, and religion and some spiritual practices are currently the subject of rigorous public debate, particularly due to their association with cultures of violence. While we believe that a critical approach to studying religion and spiritual traditions is necessary, and acknowledge the capacity of religious and some spiritual movements to inspire direct and structural violence, through competing superiority claims and texts which promote anthropocentrism, gender and sexuality inequality as discussed briefly above, the wisdom that diverse religious and spiritual traditions provide in terms of how to confront personal and global crises is often overlooked. It can be argued that with many pressing global risks confronting us, be they economic, environmental or social, this wisdom is needed, now more than ever.

It is therefore possible to argue that education about diverse worldviews, incorporating religious, spiritual and non-religious perspectives, could assist students in making sense of personal and global issues, as long as it was delivered critically and inclusively. At the same time the question persists: Can learning about religion and spirituality, and nurturing spiritual development and wellbeing, be included in secular education systems?

Here we briefly examine the case of the Australian state of Victoria, where both the authors reside. 61.1 per cent of Australia's population identified as Christian, 22.3 per cent as having No Religion, 2.5 per cent as Buddhists, 2.2 per cent as Muslims, 1.3 per cent as Hindus, 0.5 per cent as Jews and 0.8 per cent as from Other non-Christian Religions in the 2011 Census. Christian affiliation is declining while those declaring no religion and identifying with so-called minority faiths is increasing dramatically (ABS, 2011). Policies of multiculturalism have affirmed and continue to affirm respect for cultural and, more recently, religious diversity since the 1980s. Despite this, Australia has experienced widespread attacks on multiculturalism, and a rise of Islamophobia and xenophobia since the 1990s and particularly after the events of 11 September, 2001, and the London and Bali bombings of 2005 and 2002 respectively (Bouma et al., 2007). These events have catapulted religion into the public sphere, with some theorists claiming that we are now living in a post-secular age (see, for instance, Habermas, 2006, 2008; Habermas et al., 2011; King, 2009).

In Australia, discrimination, based on skin colour, ethnic origin or religion, remains a persistent and increasing problem up from 9 per cent in 2007 to 15 per cent in 2015 (Markus, 2015). Narrow nationalistic movements such as Reclaim Australia, and the political party One Nation now also have a prominent voice in the public and political sphere. These developments reflect similar and deeply disturbing global trends, evident in the Brexit vote and the Presidential election of Donald Trump in the United States. What is evident is that diversity, or even super-diversity, is the new normal, yet a significant proportion of the population are vehement in their resistance to it. Such diversity, and resistance towards it, certainly highlights the need for people to understand one another and it has given rise to a wide range of intercultural, interfaith and interreligious activities at all levels in society, from governing bodies, including some education systems, to grassroots citizenry.

In terms of education, Victorian government schools were established as secular in the 1870s, which prohibited the teaching of any mainstream curriculum content related to religion. However, religious instruction programs have been offered by Christian and Jewish volunteers in school time since the 1950s, and by additional minority faith instructors from the 1990s. As well, with the introduction of the new Victorian Certificate of Education (VCE) in 1991, some religion-based subjects were introduced into Years 11 and 12: Religion and Society, and Texts and Traditions. It wasn't until the 2006 *Education and Training Reform Act* that General Religious Education was permitted in Victoria, taught by qualified teachers, yet other than the elective VCE subjects, which seldom receive enough interest to be offered in state schools, GRE programs from Foundation to Year 10 did not begin to be developed until 2015 (Halafoff, 2015).

In response to some concern and movement from interested advocates, a new emphasis on 'Learning about Worldviews and Religions' was introduced into the Victorian iteration of the new national Australian Curriculum, across the curriculum in 2015, including the Civics and Citizenship and History learning areas, and in Ethical, Intercultural and Personal and Social Capabilities. It includes an emphasis on Buddhism, Christianity, Hinduism, Islam, Judaism, Secular Humanism and Rationalism. A word search in the Victorian Curriculum shows 70 instances for 'religious' and 47 for 'religion' across the Capabilities, and in learning areas of Languages and the Humanities. By contrast 'spiritual' returns only 20, and 'spirit' only 3, results spread more widely across the Capabilities, English, Health and Physical Education, Languages, The Arts and Humanities learning areas (VCAA, n.d.). However, it must be noted, that while the situation continues where religion is to be addressed across the curriculum, it is very likely that the translation into practice will depend heavily on the knowledge and background of the teachers, most of whom will not be trained in the subject. This could result in the topic being included in a less than methodical approach which could reduce it to a less than meaningful study for a large number of students.

More importantly, while a rigorous debate has ensued in Australia on the role of religion in education, spirituality hasn't typically featured prominently in these arguments. One clear reason for this is the fact that for many, religion and spirituality are seen as interchangeable. Therefore, while Religious Education as a subject in faith-based schools is not part of the debate, the focus has been on whether confessional religious instruction should be continued in government secular schools as an elective program, and whether education about diverse religions and non-religious worldviews should become a learning area in the wider curriculum, particularly given the changing religious and non-religious composition of our society, and the rise of anti-religious sentiments, often fuelled by the media and political discourses. Broadly speaking, religious instruction is viewed as undermining secular principles, while learning about diverse religious and non-religious worldviews is seen to be in line with secular principles, as long as no religion receives preferential treatment and confessional approaches and proselytising is forbidden (Byrne, 2014; Halafoff, 2013a, 2015: Maddox, 2014). Learning about diverse worldviews is also seen as contributing to socially inclusive societies, religious literacy, and therefore to fostering global citizenship (Halafoff, 2015). The situation with spirituality and spiritual wellbeing is however more complex.

The 1999 *Adelaide Declaration on National Goals for Schooling in the Twenty-First Century* first called for schools to attend to the spiritual development of students, alongside their intellectual, physical, social, moral and aesthetic development (The Adelaide Declaration, 1999). Yet the *Adelaide Declaration* gave scant attention to religion, stating only that schools should be 'free from the effects of negative forms of discrimination based on sex, language, culture and ethnicity, religion or disability' (The Adelaide Declaration, 1999).

*The Melbourne Declaration on Educational Goals for Young Australians*, published in 2008, which was referred to earlier, shaped the drafting of the Australian Curriculum. The *Melbourne Declaration* (MCEETYA, 2008, p. 4) highlighted the need for schools to 'play a vital role in promoting the intellectual, physical, social, emotional, moral, spiritual and aesthetic development and well being of young Australians'. It stressed the importance of assisting students to 'have a sense of self-worth, self-awareness and personal identity that enables them to manage their emotional, mental, spiritual and physical wellbeing' (p. 9). It also stated that globalisation has created 'the need to nurture an appreciation of and respect for social, cultural and religious diversity, and a sense of global citizenship'. The *Melbourne Declaration* (p. 7) also committed Australian schools to providing education 'that is free from discrimination based on gender, language, sexual orientation, pregnancy, culture, ethnicity, religion, health or disability, socioeconomic background or geographic location' and ensuring 'that schooling contributes to a socially cohesive society that respects and appreciates cultural, social and religious diversity'.

One problem, however, was that even though the *Melbourne Declaration* has a strong emphasis on both nurturing spiritual development and wellbeing, and on promoting respect for religious diversity, the Australian Curriculum does not clearly define spiritual development and wellbeing and nor does it include a specific learning area or capability dedicated to either religion or spirituality. Consequently, it remains unclear how and where, precisely, this is to occur within Australian schools (Donnelly & Wiltshire, 2014; Halafoff, 2015). Victoria has now included specific sections and some guidelines on 'Learning about Worldviews and Religions' in its current Curriculum, but, again, there are no clear guidelines on what is meant by spirituality. The Personal and Social Capability Rationale state that students should be enabled

> to manage their emotional, mental, spiritual and physical wellbeing, with a sense of hope and optimism about their lives and the future. On a social level, it helps students to form and maintain healthy relationships and prepares them for their potential life roles as family, community and workforce members.
>
> (VCAA n.d.)

Yet, spirituality or spiritual wellbeing isn't mentioned at all in the Structure, Learning or Scope and Sequence of the Personal and Social Capability. Indeed, most references to spiritual and spirituality in the Victorian Curriculum relate to places, cultures and languages. So while significant progress has been made when it comes to education about religions and worldviews within the policy documents, the issue of how to nurture spiritual development and wellbeing within Victoria's schools, and in other Australian states, is yet to be fully expounded.

## Conclusion

Having examined the concept and significance of spiritual wellbeing and acknowledged the current situation, particularly in Australia, but also internationally, drawing on issues and insights raised by other contributors to this volume, we have come away with several important queries that we suggest should be addressed by all stakeholders when considering how best to address student wellbeing, and spiritual wellbeing in particular. These are:

- What is the historical and current spiritual, religious and non-religious composition of your society and how are current educational policies and practices adapting to these changes?
- In hard secular,[12] non-religious societies and schools, what possibilities and resources are there for educators to assist children and young people as they grapple with the big questions of how to live a good, ethical life personally and collectively?
- In softer secular societies and schools, where respect for religious and spiritual diversity is promoted, are there possibilities and resources for educators to assist children and young people as they grapple with the big questions of how to live a good life personally and collectively, from religious, spiritual and non-religious perspectives?

- And in such cases, when diverse religious, spiritual and non-religious perspectives are incorporated into the current curriculum, how well balanced are they and what factors assist or impede their inclusion?
- To what degree might Educational Acts and policies need to be changed in order to reflect societal changes? Perhaps in some contexts, they may need to become more secular, limiting spiritual and religious content, while in others they may need to adapt to post-secular realities, which allow for spirituality and religion to be acknowledged as a central and/or peripheral part of many people's lives.

We conclude, in contrast to many volumes on spirituality, wellbeing and education, that there is no easy answer to any of these questions. Contemporary society's relationship with spirituality is deep and complex and ever changing, and education systems need to be aware of and responsive to this reality. While we argue that context is the most important factor in determining what should work best in each setting, we can recommend that in all contexts these changes be considered through deliberate, democratic, consultative processes, involving young people, scholars, educators, policy makers and curriculum writers. In some contexts, spiritual and/or religious community leaders may also be included in these discussions. We also suggest that where content from diverse religious, spiritual and non-religious perspectives can be incorporated in curricula, that it be done so equitably and with respect for human and non-human rights. Finally, we would encourage educators nurturing spiritual wellbeing, or providing quality of life education to stress relationality and connectedness, not only with human but also with more than human life, given that we inhabit this world with myriad beings, and must learn how to live together harmoniously and sustainably.

In the end, we would like to suggest that to address the current challenges and threats we are collectively facing, which are of our own making, we may well need to turn to all of the wisdom traditions available to us, be they spiritual, religious or non-religious, to re-enchant education and learn how to live a good, ethical life, both individually and collectively, on the one planet that we all share together.

## Notes

1 Sociologist David O. Moberg (2001) and healthcare expert Harold Koenig (see, for instance, his recent publication in 2013) have both contributed extensively to research in spirituality and health. As well, there is research by Robert Coles (1990) and Jerome Berryman (1991) in the USA into the spirituality of children and the spiritual dimension of religious education respectively. Ron Best (1996) and Jane Erricker, Clive Erricker and Cathy Ota (1997) (the original co-editors of the *International Journal of Children's Spirituality*) were instrumental in raising awareness about spirituality and education in Britain and internationally through the convening of many conferences, publications and research. Also in Britain, David Hay and Rebecca Nye (1998) introduced the concept of relational consciousness which inspired much research into children's spirituality, and Andrew Wright (2000) investigated spirituality and education. In Australia, Graham Rossiter and Marisa Crawford brought many years of research into religious, moral and spiritual education

together in a volume *Reasons for Living* published in 2006, Brian Hill (1991) examined values education in Australian schools and later discussed aspects of spirituality in education, and John Fisher (1998) began his research into spiritual health and education and has built a solid foundation for studies in this field over the past twenty years.

2  See for instance, *Education and Spirituality for the Whole Child*, edited by R. Best, 1996 and *The International Handbook of the Religious, Moral and Spiritual Dimensions of Education*, edited by M. de Souza, K. Engebretson, G. Durka, R. Jackson and A. McGrady (2006), among others.

3  A Google search of the combined words around children and young people's wellbeing revealed about 48,300,000 hits. A more specific search for 'young Australian's mental health' revealed 1,440,000 hits and for 'children's mental health Australia' there were 12,300,000 hits.

4  See http://mindblank.org.au/about-mindblank

5  See http://au.reachout.com

6  See https://headspace.org.au/

7  See https://youthbeyondblue.com

8  For further information, references and links see: https://youthbeyondblue.com/footer/stats-and-facts

9  See https://missionaustralia.com.au/what-we-do/research-evaluation/youth-survey for further findings from the 2016 Youth Survey.

10  The report is available on the website: https://health.gov.au/internet/main/publishing.nsf/Content/9DA8CA21306FE6EDCA257E2700016945/$File/child2.pdf

11  The Manifesto for Wellbeing was launched in Melbourne on 14 June, 2005. It was one of the projects of the Australian Institute, an influential progressive think tank in Australia. See the website: http://clivehamilton.com/speech-at-the-launch-of-the-wellbeing-manifesto/

12  A 'hard' secular position sees religion as belonging to the private sphere and demands a complete separation of church and state (i.e. France), while a 'soft' secular stance respects religious pluralism and religion's role in the public sphere, as long as no one religion is dominant (i.e. Canada and Australia) (Byrne, 2014; Kosmin, 2007).

# References

ABS 2011: www.abs.gov.au/websitedbs/censushome.nsf/home/CO-61

*The Adelaide Declaration on National Goals for Schooling in the Twenty-First Century*: Accessed July 22nd, 2017 http://www.scseec.edu.au/archive/Publications/Publications-archive/The-Adelaide-Declaration.aspx

Ammerman, N. T. (2013). Spiritual but not religious? Beyond binary choices in the study of religion. *Journal for the Scientific Study of Religion, 52*(2), 258–278.

Armstrong, K. (2009). *The case for god: What religion really means*. London: The Bodley Head.

Bache, I., & Reardon, L. (2016). *The politics and policy of wellbeing: Understanding the rise and significance of a new agenda*. Cheltenham: Edward Elgar Publishing.

Beck, U. (1992). *Risk society: Towards a new modernity*. London: Sage Publications.

Beck, U. (1999). *World risk society*. Cambridge: Polity Press.

Berryman, J. (1991). *Godly play, a way of Religious Education*. San Francisco: Harper.

Best, R. (ed.). (1996). *Education, spirituality and the whole child*. New York: Continuum International Publishing.

Bouma, G., & Halafoff, A. (2009). Multifaith education and social inclusion in Australia. *Journal of Religious Education, 57*(3), 17–25.

Bouma, G. D., Pickering, S., Halafoff, A., & Dellal, H. (2007). *Managing the impact of global crisis events on community relations in multicultural Australia*. Brisbane: Multicultural Affairs Queensland.

Byrne, C. (2014). *Religion in secular education: What in heaven's name are we teaching our children?* Leiden: Brill.

Coles, R. (1990). *The spiritual lives of children.* Boston: Houghton Mifflin Company.

Crawford, M., & Rossiter, G. (2006). *Reasons for living: Education and young people's search for meaning, identity and spirituality – A handbook.* Camberwell, Vic: ACER Press.

Csikszentmihalyi, M. (1992, 2002). *Flow: The classic work on how to achieve happiness.* London: Rider.

de Souza, M. (2001). Addressing the spiritual dimension in education: Teaching affectively to promote cognition. *Journal of Religious Education, 49*(3), 31–41.

de Souza, M. (2003). Contemporary influences on the spirituality of young people: Implications for education. *International Journal of children's Spirituality, 18*(3), 269–279.

de Souza, M. (2004). Teaching for effective learning in religious education: A discussion of the perceiving, thinking, feeling and intuiting elements in the learning process. *Journal of Religious Education, 52*(3), 22–30.

de Souza, M. (2005). Engaging the mind, heart and soul of the student in religious education: Teaching for meaning and connection. *Journal of Religious Education, 53*(4), 40–47.

de Souza, M. (2012). Connectedness and *connectedness*. The dark side of spirituality: Implications for education. *International Journal of children's Spirituality, 17*(3), 291–304.

de Souza, M. (2016). *Spirituality in education in a global pluralized world.* Abingdon, Oxon: Routledge.

de Souza, M., & Watson, J. (2016). Understandings and applications of contemporary spirituality – Analysing the voices. In M. de Souza, J. Bone & J. Watson (eds), *Spirituality across disciplines – Research and practice: Perspectives from mysticism and secular cultures, education, health and social care, business, social and cultural studies* (pp. 331–347). Switzerland: Springer International Publishing.

de Souza, M., Engebretson, K., Durka, G., Jackson, R., McGrady, A., (eds). (2006). *International Handbook of the Religious, Moral and Spiritual Dimensions of Education.* 2 volumes. Dordrecht, The Netherlands: Springer Academic Publishers.

de Souza, M., Bone, J., & Watson, J. (eds). (2016). *Spirituality across disciplines – Research and practice: Perspectives from mysticism and secular cultures, education, health and social care, business, social and cultural studies.* Switzerland: Springer International Publishing.

de Souza, M., Francis, L., O'Higgins-Norman, J., & Scott, D. (Eds). (2009). *International handbook of education for spirituality, care and wellbeing.* Volumes 1 and 2. Dordrecht, The Netherlands: Springer Academic Publishers.

Donnelly, K., & Wiltshire, K. (2014). *Review of the Australian Curriculum – final report.* Canberra: Australian Government Department of Education.

Eckersley, R. (2007). The politics of happiness. *Living Now*, March, issue 93, pp. 6–7. Retrieved 16 November 2016 from http://richardeckersley.com.au/attachments/Living_now_happiness.pdf

Ellison, C. G., & Levin, J. S. (1998). The religion health connection: Evidence, theory, and future directions. *Health Education and Behaviour, 25*(6), 700–720.

Ellison, C. W. (1983). Spiritual wellbeing: Conceptualization and measurement. *Journal of Psychology and Theology, 11*, 330–340.

Erricker, C., Erricker, J., Ota, C., Sullivan, D., & Fletcher, M. (1997). *The education of the whole child.* London: Cassell.

Ezzy, D., & Halafoff, A. (2015) Spirituality, religion and youth: An introduction. In J. Wyn & H. Cahill (eds), *Handbook of Children and Youth Studies* (pp. 845–860). Dordrecht: Springer.

Fisher, J. (1998). *Spiritual health: Its nature and place in the school curriculum.* PhD thesis. University of Melbourne: Melbourne University Bookshop.

Habermas, J. (2006) Religion in the public sphere. *European Journal of Philosophy, 14*(1), 1–25.

Habermas, J. (2008). *Notes on a post-secular society.* Retrieved on 20 April 2015 from http://signandsight.com/features/1714.html

Habermas, J., Brieskorn, N., Reder, M., Ricken, F., & Schimdt, J. (2011). *An awareness of what is missing: Faith and reason in a post-secular age.* Cambridge: Polity Press.

Halafoff, A. (2013a) Education about religions and beliefs in Victoria. *Journal for the Academic Study of Religion,* 26(2), 172–197.

Halafoff. A. (2013b). *The multifaith movement: Global risks and cosmopolitan solutions.* Dordrecht: Springer.

Halafoff, A. (2015). Special religious instruction and worldviews education in Victoria's schools: Social inclusion, citizenship and countering extremism. *Journal of Intercultural Studies, 36*(3), 362–379.

Hay, D. (2006). *Something there: The biology of the human spirit.* London: Dartman, Longman & Todd Ltd.

Hay, D., & Nye, R. (1998/2006). *The spirit of the child.* rev. ed. London: Jessica Kingsley.

Hill, B. (1991). *Values education in Australian schools.* Hawthorn, Vic: ACER.

King, M. (2009). *Postsecularism: The hidden challenge to extremism.* Cambridge: James Clark & Co.

Knitter, P. F. (1995). *One earth, many religions: Multifaith dialogue and global responsibility.* Maryknoll: Orbis Books.

Koenig, H. G. (2013) *Spirituality in patient care: Why, how, when and what.* 3rd Ed. West Conshohocken, PA 19428 USA: Templeton Foundation Press.

Kosmin, B. (2007). Contemporary secularity and secularism. In B. Kosmin & A. Keysar (eds), *Secularism and secularity: Contemporary international perspectives* (pp. 1–13). Hartford: Institute for the Study of Secularism in Society and Culture.

Maddox, M. (2014). *Taking god to school: The end of Australia's egalitarian education?* Sydney: Allen & Unwin.

Markus 2015: http://scanlonfoundation.org.au/wp-content/uploads/2015/10/2015-Mapping-Social-Cohesion-Report.pdf - accessed 22nd July 2017

McGuire, M. (2008). *Lived religion, faith and practice in everyday life.* Oxford: Oxford University Press.

Moberg, D. O. (ed.). (2001). *Ageing and spirituality.* Binghamton, NY: The Haworth Pastoral Press.

Nelson, J. M. (2009). *Psychology, religion and spirituality.* New York, USA: Springer Science + Business Media.

Office for Standards in Education (Ofsted) (1994). *Handbook for the inspection of schools.* UK: Ofsted.

O'Múrchú, D. (1997). *Reclaiming spirituality.* New York: Crossroad Publishing Company.

Schmidt-Leukel, P. (2004). Part of the problem, Part of the solution: An introduction. In P. Schmidt-Leukel (ed.), *War and peace in world religions* (pp. 1–10). London: SCM Press.

Seligman, M. (2011). *Authentic happiness. Using the new positive psychology to realize your potential for lasting fulfilment.* First edition Simon & Schuster 2002. This edition Sydney, NSW: William Heinemann.

Thorenson, C. E., Harris, A., & Oman, D. (2001). Spirituality, religion and health: Evidence, issues and concerns. In T. Plante & A Sherman (eds), *Faith and health: Psychological perspectives* (pp. 15–52). New York: Guildford.

Ministerial Council on Education, Employment, Training and Youth Affairs (MCEETYA) (1999). *The Adelaide declaration on national goals for schooling in the twenty-first century.* Melbourne: Ministerial Council on Education, Employment, Training and Youth Affairs.

Ministerial Council on Education, Employment, Training and Youth Affairs (MCEETYA) (2008). *Melbourne declaration on educational goals for young Australians*. Melbourne: Ministerial Council on Education, Employment, Training and Youth Affairs.

Vendley, W., & Little, D. (1994). Implications for religious communities: Buddhism, Islam, Hinduism, and Christianity. In D. Johnston & C. Sampson (eds), *Religion, the Missing Dimension of Statecraft* (pp. 306–315). Oxford: Oxford University Press.

Victorian Curriculum and Assessment Authority (n.d.). Victorian curriculum: Foundation-10. Retrieved 28 November, 2016 from: http://victoriancurriculum.vcaa.vic.edu.au

Watson, J., de Souza, M., & Trousdale, A. (eds). (2013). *Global perspectives on spirituality and education*. Abingdon, Oxon: Routledge.

Wright, A. (2000). *Spirituality and education*. London: Routledge-Falmer.

# 3

# BEYOND FAITH? RECENT TRENDS IN RELIGION AND SPIRITUALITY AMONG TEENAGERS

*Andrew Singleton*

## Introduction

In 1959 American evangelist Billy Graham staged a series of revival crusades across Australia. One crusade drew the largest-ever crowd to Australia's biggest sporting stadium, the Melbourne Cricket Ground. Thousands of young people heeded Graham's altar call and came forward to devote their lives to Christ. According to Judith Smart (1999, p. 167), in that 1959 tour, 'decisions for Christ . . . numbered about 130,000 in Australia (representing about 1.24 per cent of the total population.)'. Just five years later, the Beatles toured Australia and were greeted by 300,000 screaming young fans in the streets of Adelaide (Safioleas, 2016, p. 16). The Beatles tour represented something of a watershed in Australian society. Among young people, the church was seemingly giving way to other interests. As Safioleas (2016, p. 17) observes, 'Australia [in the 1960s] . . . was slowly turning into a remarkably different place'. Australia was not alone. The popularity of the Beatles signified the emergence of a new and at times rebellious youth culture across the West, one that challenged existing institutions, particularly the church and state (Catto, 2014, p. 3).

In the 1950s and early 1960s, countries like Great Britain, the United States, Canada, New Zealand and Australia were abidingly 'Christian'. In all of these places the overwhelming majority of the population identified with a Christian denomination, and a large minority attended church regularly (see Brown, 2012; McLeod, 2007; Putnam & Campbell, 2010). Most people professed belief in God. Since the late 1960s there has been an appreciable drift away from the Christian Churches. Across all Christian traditions attendance and participation has decreased. Recent research reveals that it is the youngest age cohorts who are at the forefront of this turn away from Christianity (see Crockett & Voas, 2006; Voas, 2010). Once, most young people in the West were inculcated into the Christian faith; this can no longer be assumed.

While Christianity is waning, the number of Buddhist, Hindu, Muslim or Sikhs living in the West has grown substantially (ABS, 2013; Pew Research Center, 2015a). The age profile of these faith communities is younger than that of the Christian churches. Additionally, a small minority of teens are interested in alternative spiritualities. All of these changes mean that greater pluralism, choice and diversity characterises religion and spirituality in the West, particularly among teens.

This chapter explores and explains these 'big picture' religious transformations. It then describes some of the key religious and spiritual trends found among young people. Such an evaluation – which recognises the diverse ways in which young people find meaning in contemporary society – opens the space for dialogue about the place of spirituality in education.[1] I begin by placing current trends in historical context.

## Religious transformations in the west: from Christian to religiously plural

In this section I describe how these societies have moved from being predominantly Christian to religiously and non-religiously diverse since the 1960s. As will be demonstrated, today's young people are most affected by this profound social shift.

This chapter began with the example of Billy Graham's enormously successful 1959 tour of Australia. At that time, families were increasing in number and size; there were booming suburbs and increased prosperity. After the chaos of the war, people craved stability and certainty. Graham found a country receptive to his message. The 1950s was a high watermark for the Christian faith in Australia. Churches enjoyed strong attendances, and with their social activities, they played a role in the community that went beyond simply meeting people's religious needs (Singleton, 2014, p. 96). Data from the Australian census in 1961 indicated that almost nine out of ten Australians identified themselves as Christian. A Gallup poll taken in 1961 found that 43 per cent of the adult population (then counted as 21 or above) attended services of worship at least monthly or more often (author's calculations of the original data).

Likewise, the 1950s churches in Europe, Great Britain and North America enjoyed strong attendances and were a focal point of the community (see Brown, 2012; Hervieu-Léger, 2000; Putnam & Campbell, 2010). Writing about America, for example, Putnam and Campbell (2010, p. 83) note: 'Virtually all experts agree . . . that the period from the late 1940s to the early 1960s was one of exceptional religious observance in America.' At this time, children and teenagers in all of these countries were counted among those who went to church regularly.

Since the mid-1960s onwards, however, this pattern of broad Christian participation and affiliation has slowly changed. Across almost every Western nation, the proportion of the population identifying as Christian has declined, and regular attendance at worship has dropped (see Brown, 2012; Eagle, 2011; Sherkat, 2014; Singleton, 2014). Concomitantly, the proportion of those who claim no religious affiliation – the 'nones' – has increased dramatically (see Singleton, 2015), and now in many countries nones are the single largest grouping among 'religious' categories (i.e. Catholic; Anglican etc.).

The most recent research finds that this turn from Christianity is largely a *birth cohort* or *generational* effect, driven by the youngest members of society (see Crockett & Voas, 2006; Pew Research Center, 2015a; Sherkat, 2014). Sociologist David Voas (2010, p. 32) puts it this way: 'Society is changing religiously not because individuals are changing, but rather because old people [who tend to be more religious] are gradually replaced by younger people with different characteristics.' The youngest members of society are eschewing Christianity, whereas the older members of society remain largely devoted to the churches. For example, writing about Great Britain, sociologists Alasdair Crockett and David Voas (2006, p. 581) find: 'Religious decline in twentieth-century Britain was overwhelmingly generational in nature; decade-by-decade . . . each birth cohort was less religious than the one before.' Sociologist Darren Sherkat (2014, p. 48) detects a similar pattern in America, finding the biggest declines have occurred in mainline Christian denominations, largely because 'younger generations are more likely to reject religious identification'.

Most commentators agree that this drift away from Christianity has its roots in the profound cultural and demographic changes that took place in the 1960s. These changes particularly affected the young people of that time: the generation known as the 'Baby Boomers' (see Brown, 2012; Mason, 2010; Mason et al., 2010; Putnam & Campbell, 2010). Callum Brown (2012, p. 30), notes that important cultural trends of the 1960s included: 'the sexual revolution; the rise of drug taking . . . the loss of respect for civic institutions . . . and the resulting challenge to authority (notably by youth in a so-called generation gap) . . . [and] the emergence of a new women's activism.' Church had little appeal for the swelling ranks of Boomers. As the Boomers became parents, and having drifted from organised religion, their children have also drifted away at an even greater rate (Crockett & Voas, 2006; Mason et al., 2010).

This drift away from Christianity is only one important religious change that has taken place since the 1960s. Western societies have become far more religiously diverse. The Muslim, Sikh, Buddhist and Hindu populations living in the West have grown remarkably. In Australia, approximately 8 per cent of the population identifies with one of these religions; in England and Wales it is approximately 8 per cent and in America, 6 per cent of the population is Buddhist, Hindu, Sikh, Muslim or another faith (ONS, 2011; Pew Research Center, 2015a; Singleton, 2014). All the projections suggest that these proportions will increase (see Pew Research Center, 2015b). The growth of these religions is almost entirely due to migration, and high birth rates among these groups (Singleton, 2014, p. 94).

In sum, religion in the Western world has changed rapidly in the span of 50 years. Christianity is in decline and the proportion of 'nones' and those who affiliate with world faiths is increasing. This is largely due to shifting societal patterns, both demographic and cultural. Moreover, since the 1960s, societal and cultural change has continued apace, with the spread of global capital, increased social mobility, and global forms of communication. The net effect is that today's young people are coming of age in a time of religious choice, individualisation and secularity.

## The everyday religious and spiritual lives of teenagers

Having established the historical context, this section offers an overview of the religious and spiritual lives of today's Western teenagers. Helpfully, this has been rich area of inquiry for social scientists in the past decade. There have been several major national research projects on the religious and spiritual lives of teenagers in the West. American projects include the *National Study of Youth and Religion* (Pearce & Denton, 2011; Smith & Denton, 2005). British projects include the *Youth on Religion* (Madge et al., 2014), *Teenage Religion and Values* (Robbins & Francis, 2010) and the *Young People's Attitudes to Religious Diversity* (Arweck, 2017) studies. Elsewhere is the Australian *Spirit of Generation Y* project (Mason et al., 2007) project and the Canadian *Project Teen Canada* (Bibby, 2009) studies. Additionally, there have been numerous high quality, smaller qualitative projects that have explored more deeply the ways in which religious, spiritual and non-religious youth live their everyday lives (see Collins-Mayo and Dandelion, 2010).

While these studies reveal important national differences (i.e. a greater proportion of teens in America are practising Christians; there are more devoted Muslim youth in England than Australia) many similar themes emerge. These common threads are the focus of this section.

Invariably, the research finds religiously devoted young people are in the minority. The majority of young people are variously religiously disengaged, entirely non-religious, or spiritual. These perspectives are discussed below.

### Christian youth: devoted and disengaged

Most of the research finds that only a small proportion of young people *who identify as Christian* are very committed to their faith (i.e. attending church regularly; regular religious practice). (While America has a higher proportion of these kinds of teens than elsewhere, they are still the minority.) Across the West, the young people who go to church regularly are most likely to be found in conservative Protestant denominations (Mason et al., 2007; Smith & Denton, 2005; Smith & Snell, 2009).

In terms of influences on faith development, the research finds invariably that family religiosity is the single most important influence on young people's religious outlook. Mason et al. (2007, p. 156), for example, found that regular attendance of parents at religious services, along with enthusiastic family talk about religion, increased the probability of a teen being highly religious. The most religious teens also tend to have a close network of peers who are similarly devoted to their faith.

Beyond the most devoted Christian teens, a much larger group retain looser ties to the churches, mainly expressed through affiliation to their parent's denomination and belief in God. Most affiliate with a religion because their family does;

they attend services sporadically and they tend to have a 'pick and choose' attitude to their beliefs (see Mason et al., 2007; Pearce & Denton, 2011; Smith & Denton, 2005).

The plight of Catholic youth has been a particular focus of many of the large-scale national studies of youth religion. While there is a small proportion of Catholic youth who are highly devoted (particularly migrant youth or the children of migrants) the majority of young Catholics are religiously disengaged (Mason et al., 2007; Smith et al., 2014). Smith and colleagues (2014, p. 60) note: 'Previous research shows that younger Catholics in the U.S. are less involved in the Church, more likely to pick and choose their beliefs, more individualistic, and less distinctively Catholic than older Catholics.' A reasonable proportion have left the church entirely.

Overall, the research finds that the *majority* of teens who affiliate with a Christian denomination are not especially devoted to their faith.

## 'Nones . . .'

As noted above, compared with earlier generations of youth, a greater proportion of young people today do not affiliate with a religion: the so-called 'religious nones'. Some of the nones were never raised in a religious tradition, while some were 'raised religious' as children but have abandoned this affiliation by their teen years (Mason et al., 2010, p. 94).

While some of the 'nones' hold religious beliefs, or believe in things such as reincarnation or spirit communication, most are indifferent to religion, although they do not reject it out of hand. A small proportion identify as atheist. The Australian *Spirit of Generation Y* research, for example, found most 'nones' to be tolerant of religion, but 'pay it very little regard' (Mason et al., 2007, p. 217). Their orientation to life is typically 'this-worldly' or secular, rather than spiritual.

To be sure, not that much is known about this group, even though they are increasing in number. Most of the research has emphasised what nones do not believe, and has paid insufficient attention to their commitment to secular or non-religious ideals. Studies are only just appearing that examine the ways in which non-religious youth engage in sense making about life matters (see Arweck, 2013; Catto & Eccles, 2013).

## Muslim, Hindu, Sikh and Buddhist teens

As noted above, the proportion of young people in the West who identify with faiths apart from Christianity is increasing. This includes Muslim, Hindu, Sikh and Buddhist teens. This section explores some of the recent research on their religious experiences.

Amid public discussion of banning burkas and Islamist radicalisation, Muslim youth in the West must contend with rising Islamophobia (see Singleton, 2014). Additionally, as a group with a large proportion of its members born in another country, there is a close relationship between ethnic and Muslim identity (see

Hopkins, 2004). The experience of both religious intolerance and racism is thus a common thread in the lives of Muslim teens, many of whom are first or second-generation migrants. (This is also true of Hindu, Buddhist and Sikh teens.)

Additionally, Muslim youth must also contend with other negative public assumptions about them. For Muslim girls and women who wear the hijab or niqab, they are often seen as '"passive victims of oppressive cultures" and as the "embodiment of a repressive and fundamentalist religion"' (Dwyer, 1998, p. 53 in Hopkins, 2004, p. 258). In like manner, Muslim boys and men 'often appear in the dominant imagination as violently patriarchal, unemployed and involved in crime' (Hopkins, 2006, p. 338). Further, the radicalisation of a tiny proportion of Muslim youth has been something of a flashpoint in Muslim and non-Muslim relations.

It is in this broader context that Muslim youth live their everyday religious lives. Beyond public attitudes to Islam, these young people also have to negotiate family and cultural expectations about living their faith (see Mansouri & Percival-Wood, 2008). The large-scale Australian and American quantitative studies on youth religion have little to say about Muslim teens, given that so few are uncovered in their random samples, and thus it is not possible to generalise to the larger Muslim population in those countries. In contrast, the British *Youth on Religion* (YOR) project sought to overcome this deficiency by deliberately surveying large numbers of Muslim youth using a non-random, purposive sample that looked at youth in two religiously diverse regions of England. They found that Muslim youth had the highest levels of religious salience, practice and belief among all of the religious youth they surveyed (see Madge et al., 2014). Not all Muslim youth are devout, however, and like followers of all religions, young people vary in the degree to which they seriously practice their faith.

Arguably, it is qualitative studies have provided the richest accounts of the religious lives of Muslim youth. These have provided useful insights into the family transmission of faith and young women's choices around religious dress. This kind of research has challenged simplistic understandings of the Muslim faith, particularly as it pertains to young people.

Because such a large proportion of Muslims in the West are first or second-generation migrant families, it is very difficult to disentangle the cultural and religious threads in the experience of being raised Muslim in the West. Consequently, a common theme that emerges from accounts of young Muslim lives is tensions between the older and younger generations (see Madge et al., 2014). Writing about being raised Muslim in America, Chaudry (2016, p. 75), observes: 'Part of the preservation of [our] culture . . . was insisting on their [cultural] cultural norms for their American-born-and-raised kids.' Some Muslim youth pull away from these restrictions (or live double lives to some extent) while others embrace them. Notwithstanding, the strength of family and community ties is apparent in the lives of most Muslim youth. The British YOR study found that Muslims reported the highest level of similarity between the religion of mother and child (Madge et al., 2014, p. 147). Confirming this finding, Scourfield et al. (2012), in a representative study of England and Wales, found the highest rates of intergenerational transmission of religion was among Muslims.

The wearing of the hijab is another often-misunderstood aspect of Muslim life in the West. The popularity of hijab-wearing has waxed and waned over the past 100 years. It has made a comeback in recent decades, and is now worn extensively throughout the Muslim world. Many people, particularly non-Muslim Westerners, view the hijab as evidence of 'Islamic patriarchy and oppression of women' (Ahmed, 2011, p. 8), and it has been a flashpoint for debate about religious freedom (Singleton, 2014, p. 162).

The British YOR study is one of the few projects that asked Muslim teens their own thoughts about religious dress. Their findings present a complex picture of personal agency and cultural and familial expectation. On the one hand, they find that among their participants, there 'was a prevailing feeling that wearing a hijab was a personal decision and something that should be done only from choice' (Madge et al., 2014, p. 133). On the other, they detected something of an 'illusion of choice' when it comes to hijab wearing by dint of the fact that 'parents, particularly mothers, [expect] that daughters would at some point wear the hijab' (Madge et al., 2014, p. 133).

The literature on Hindu, Buddhist and Sikh youth is arguably sparser than that on Muslim youth. Singh's qualitative research on the role of the turban among contemporary Sikhs reveals similar findings to that on the religious dress of young Muslims (see Singh, 2010, 2012). Many Sikh youth report facing 'racism and ridicule . . . in maintaining [this conspicuous aspect of] Sikh identity' (Singh, 2010, p. 131). The British YOR research found that the reasons for wearing the turban are many, including: 'to be like their friends, to act as an ambassador for their culture and religion, because it makes them feel more like a Sikh, to keep their families happy, or because they feel comfortable with it' (Madge et al., 2014, p. 128). By contrast, these studies show other British Sikh youth feel sufficiently empowered to not wear it or do not want to be conspicuously Sikh.

This theme of tension between wider culture and faith is evident in other research on religious minority youth. Sociologist Kim Lam (2010), for example, conducted research into the lives of second-generation Vietnamese Buddhist youth in Australia. She found that they 'do not always adhere to the rituals taught to them by their parents and have different standards for accepting teachings and practices than their parents' (Lam, 2010, p. 1). Lam (2010, p. 51) concludes that this is evidence that 'contemporary forces of individualisation and detraditionalisation are also shaping the religious paths of Vietnamese Buddhists youths'.

To summarise, similar patterns are found in the lives of all religiously devout youth – Christian, Muslim, Hindu, Sikh and Buddhist. Even as many retain very strong family and communal support for their faith, they do so in a society that increasingly emphasises individual choice, freedom and agency. There are many external, secularising pressures on them when it comes to living out their faith; there are also internal religious pressures exerted by their families and members of the older generations. Being faithful in religiously diverse societies is not always straightforward.

In addition to exploring the everyday religious lives of teenagers, scholars have identified particular trends and patterns in the ways teens approach matters of faith and spirituality. Some of the most significant themes are explored in the next section. This includes the rise of religious individualism and spiritual seeking, among other cognate concepts.

## Themes in teen religion and spirituality

Much of the public interest that followed the release of the first wave of findings from the American *National Study of Youth Religion* project (Smith & Denton, 2005) was around the concept of 'moral therapeutic deism' (MTD). Authors Smith and Denton claimed that this was a 'de facto' or implicit religious perspective held by many American teens across all Christian traditions (see Smith & Denton, 2005; Smith, 2010). According to Smith (2010, p. 41), 'this "religion" . . . consists of [a belief in] a God who created and orders the world . . . This God wants people to be good, nice, and fair to each other, but does not need to be particularly involved in their lives'. Additionally, the main aim of life is 'to be happy and feel good about oneself' (Smith & Snell, 2009, p. 155). Smith and Denton (2005) argue that this worldview did not emerge in a vacuum, but is a consequence of broader social forces, particularly the rise of a therapeutic culture that emphasises personal well-being and fulfilment (Singleton, 2014, p. 213).

While MTD might be a de facto faith among American teens, it is probably less prevalent in countries like Great Britain, Canada or Australia, where a smaller proportion of teens believe in God or have connections to church (see Mason et al., 2010). Bibby (2009, p. 183), for example, finds 'little support for Smith's argument in Canada . . . those most likely to be into [MTD are] . . . occasional [church] attenders'.

A broader theme that underpins MTD – that the purpose of life is to be happy – was evidenced in research on British teens. Savage and colleagues (Savage et al., 2006) describe an implicit, more secular worldview they call the 'happy midi-narrative'. This is the belief that the 'universe and social world are essentially benign and life is OK' (Savage et al., 2006, p. 37), and that it is an individual's responsibility to 'create a meaningful and happy life' (Savage et al., 2006, p. 39). This happiness is achieved through successful relationships, engaging work and the resources of popular culture. The Australian and Canadian research suggests that this, rather than the more theocentric MTD worldview, is probably the default worldview of teens in those countries (see Bibby, 2009; Mason et al., 2007).

Both MTD and the happy midi-narrative worldviews share in common the idea that it is the *individual's* responsibility to pursue a path in life that leads to happiness and fulfilment (see Collins-Mayo et al., 2010, p. 19). This is emblematic of the individualism that characterises late-modern society. According to Collins-Mayo and colleagues (2010, p. 17): 'Young people are charged with the responsibility of finding their own way through life in an . . . uncertain world.'

Looping back to teens and religion, this individualism has been shown to inform the ways in which many Christian teens approach matters of faith. On this topic, the Australian *SGY* researchers found that: 'In matters of religion, "truth" means what it means for *me*; what is true for someone else may be quite different, and has its own perfect right to exist independently, without being constrained by any standard external to the individual' (Mason et al., 2007, p. 324). Collins-Mayo et al. (2010, p. 17) suggest young people treat religion as a 'cultural resource that young people . . . choose to draw upon [if it suits them]'. Smith and Denton (2005, p. 147) argue too that most American teens believe 'each individual is uniquely distinct from all others and deserves a faith that fits his or her singular self; that individuals must freely choose their own religion; that the individual is the authority over religion and not vice versa'. For many, faith is a resource for feeling good about everyday life, and can be adjusted in ways that suit the individual's purposes.

And what of teens who do not have any kind of Christian faith? We know that many probably tacitly follow a happy midi-narrative. Do some search for more to life than this? Are many spiritual? Most social researchers agree that there is a widespread societal interest in spiritualties that exists outside the bounds of organised religion. Certainly, Westerners can now happily conceive of a non-religious spiritual life-world and have an ever-expanding array of spiritual resources on which to draw, whether that is New Age themes, alternative religions or Buddhist ideas (Singleton, 2014, p. 214). In practical terms, this might entail a dedication to an alternative spiritual practice, like tarot or yoga (if the practitioner decides that this is spiritual), or an alternative religion, like Wicca or Spiritualism. To be sure, the research reveals that only a very small minority of young people are dedicated to such alternatives (see Berger & Ezzy, 2007; Mason et al., 2010).

Spirituality can also take more eclectic forms, what has been dubbed as the 'mix and match' approach to spiritual matters. In this mode, people can 'mix and match' 'unbundled' components of spirituality from a very wide range of sources – like a belief in astrology or reincarnation – rather than having to accept one complete 'package' (Mason et al., 2007, p. 36).

Some of the research into teens has examined the prevalence of this kind of 'spiritual seeking' or 'questing' among young people, if this is understood to be those who are drawing on a range of seemingly eclectic spiritual resources. The American *National Study of Youth Religion* found only a small proportion of teens that 'think of themselves as spiritual but not religious or incorporate spiritual practices from other faiths' (Smith & Denton, 2005, p. 83). British research by Collins-Mayo and colleagues (2010, p. 15) found 'relatively little evidence of "pick-and-mix" spirituality'. The Australian *Spirit of Generation Y* project studied this issue very carefully, and found that approximately 17 per cent of teens and emerging adults blended spiritual beliefs and practices (Mason et al., 2007). To be sure, these approaches define 'spirituality' very narrowly; it may not centre on alternative spiritual practices or beliefs at all, or many not be constituted by 'picking and choosing' disparate elements. We might be looking in the wrong places when it comes to finding spirituality, by dint of the way it is defined.

To that end, it is apposite to define spirituality more expansively. One view is that spirituality:

> Can easily be understood to refer to whatever *inspires* someone – the vision of reality from which [people] derive their zest for life, their sense of meaning and purpose, their basic worldview and fundamental values. It can also be stretched beyond its religious origins to cover non-religious sources of inspiration such as the vision of care for the earth and the search for the true self.
>
> (Mason, 2010, p. 56)

Understood this way, it is possible to argue that a large proportion of teens might be engaged in a spiritual 'search for meaning' (see Tacey, 2010). Now, in a plural, religiously diverse and secular age, it is possible that teens will find that meaning in many different places, and often fragmentary ways. For some young people, this is a deliberate effort, like a commitment to a political or environmental philosophy. Others may uncritically accept a default cultural narrative, whether this is MTD, the happy midi-narrative or consumerism.

## Conclusion: what does it all mean?

This chapter has told the story of how Western societies have moved from being abidingly Christian to religiously plural, non-religious and increasingly individualistic. Teens come from many backgrounds and hold a wide range of worldviews. This clearly has implications for the ways in which educators might approach matters of spirituality and education in school settings.

When it comes to their personal spiritual or religious orientation, students in any given classroom or school setting are now likely be in very different places: some will follow a faith tradition, others will be indifferent to religion, while others might be interested in spirituality. For the most part, however, Western teens are coming from a low base when it comes to 'religious literacy', that is, knowledge of their own faith tradition, the faith tradition of their family heritage or the faith traditions of others (see Moore, 2007; Prothero, 2007).

To that end, school-based education *about* religion and spirituality is arguably best served by raising awareness about the realities of religious diversity, and teaching about the worldviews and perspectives of others. In so doing, research suggests educators will be able to foster religious and spiritual tolerance and understanding among those they teach (see Halafoff, 2013; Jackson, 2012).

Additionally, no matter how one personally feels about religion or spirituality, with the decline of community organisations (i.e. scouts) and churches (see Putnam, 2000), schools and educators are increasingly relied upon to help foster values and a sense of personal meaning for today's teens. Schools, in a sense, are the 'new church' for many teens. While students (and educators) may hold diverse perspectives, it is still possible to nurture a non-partisan spiritual ethic, if this is understood to refer to an ethical, purposeful and meaningful life, characterised by altruism and a concern for others. Moreover, rather than difference and diversity being a hindrance to the nurturing of this kind of spiritual wellbeing in school settings, it offers the vital opportunity to learn from the insights of others.

## Note

1  The remit of this chapter is Western, English-speaking countries; I have described global trends elsewhere (Singleton, 2014).

## References

Ahmed, L. (2011). *A quiet revolution: The veil's resurgence, from the Middle East to America*. New Haven, CT: Yale University Press.

Arweck, E. (2013). 'I've been christened, but I don't really believe in it': How young people articulate their (non-)religious identities and perceptions of (non-) belief. In A. Day, G. Vincett & C. Cotter (eds), *Social identities between the sacred and the secular* (pp. 103–126). Farnham: Ashgate.

Arweck, E. (ed.). (2017). *Young people's attitudes to religious diversity*. London: Routledge.

Australian Bureau of Statistics (ABC) (2013). *Australian social trends*. Canberra: ABS, cat no. 4102.0.

Berger, H., & Ezzy, D. (2007). *Teenage witches: Magical youth and the search for the self*. New Brunswick, NJ: Rutgers University Press.

Bibby, R.W. (2009). *The emerging millennials: How Canada's newest generation is responding to change and choice*. Lethbridge, AB: Project Canada Books.

Brown, C. G. (2012). *Religion and the demographic revolution: Women and secularisation in Canada, Ireland, UK and USA since the 1960s*. Woodbridge: Boydell Press.

Catto, R. (2014). What can we say about today's British religious young person? Findings from the AHRC/ESRC Religion and Society Programme. *Religion, 44*(1), 1–27.

Catto, R., & Eccles, J. (2013). (Dis)Believing and belonging: Investigating the narratives of young British atheists. *Temenos, 49*(1), 37–63.

Chaudry, R. (2016). *Adnan's story*. London: Century Books.

Collins-Mayo, S., & Dandelion, P. (eds). (2010). *Religion and youth*. Farnham: Ashgate.

Collins-Mayo, S., Mayo, B., Nash, S., & Cocksworth, C. (2010). *The faith of generation Y*. London: Church House Publishing.

Crockett, A., & Voas, D. (2006). Generations of decline: Religious change in 20th-century Britain. *Journal for the Scientific Study of Religion, 45*(4), 567–84.

Eagle, D. (2011). Changing patterns of attendance at religious services in Canada, 1986–2008. *Journal for the Scientific Study of Religion, 50*(3), 187–200.

Halafoff, A. (2013). Education about religions and beliefs in Victoria. *Journal for the Academic Study of Religion, 26*(2), 172–197.

Hervieu-Léger, D. (2000). *Religion as a chain of memory*. New Brunswick, NJ: Rutgers University Press.

Hopkins, P. (2004). Young Muslim men in Scotland: Inclusions and exclusions. *Children's Geographies, 2*(2), 257–72.

Hopkins, P. (2006). Youthful Muslim masculinities: Gender and generational relations. *Transactions of the Institute of British Geographers, 31*, 337–352.

Jackson, R. (ed.). (2012). *Religion, education, dialogue and conflict: Perspectives on religious education research*. London: Routledge.

Lam, K. (2010). *Second generation Vietnamese Buddhists in Australia: An intergenerational study* (Unpublished honours thesis). Melbourne: Monash University.

McLeod, H. (2007). *The religious crisis of the 1960s.* Oxford: Oxford University Press.

Madge, N., Hemming, P. J., & Stenson, K. (2014). *Youth on religion: The development, negotiation and impact of faith and non-faith identity.* London: Routledge.

Mansouri. F., & Percival-Wood, S. (2008). *Identity, education and belonging: Arab and Muslim youth in contemporary Australia.* Melbourne: MUP.

Mason, M. (2010). The spirituality of young Australians. In S. Collins-Mayo & P. Dandelion (eds), *Religion and youth* (pp. 55–63). Farnham: Ashgate.

Mason, M., Singleton, A., & Webber, R. (2007). *The spirit of generation Y: Young people's spirituality in a changing Australia.* Melbourne: John Garratt Publishing.

Mason, M., Singleton, A., & Webber, R. (2010). Developments in spirituality among youth in Australia and other western societies. In G. Giordan (ed.), *Annual review of the Sociology of Religion, Youth and Religion* (Vol. 1, pp. 89–114). Leiden: Brill.

Moore, D. L. (2007). *Overcoming religious illiteracy: A cultural studies approach to the study of religion in secondary education.* New York: Palgrave Macmillan.

Pearce, L. D., & Denton, M. L. (2011). *A faith of their own: Stability and change in the religiosity of America's adolescents.* New York: Oxford University Press.

Pew Research Center (2015a). *America's changing religious landscape.* Washington, DC: Pew Research Center.

Pew Research Center (2015b). *The future of world religions: Population growth projections, 2010–2050.* Pew Research Center, Washington, DC.

Prothero, S. (2007). *Religious literacy: What every American needs to know – and doesn't.* New York: HarperCollins.

Putnam, R. (2000). *Bowling alone.* New York: Touchstone Books.

Putnam, R., & Campbell, D. (2010). *American grace: How religion divides and unites us.* New York: Simon and Schuster.

Robbins, M., & Francis, L. (2010). The teenage religion and values survey in England and Wales. In S. Collins-Mayo & P. Dandelion (eds), *Religion and youth* (pp. 47–53). Farnham: Ashgate.

Safioleas, A. (2016). Bigger than Jesus. *The Big Issue*, 518, 14–17.

Savage, S., Collins-Mayo, S., Mayo, B., & Cray, G. (2006). *Making sense of generation Y: The world view of 15–25 year-olds.* London: Church House Publishing.

Scourfield, J., Taylor, C., Moore, G., & Gilliat-Ray, S. (2012). The intergenerational transmission of Islam in England and Wales: Evidence from the citizenship survey. *Sociology, 46*(1), 91–108.

Sherkat, D. (2014). *Changing faith: The dynamics and consequences of Americans' shifting religious identities.* New York: New York University Press.

Singh, J. (2010). British Sikh youth: Identity, hair and the turban. In S. Collins-Mayo & P. Dandelion (eds), *Religion and youth* (pp. 131–138). Farnham: Ashgate.

Singh, J. (2012). Keeping the faith: Reflections on religious nurture among young British Sikhs. *Journal of Beliefs & Values, 33*(3), 369–383.

Singleton, A. (2014). *Religion, culture and society: A global approach.* London: Sage.

Singleton, A. (2015). Are religious 'nones' secular? The case of the nones in Australia. *Journal of Beliefs & Values, 36*(2), 239–243.

Smart, J. (1999). The evangelist as star: The Billy Graham crusade in Australia, 1959. *Journal of Popular Culture, 33*(1), 165–175.

Smith, C. (2010). On 'moralistic therapeutic deism' as US teenagers actual, tacit, *de facto* religious faith. In S. Collins-Mayo & P. Dandelion (eds), *Religion and youth* (pp. 41–46). Farnham: Ashgate.

Smith, C., & Denton, M. L. (2005). *Soul searching: The religious and spiritual lives of American Teenagers*. New York: OUP.

Smith, C., & Snell, P. (2009). *Souls in transition: The religious and spiritual lives of emerging adults*. New York: OUP.

Smith, C., Longest, K., Hill, J., and Christoffersen, K. (2014). *Young Catholic America: Emerging adults in, out of, and gone from the church*. New York: OUP.

Tacey, D. (2010). What spirituality means to young adults. In S. Collins-Mayo & P. Dandelion (eds), *Religion and youth* (pp. 65–72). Farnham: Ashgate.

Voas, D. (2010). Explaining change over time in religious involvement. In S. Collins-Mayo & P. Dandelion (eds), *Religion and youth* (pp. 25–32). Farnham: Ashgate.

# 4

# SPIRITUALITY IN AUSTRALIAN EDUCATION

## A legacy of confusion, omission and obstruction

*Terence Lovat*

## Introduction

The role that spirituality has been allowed to play in public life in Australia is enigmatic, to say the least. The fact that the then colony was being normalised towards eventual federation throughout the high water mark of nineteenth-century secularism no doubt contributed to a measure of zeal, counter zeal and downright confusion about spirituality, not all of which has been satisfactorily dealt with to this day. I argue that we see this in an array of educational public policies concerned with matters like the place of theology in higher education and religious education in public schools (Byrne, 2012; Fleming et al., 2015). While, in both cases, customary nineteenth-century attempts towards separation of church and state can be seen, nonetheless they took quite different forms in the two sectors, creating further confusion and ultimately obstruction of a rational pathway for spirituality to be addressed educationally (de Souza, 2010). This suggests that secularism was never an organised, reified movement but rather a series of movements and trends taking different forms depending on the exact nature of the issue and the reaction of purported adversarial forces. In these cases, a clear difference is seen in the politick of advancing the cause of mass public schooling in the context of an extant religious system, or systems, and that of higher education as an elite and innovative development. In neither case was the place of spirituality and spiritual education clearly considered and a rational way forward proposed. The chapter will utilise New South Wales (NSW) instances, primarily, in appraising these issues historically and describing and evaluating late-twentieth into twenty-first-century attempts to counter them in ways that are more suited to contemporary philosophies of education, human development and societal need. As above, the focus will be especially on the school context, with some reference to the university context as an earlier relevant background to what transpired in the schools.

## Religious education in public schooling

Australia's first university, The University of Sydney, founded in 1851, constitutionally excluded theology from its curriculum (Breward, 1997). Reasons for the exclusion were complex but it seems explained best by the context of nineteenth-century secularism and the unease between the churches and public authorities concerning the role that churches should continue to play in a public domain like education (Davis, 1966). Targeting theology as a discipline of learning clearly seemed to be the best way of achieving this, at least in the minds of the relevant decision-makers. Keeping the churches at bay was naturally not an issue on which religious and public officials tended to agree, with hostility from both sides apparent. Certainly, the action on the part of Anglican Bishops Broughton of Sydney and Tyrrell of Newcastle, '. . . trenchantly arguing a case against a "godless university"' (Davis, 1966, pp. 49–50) was bound to heighten tension. In turn, the justification coming from the Academic Senate of the university that the ban was to '. . . prevent sectarian interests from contaminating academic pursuits' (Breward, 1997, p. 8) was equally non-conciliatory. Australia was off to a dubious start in terms of finding a place for spiritual considerations in the public curriculum.

Like the university system, Australian public schooling also began in the nineteenth century, the NSW Public Instruction Act (1880) (NSW, 1912) being just one of the many Colony State Acts that marked its formal beginnings. In the case of schooling, we find much of the same resistance on the part of the churches, as exhibited towards the foundation of the university system. Indeed, resistance especially from the Catholic Church was considerably more vigorous because, by the time of the Act, it had a huge stake in school education (O'Farrell, 1985, 1993). So, whereas resistance to the shape of university education was somewhat academic, in the case of school education, it was considerably more about property, possession and power. There was also a far greater public sensitivity to school education than to university education. While a lack of theology in the university might have been judged to be something of a non-issue for parents of university-aged children, the lack of religious formation in schools was an issue of considerable concern for parents faced with choice in where they sent their children to school. As such, the two stories are different, albeit both being shrouded in duplicity, omission and obstruction, and much of it continuing to cause confusion up to the present day.

Granted the greater sensitivity, we tend to find a greater level of judiciousness being exercised by those establishing public schooling than was always evident among the founders of the universities (NSW, 1912). The founders of public schooling in NSW were sufficiently pragmatic to know that its success relied on its charter being in accordance with public sentiment. Part of the pragmatism was in convincing those whose main experience of education had been through some form of church-based education that public schooling was capable of meeting the same ends. Among these ends was a religious (and, by dint of reference, moral) perspective that had been at the heart of all forms of church-based education, arguably most markedly within Catholic education where religious orders increasingly made up the major part of the teaching force (O'Farrell, 1985). For Mary MacKillop, for instance, the Scottish Catholic founder of the Sisters of St Joseph, now Australia's first Catholic 'saint', teaching young people to deal with the religious and moral dimension was a very explicit part of the mission of her Catholic schools in colonial Australia (cf. Lovat, 2005; Modystack, 2000). Hence, if the new public schooling was to have any hope of convincing its adherents that it could do the same job as church-based education, then part of the case it put had to be around safeguarding the religious and moral perspective.

The 1880 Act that contained the charter of NSW public schooling reveals therefore a vision about the scope of education quite beyond what would be characteristic of much of the twentieth century's practical approach to public schooling (NSW, 1912). Beyond the standard goals of literacy and numeracy, education was said, among other things, to be capable of assuring religious under-standing and personal morality for each individual, and so to assist in forming a suitable citizenry for the soon-to-be new nation. Under the rubric of 'General Religious Teaching', it stressed the need for students to be inculcated into the values that underpinned their society, including understanding the role that religious values had played in forming that society's legal codes and social ethics. This facet of the curriculum was to be in the hands of the school's regular teachers, whatever their curriculum specialisation. The idea therefore that public schooling is part of a deep and ancient heritage around religious and moral neutrality is clearly a misconception. The evidence suggests that public schooling's initial conception was of being the complete educator, not only of young people's minds but of their inner character, including their religious and moral character and that it was principally on this basis that public schooling could claim to be formative of good citizenship (NSW, 1912). In this sense, more than the germ of a spiritual perspective was present from the beginning, at least in latent form.

The other dimension of religious education endorsed in the 1880 Act was the denominational form, known initially as 'Special Religious Instruction' (SRI) which, unlike 'General Religious Teaching', was to be staffed voluntarily by the various churches and religious bodies (NSW, 1912). Also unlike 'General Religious Teaching', students and their parents would be free to opt in or out of this denominational offering. It was not seen as inextricable to the public school, in the way that 'General Religious Teaching' was framed and, I would argue, was only ever likely to be successful if it found its home in 'General Religious Teaching'. If this latter failed to saturate the ambience of learning as it was designed to do, then inevitably denominational-based religious education would struggle. Hence, I argue that, in this 'twin' approach, there was a dominant twin, and that was 'General Religious Teaching'. Unfortunately, the dominant twin was still-born and the twin that survived did so only awkwardly. This in itself is part of the sad story of any analysis of spiritual education in Australia.

For all the attempts to position public schooling as the comprehensive educator, thereby supplanting the role played by church-based education in the religious and moral domain, the history of both the country and the times was against it. The late nineteenth century was, as illustrated above, a time of sharp division between secular and religious forces and, within the religious forces, between Protestantism and Catholicism. For the Catholic Church, the fact that the Protestant churches largely surrendered their education systems to the State would simply have confirmed the view that the Protestant churches were overly disposed to establishment agendas. As a result, the Catholic system of education went forward on its own, with the Catholic Archbishop of Sydney of the time, Roger Vaughan, declaring that the new public education system was a godless, secularist option that would become the seed plot of future immorality and lawlessness, and would see Catholic parents eternally damned if they dared even consider sending their children there (cf. O'Farrell, 1985). In the very sectarian late nineteenth century, this view which had the power to skew the way of all education, including public schooling, developed. For one thing, Catholic education was the single largest educational force of the day, with heavy purchase on the approximately 20 per cent of the population that was Catholic at the time but, with a far wider reach into the general population (ABS, 2008). As well, its loud self-proclamation as the only legitimate religious and moral force in education was bound to affect the charter that developed around public schooling. Among many practical effects, it seemed that public educators moved away deliberately from their charter around religious and moral content and awareness, preferring to leave this to the churches. Hence, the public school became, in effect, a bastion of religious neutrality and a wasteland as a nurturer of spirituality.

Nonetheless, the important point of this historical recount is that public schooling's initial conception of itself, at least as evidenced in NSW through the 1880 Act (NSW, 1912), was of providing an ambience in which spiritual content and literacy development should have a central place. Furthermore, in spite of the slippage in this understanding throughout much of the twentieth century, as referred to above, it was in many ways the 1880 conception that was revived exactly a century later when, in 1980, the NSW Rawlinson Report (NSW, 1980) commended its own version of a 'twin' approach to religious education in public schools. On the one hand, 'General Religious Education' (GRE) was to be available as a public curriculum, taught by regular teachers and, where appropriate, integrated into other mainstream curricula; on the other hand, 'Special Religious Education' (SRE) was to be preserved for denominational enfaithing, taught by volunteers from the various faiths and sitting outside the mainstream curriculum. As suggested, this is essentially a re-statement of the 'twin' approach to religious education to be found in the 1880 Act. While there has been continued controversy about the SRE 'twin', the less heralded but arguably far more important GRE twin is the one that proffers that the NSW public curriculum should include broad-based, inter-denominational religious knowledge and formation reflective of the cultural underpinnings of the society into which students are being inducted as citizens. This is the same twin that was lost at birth throughout the exaggeratedly secularist nineteenth and twentieth centuries, predictably leaving SRE without its necessary sibling in an environment that was non-conducive if not quite hostile to the very idea that matters concerned with spirituality should have a role of any kind in the public school.

## Rediscovering spirituality in public schooling

The re-discovery of the role of spirituality, specifically in the forms of religious and moral content, has been the subject of the re-appraisal of the goals of schooling for the twenty-first century. For a start, it has taken the form of some powerful statements elicited from senior bodies about public schooling as sites of spiritual and moral nurture, of the sort that point to serious revision of the form of secularism that dominated public schooling in the twentieth century. For example, in the Adelaide Declaration on National Goals for Schooling in the Twenty-first Century (MCEETYA, 1999), we read: 'Schooling provides a foundation for young Australians' intellectual, physical, social, moral, spiritual and aesthetic development' (Preamble). Such a statement appears to represent a radical shift in the ethos of public schooling about this matter, at least at the level of government and bureaucracy, if not the hearts and minds of public school personnel. If, as some suggested in 1999, this was a momentary lapse, an aberration in an otherwise steely secularism about the central purpose of public schooling or, as some suggested strongly, a function of the then conservative Liberal/National Government, then the Melbourne Declaration on Educational Goals for Young Australians (MCEETYA, 2008), overseen by the succeeding Labor Government, showed that indeed there was a purposeful change of thinking about that steely secularism and its appropriateness to twenty-first century schooling. The Melbourne Declaration represented an update on the Adelaide Declaration and, around the issue of spiritual and moral nurture, was considerably more explicit and expansive than its predecessor. For example, the Preamble to the Document states:

> Schools play a vital role in promoting the intellectual, physical, social, emotional, moral, spiritual and aesthetic development and wellbeing of young Australians. (p. 4)

Among the goals is one that states:

> . . . (students should) have a sense of self-worth, self-awareness and personal identity that enables them to manage their emotional, mental, spiritual and physical wellbeing. (p. 9)

Meanwhile, in terms of the curriculum actions that should ensue from the aforesaid perspectives, it states:

> The curriculum will enable students to develop knowledge in the disciplines of English, mathematics, science, languages, humanities and the arts; to understand the spiritual, moral and aesthetic dimensions of life; and open up new ways of thinking. (p. 13)

In a word, the Melbourne Declaration makes it plain that public schooling should be constituted of an environment that encourages, supports and nurtures the spiritual and moral development of its students. One senses there is more than the mere expediency of a changing society behind this, although this clearly would have been a motivating factor. Moreover, one sees the influence of a spate of recent research in neuroscience, neuropsychology and neurobiology pertaining to learning and development that makes explicit reference to spiritual intelligence, moral intelligence, spiritual awareness and even mystical consciousness as inherent features of overall human development even among those most seemingly opposed to religion and religiousness (Beauregard & O'Leary, 2007; Emmons, 1999, 2000, 2003; Han et al., 2008; Heelas, 2011; Mayer, 2000; Sternberg, 2004; Walach, 2007). Added to this is the increasing sense that exposure to spiritual and moral exploration is an especially powerful way in which the vital cognitive function of imagination is impelled. Imagination is seen increasingly by neuroscientists as the key to fostering the emotional regulation necessary to sound reasoning, and hence to academic achievement (cf. Narvaez, 2013).

Whatever the precise motivations behind this renewed appreciation of the role that spiritual and moral exploration can play in holistic learning, the challenge remains to find structures and pedagogies that facilitate such an ambience. Some of it can be achieved through having available appropriate curricula and this much has been achieved through a raft of new syllabuses and initiatives at both NSW and national levels that have brought renewed focus on such exploration (e.g. DEEWR, 2008; DEST, 2005, 2006; NSW, 1991, 2000). The challenge however of re-capturing the original vision of General Religious Teaching (envisioned in the 1880 Act) is clearly more profound than one concerned merely with academic content and assessment, especially if the revived importance of spiritual and moral exploration, signalled in the neuroscientific research perspectives noted above, is to be addressed. The real challenge is to create an ambience entailing principal and teacher knowledge, attitudes and skills, as well as a physical environment and formal and informal curricula that allow and facilitate spiritual and moral nurture. It entails new forms of training and in-service, enhanced intercultural and interfaith awareness and heightened sensitivity to building the kind of environment wherein, alongside all the other goals of schooling, spiritual and moral development can be endorsed and supported.

The wider and more interesting area for ongoing exploration is whether the public syllabus could also accommodate informed personal faith exploration in a way that would facilitate, or possibly supersede the likes of SRE, an ongoing area of contention (Knight, 2010) and with dubious enfaithing credentials. In a separate paper (Lovat, 2012), I have argued that a comprehensive phenomenological method has potential to serve the agendas of religious literacy and personal exploration without inherent contradiction and in a way that retains the integrity of the public curriculum. Indeed, this notion is accommodated in some of the public curricula noted above. An example is seen in the original NSW Higher School Certificate subject, *Studies of Religion* (NSW, 1991), a subject designed largely as a social scientific probe but at the same time incorporating among its objectives one that speaks of '. . . the ability to reflect upon the development of (their) own beliefs and values' (p. 11).

Hence, there would seem to be ample scope for general RE's twin, SRE, to function in unison and with some synergy within the context of a subject of this kind. This would be at least one way in which the more difficult of the twins, that which is attempting a form of enfaithing, however mildly, could operate with some meaning. In this case, space for spiritual development would be within the bounds of the public syllabus and the control of the regular teacher, perhaps with ancillary support from religious bodies. Such learning space would seem to fit well with the challenge around learning wrought by the neurosciences, as above. The challenge for public schooling in all this would be in taking the wider view of its role, together with the substantial teacher re-orienting required. In this regard, couching it in terms of a re-discovery of its original charter around religious and moral literacy would be a helpful conceptual starting point. The concomitant challenge for the churches and other religious bodies would be in foregoing some of the political and legal power they have over SRE in order to allow for this wider learning space to be realised in the public school.

Many teachers in public schools will inevitably assume that addressing spiritual and moral development is of little or no significance in the secularised state in which they assume to be living, and least of all in the public school which, they will maintain, has no charter or responsibilities around such development. If ever this was true, it is clearly not true today, granted the increasing presence of young people, families and whole communities, both home-grown and immigrant, for whom faith matters, and matters a great deal. For them, it is expected that any school will accommodate their spiritual and moral needs and demands. Some of these needs and demands are obvious, pertaining to the range of food available in the canteen, the type of dress that is tolerated within the uniform regime, flexibility of schedules that allow for mandatory prayers and festival celebrations, and a host of other such practical accommodations. Some of the demands are more subtle, however, and are therefore arguably more challenging. Research carried out on this issue within some of the populations representing the most significant changes in the Australian population mix might serve to illustrate the point.

## Researching the spiritual imperative

For instance, research was carried out within one of Australia's largest Hindu and Hindu-related populations (Lovat, 1995a, 1995b, 1997, 2006; Lovat & Morrison, 2000). Hinduism and its derivative traditions expressing religious spirituality has had the largest population growth in the national census of the past two decades (ABS, 2012). The research revealed a subtle but vital difference in the priorities assumed of the school's role from what might have been seen as the norm among a dominantly Anglo-Celtic, pseudo-Christian clientele. For this population, among those both overtly religious and otherwise, the role of the school, religious, private or public, encompassed the addressing of religious and moral content and their concomitant formation. By and large, this was not seen as enfaithing as such, but rather as an indispensable component of adequate enculturation. In fact, there was some concern expressed about religious education in its traditional denominational forms because, it was said, it is the religiousness of life that matters rather than its particular expression. Indeed, an over emphasis on enfaithing of a narrow denominational kind was said to have potential to distract and even undermine the far more important work of education in drawing its students into an understanding and appreciation of the ingrained spiritual dimension of life (Lovat, 1995a).

In these research findings, the demand that all schools should address and offer elements of formation around religious and moral content was present but the distinction between this routine feature of the curriculum and dealing with the spiritual was more strongly pressed. The distinction was largely based on the difference between cognitive and affective learning. 'Religion and morality could be studied but spirituality had to be experienced' constituted a common kind of response (Lovat, 1995b). Hence, quite beyond incorporating into the public school the potential for religious education of either or both the general and denominational kind was the more important incorporation of moments that allow, support and encourage student contemplation of their own and the world's nature as inherently spiritual. For the Hindu, this is where God is to be found and only on this understanding and appreciation can a firm and sustainable personal and communal morality be formed (Lovat, 1995b). This perspective seems clearly to be in accordance with the spirit of General Religious Teaching from the 1880 Act and General Religious Education from the 1980 Rawlinson Report.

Research on Australian populations like this, with the strong emphasis on moral formation as an artefact of spiritual development, leads naturally to some consideration of modern forms of values education and their potential to deal with the spiritual demands of contemporary schools' populations. The various projects of the Australian Values Education Program (DEEWR, 2008; DEST, 2006) have been shown to have significant impact on a range of educational measures (Lovat et al., 2009; 2010a). Among these measures were ones concerned with overall student wellbeing, school ambience and indeed academic achievement, seeming to confirm something of the neuroscientific theses above. Underlying these measures lay issues surrounding self-esteem, moral choice and self-regulation, and findings included strong indications of enhancement of such facets of human development. In a word, there were indications that students' understanding of self and internal comfort (inner peace) with being one's self could be enhanced by the practices entailed in certain approaches to values education.

Among the projects that yielded these findings were ones that dealt explicitly with spiritual and moral content and enhanced understanding of the importance of these dimensions of self and other (Lovat et al., 2010b). For example, there was a project that dealt with the importance of ascertaining the spiritual and moral aspects of religious difference and ways of overcoming fear and conflict through entering into the world of the 'other' via their spiritual beliefs, perceptions and values (DEEWR, 2008, p. 67). In this case, the particular emphasis was on Muslim and non-Muslim difference, with Muslim and public schools involved. In another project, the importance of spiritual and moral values was explored through students from a range of different religious and public schools being introduced to and experiencing each other's major festivals, religious and secular (DEEWR, 2008, pp. 28–29):

> At each of these gatherings, the values of understanding, tolerance and inclusion, freedom, respect and responsibility were foregrounded. The nature of the interfaith and intercultural student mix combined with the method- ology of the Socratic circle gave everyone involved the chance to express their opinions respectfully, to develop understanding of the issue and the other people involved, and to behave responsibly and inclusively . . . It would therefore seem that the Socratic circles technique plays a role in improving students' communicative abilities as well as deepening their understanding of different world views and different values perspectives.
>
> (DEEWR, 2008, p. 121)

## Conclusion

Work such as cited herein illustrates, on the one hand, the potential of the public curriculum to engage meaningfully with spiritual development in the way that the Adelaide and Melbourne Declarations enjoin and, on the other hand, for such engagement to enrich and enhance the other areas of human development, social, emotional, moral, aesthetic and intellectual, as also enjoined in these declarations about the scope of twenty-first-century schooling. Clearly, such a view of learning fits well with the neuroscientific perspectives noted above. So, one senses that spiritual education done well, in a way that exploits wonder and imagination and impels self-reflectivity, could one day come to be seen as possessing especially facilitative potential to impel sound reasoning and good overall learning. One might suggest that the vision of those nineteenth-century educational founders around the comprehensiveness of public education would then have been vindicated. Also vindicated would be the implicit conception that General Religious Teaching (or Education) and the attention to the spiritual and moral dimensions of life that it implied can serve as a means of fortifying the broader goals of education. Well balanced, integrated, neuroscientifically inspired and essentially non-denominationally bound spiritual education would seem to have much to contribute to Australia's healthy growth as a nation.

## Acknowledgement

This chapter draws and expands on an earlier paper written by the same author and published by the Australian College of Educators as:

Lovat, T. (2010). Spirituality and the public school. In M. de Souza & Julie Rimes (eds), *Meaning and connectedness: Australian perspectives on education and spirituality* (pp. 19–30). Canberra: The Australian College of Educators.

# References

ABS (Australian Bureau of Statistics) (2008). *Cultural diversity.* Year Book Australia, 2008. Canberra: Australian Bureau of Statistics. Available at: http://abs.gov.au/ausstats/abs@.nsf/7d12b0f6763c78caca257061001cc588/636F496B2B943F12CA2573D200109DA9?opendocument

ABS (Australian Bureau of Statistics) (2012). *Reflecting a nation: Stories from the 2011 census, 2012–2013.* Canberra: Australian Bureau of Statistics. Available at: http://abs.gov.au/ausstats/abs@.nsf/Lookup/2071.0main+features902012–2013

Beauregard, M., & O'Leary, D. (2007). *The spiritual brain: A neuroscientist's case for the existence of the soul* (1st ed.). New York: HarperOne.

Breward, I. (1997). Historical perspectives on theological education in Australia. In G. Treloar (ed.), *The furtherance of religious beliefs: Essays on the history of theological education in Australia* (pp. 8–23). Macquarie University, Sydney: Centre for the Study of Australian Christianity.

Byrne, C. (2012). Ideologies of religion and diversity in Australian public schools. *Multicultural Perspectives, 14*(4), 201–207.

Davis, R. (1966) *The Morpeth Papers: A collection of papers read at the Bishop of Newcastle's Conference on Theological Education held at St John's College, Morpeth, NSW, February 14–17, 1966.* Newcastle, Australia: Anglican Diocese of Newcastle.

DEEWR (2008). *At the heart of what we do: Values education at the centre of schooling.* Report of the Values Education Good Practice Schools Project – Stage 2. Melbourne: Curriculum Corporation. Available from: http://curriculum.edu.au/values/val_vegps2_final_report, 26142.html

de Souza, M. (ed.). (2010). *Meaning and connectedness: Australian perspectives on education and spirituality.* Canberra: The Australian College of Educators.

DEST (2005). *National framework for values education in Australian schools.* Australian Government Department of Education, Science and Training. Available at http://curriculum.edu.au/verve/_resources/Framework_PDF_version_for_the_web.pdf

DEST (2006). *Implementing the national framework for values education in Australian schools: Report of the Values Education Good Practice Schools Project – Stage 1: Final report, September 2006.* Melbourne: Curriculum Corporation. Available from http://valueseducation.edu.au/values/default.asp?id=16381

Emmons, R. A. (1999). *The psychology of ultimate concerns: Motivation and spirituality in personality.* New York: Guilford Press.

Emmons, R. (2000). Is spirituality an intelligence? Motivation, cognition and the psychology of ultimate concern. *International Journal for the Psychology of Religion, 10*(1), 3–26.

Emmons, R. (2003). *The psychology of ultimate concerns: Motivation and spirituality in personality.* New York: Guilford Press.

Fleming, D., Lovat, T., & Douglas, B. (2015). Theology in the public square of Australian higher education. *Journal of Adult Theological Education, 12*(1), 30–42.

Han, S., Mao, L., Gu, X., Zhu, Y., Ge, J., & Ma, Y. (2008). Neural consequences of religious belief on self-referential processing. *Social Neuroscience, 3*(1), 1–15.

Heelas, P. (ed.). (2011). *Spirituality in the modern world: Within religious tradition and beyond.* London: Routledge.

Knight, S. (2010). *NSW ethics course trial: Final report.* Available at http://dec.nsw.gov.au/detresources/NSW_Ethics_course_trial_BYucPDfMew.pdf

Lovat, T. (1995a). Australian Hindu perspectives on new public curricula in religious studies and values education. *British Journal of Religious Education, 17,* 168–179.

Lovat, T. (1995b). Multifaith religious and values education: Apparent or real? *Religious Education, 90,* 412–426.

Lovat, T. (1997). Patterns of religious separation and adherence in contemporary Australia. In M. Bar-Lev & W. Shaffir (eds), *Religion and the social order: Leaving religious life* (pp. 97–116). Greenwich, CT: JAI Press.

Lovat, T. (2005). Mary MacKillop: Practical mystic and contemporary educator. In P. Wicks (ed.), *Mary MacKillop: Inspiration for today* (pp. 97–109). Sydney: Trustees of the Sisters of St Joseph.

Lovat, T. (2006). The contribution of Hinduism and Hindu-inspired spirituality to Australian religious and values education. In M. de Souza, K. Engebretson, R. Jackson & G. Durka (eds), *International handbook of the religious, spiritual and moral dimensions in education* (pp. 487–499). Dordrecht, Netherlands: Springer.

Lovat, T. (2012). Interfaith education and phenomenological method. In T. van der Zee & T. Lovat (eds), *New perspectives on religious and spiritual education* (pp. 87–100). Munster: Waxmann.

Lovat, T., & Morrison, K. (2000). Disaffiliation and affiliation: Experiences of conflict in leaving Christianity and joining a new spirituality. In L. Francis & Y. Katz (eds), *Joining and leaving religion: Research perspectives.* (pp. 287–308). Leominster, UK: Gracewing.

Lovat, T., Clement, N., Dally, K., & Toomey, R. (2010a). Values education as holistic development for all sectors: Researching for effective pedagogy. *Oxford Review of Education, 36,* 1–17.

Lovat, T., Clement, N., Dally, K., & Toomey, R. (2010b). Addressing issues of religious difference through values education: An Islam instance. *Cambridge Journal of Education, 40,* 213–227.

Lovat, T., Toomey, R., Dally, K., & Clement, N. (2009). *Project to test and measure the impact of values education on student effects and school ambience.* Report for the Australian Government Department of Education, Employment and Workplace Relations (DEEWR) by The University of Newcastle. Canberra: DEEWR. Available from http://valueseducation.edu.au/values/val_articles,8884.html

Mayer, J. (2000). Spiritual intelligence or spiritual consciousness? *International Journal for the Psychology of Religion, 10*(1), 47–56.

MCEETYA (1999). *National goals for schooling in the twenty-first century.* (The Adelaide Declaration.) Available from http://dest.gov.au/sectors/school_education/policy_initiatives_reviews/national_goals_for_schooling_in_the_twenty_first_century.htm

MCEETYA (2008). *Melbourne Declaration on Educational Goals for Young Australians.* Canberra: Ministerial Council on Education, Employment, Training and Youth Affairs. Available from: http://curriculum.edu.au/verve/_resources/National_Declaration_on_the_Educational_Goals_for_Young_Australians.pdf

Modystack, W. (2000). *Blessed Mary MacKillop: A woman before her time.* Sydney: Lansdowne.

Narvaez, D. (2013). Neurobiology and moral mindset. In K. Heinrichs, F. Oser, & T. Lovat (eds), *Handbook of moral motivation: Theories, models, applications* (pp. 323–342). Rotterdam: Sense Publishers.

NSW (1912). *Public Instruction Act of 1880 and regulations.* Sydney: William Applegate Gullick.

NSW (1980). *Religion in education in NSW government schools.* Sydney: NSW Department of Education.

NSW (1991). *Studies of religion.* Sydney: NSW Board of Studies.

NSW (2000). *Society and culture.* Sydney: NSW Board of Senior Secondary Studies. http://boardofstudies.nsw.edu.au/syllabus_hsc/pdf_doc/society-culture-st6-syl-from2010.pdf

O'Farrell, P. (1985). *The Catholic Church and community in Australia: A history*. Melbourne: Nelson.

O'Farrell, P. (1993). *The Irish in Australia*. Sydney: UNSW Press.

Sternberg, R. (2004). North American approaches to intelligence. In R. Sternberg (ed.), *International handbook of intelligence* (pp. 411–444). Cambridge: Cambridge University Press.

Walach, H. (2007). Mind, body, spirituality. *Mind and Matter, 5*(2), 215–240.

# 5

# BUILDING THE FOUNDATIONS OF GLOBAL CITIZENSHIP IN YOUNG CHILDREN

*Tony Eaude*

## Introduction

This chapter discusses how young children can be helped to build the foundations of global citizenship, in the context of rapid social and cultural change. Though written in the context of England, where many of the trends discussed may be particularly strong, much of the discussion may be familiar and the implications applicable in similar contexts. The chapter argues that, as well as knowledge of varying cultures, values and qualities such as respect and empathy, flexibility and teamwork are essential elements of global citizenship (see Bourn et al., 2016); and that educational priorities should be revised to enable a broader and richer vision, focused on ensuring children's long-term wellbeing. This involves creating and sustaining inclusive learning environments which offer space for children to question and to explore, with more emphasis on children's agency and voice and a broad range of opportunities for play, the humanities and the arts and other activities associated with children's spirituality.

By young children, I mean, broadly, up to about 11 years old. Where appropriate, I try to highlight if the needs of younger and older children within this age group differ. Where I refer to primary schools, this equates with elementary schools in other systems.

The argument is not based directly on empirical research, but combines philosophical and practical perspectives, informed by a wide range of scholarly writing. This includes the author's work (Eaude, 2009, 2014, 2016) which discusses these issues in greater depth, especially the 2009 article.

The chapter's structure involves, first, discussions of the social, cultural and educational contexts, highlighting the implications for young children and those who educate them. This is followed by considerations of what global citizenship involves, children's wellbeing, children's spirituality and relevant psychological and neuroscientific research. The penultimate section indicates the implications for teachers of young children, with the conclusion summarising the argument.

## The social and cultural context

While this section tries to describe accurately social and cultural change and the implications for young children, a cautionary note is necessary. There have been both benefits and disadvantages of the changes described, though these remain matters of considerable debate. At times of rapid change, it is easy for older people to focus on problems. Therefore, this section may underplay some of the benefits of, and opportunities presented by, globalisation.

Among significant social and cultural changes in recent decades which the Cambridge Primary Review (Alexander, 2010, pp. 53–55) highlights are:

- changing patterns in the immediate and extended family and communities;
- a much improved level of physical health, though greater concern about mental health;
- a higher level of disposable income and possessions for most but not all; and
- a rapid change in types, and availability, of technology.

Thus, far fewer children live with both birth parents or close to their extended family, with greater geographical mobility because of factors such as higher rates of family breakdown, different patterns of adult relationships and migration between and within countries. Most communities, not only in cities but in previously homogeneous areas, exhibit greater ethnic, cultural, linguistic and religious diversity than even 20, let alone 50 years ago. In most industrialised countries, there has been a significant decline in religious affiliation and attendance at places of worship so that children's participation in a faith community has become less common, but, for a substantial minority, religious affiliation remains a significant marker, and maker, of identity and framework for spirituality (Astley et al., 2007). The United States may be the most prominent exception, where religious affiliation remains strong, although this has been in decline among young people there (see Smith & Denton, 2005). The structures, both religious and otherwise, which previously helped to provide a sense of belonging and identity are more fragile, in a context where many children – and adults – have multiple, and sometimes confused, identities. However, in many parts of the world, religion remains a major source of identity and spirituality for many people, and sometimes of conflict (see Astley et al., 2007). (See Eaude, 2016, Chapter 3 for a longer discussion of these issues.)

Most children in relatively rich countries are physically healthier as a result of improved health care, living conditions and nutrition, despite recent concerns about obesity, attributed partly to a more sedentary lifestyle. However, serious concerns about children's mental health, happiness and wellbeing, associated with the pressures and expectations of the society in which children grow up have been expressed (Palmer, 2006; UNICEF, 2007). While this is often a result of socio-economic deprivation, children from affluent backgrounds increasingly experience mental health difficulties in adolescence (see Claxton, 2008, pp. 2–5; Luther & Latendresse, 2005).

Most children have access to, and take for granted, a wider range of home comforts and possessions than was common 50 years ago. While many children grow up in relative security, a minority do not, leading difficult or chaotic lives, often as a result of factors such as poverty, domestic violence, neglect, and substance misuse (see Alexander, 2010, pp. 58–59).

As a result of these changes, there is greater inequality (see Dorling, 2015) with many children experiencing insecurity and confusion, though the reasons for this vary, and for significant numbers of children:

- their communities are more diverse and fragmented;
- in their home life several different factors affect their wellbeing adversely; and
- there is little structure and routine in their lives.

Computers, mobile phones and other forms of technology provide a level of access to information, music and games for most children. Even if the reliability of the information and the suitability of the entertainment were open to question, such activities occupy a significant place in young children's lives, where many spend several hours a day in front of a screen, usually on their own. (Childwise, 2015). The benefits and disadvantages of social media are hard to assess. For instance, while they enable children to communicate rapidly, they also lead to a kind of 'distant connectedness' but encourage immediate action, which can result in thoughtless, hurtful responses often becoming a means for bullying (de Souza & McLean, 2012). Such behaviour may result in some kinds of disconnectedness, linked to the shadow side of spirituality (de Souza, 2016).

There are strong social and cultural pressures towards individualism and narcissism, with the search for identity and belonging often difficult in the absence of suitable structures outside schools to support this. Accompanying these trends has been a tendency for adults to emphasise children's vulnerability and need for protection. Childhood has become increasingly scholarised (Mayall, 2010) so that children have fewer opportunities for unsupervised play and activity. The influence of the media and of sophisticated advertising, much of it targeted at young children, has helped to foster a view of success and happiness resulting from possessions, looks and celebrity. Children are encouraged from a young age to be, and see themselves as, consumers with an identity dependent on what one owns and how one looks and these messages are constantly reinforced by advertising, the media and, in particular, the urge to belong within their own peer group (see Hyde's emphasis (2008) on material pursuit as one inhibitor of children's spirituality). For example, having the 'right' brand of shoes or mobile phone has come increasingly to matter and many girls, especially in middle childhood, dress in ways associated with being sexually attractive (see Mercer, 2006).

## The educational context

While the situation varies between different educational systems, there has been an increased emphasis on what Stephen Ball (2003) describes as performativity –

concentrating on what can be measured and tested with a narrow focus, especially in reading, writing and computation, backed up by a high-stakes accountability regime. Lessons are often taught at great pace to ensure coverage of the curriculum. The curriculum for children from the age of 5 upwards has been increasingly conceptualised, and often taught, in separate subjects, with discrete programmes designed to address perceived problems.

Although legislation in England places a strong emphasis on spiritual, moral, social and cultural development, and a broad and balanced curriculum, often primary schools focus their time and energy on high attainment in tests because children are tested frequently from a young age. The pressure for success is strong, especially in affluent families, leading to growing concerns about over-testing and possible implications for children's mental health. (see Claxton, 2008).

Children have little control, or agency, over their schooling. While there have been initiatives, in England and elsewhere, to involve children in decision-making, this is usually about relatively minor issues, with little account being taken of children's voice on major issues such as the curriculum (Robinson, 2014).

One less obvious trend is an emphasis on what young children will become, focused on skills in literacy and numeracy and employability, rather than who they are. Education is seen as a frantic race to keep up, a competition, rather than children being able to enjoy the relative calm of middle childhood, before the turbulence of adolescence. Underlying all these trends is a fear of falling behind, whether at an individual, school or system level (see Ball, 2003 for an analysis and Lucas and Claxton, 2010, for an alternative view).

These trends have been increasingly strong in schools for children from the age of about 5 upwards. Accompanying them has been the marginalisation of the humanities and the arts, as in many other countries, with both these disciplines having significant potential to enhance spiritual wellbeing. In early years settings, the trends have been resisted to some extent, but the pressure to teach very young children more formally, with less opportunity for play, has been strong. Recognising these pressures, and worries about children being unhappy and behaving inappropriately, many schools have tried to develop social skills and emotional wellbeing through circle time and programmes such as Social and Emotional Aspects of Learning (SEAL) and Roots of Empathy.[1] While many teachers, parents/carers and children have welcomed these, Ecclestone and Hayes (2009) argue that they lead to brittleness and a sense of vulnerability created by an overemphasis on feelings and by the narcissism which accompanies the belief that one's own happiness is what matters most. This may be an unintended consequence, but it accords with the widespread perception that many young people are focused on themselves and lack resilience.

Ball (2003) suggests that a policy climate based on prescription and performativity means that there is little discussion of aims, since these are largely predetermined by test scores in literacy and numeracy. More worryingly, Ball (2003) argues that the 'terror of performativity' requires teachers to organise themselves in response to externally-imposed targets, indicators and evaluations and, in doing so, they set aside personal beliefs and commitments. In the race for high attainment in tests, the needs and wellbeing of the whole child are easily overlooked.

## Global citizenship

The United Nations Convention on the Rights of the Child (UNCRC), adopted in 1989, states, in Article 17, that 'children have the right to get information that is important to their health and well-being'. The UNCRC gives a greater emphasis than previous similar documents on participation, in addition to protection and provision rights (Wall, 2010, pp. 121–125). This highlights the importance of children's voices, in that 'when adults are making decisions that affect children, children have the right to say what they think should happen and have their opinions taken into account' (UNCRC, Article 12). However, Article 12 states that this should not interfere with parents' rights and responsibilities to express their views on matters affecting their children; that the level of a child's participation in decisions must be appropriate to the child's level of maturity; and that children's ability to form and express their opinions develops with age. So, while adults need to guide and support children, they also need to listen to them.

Frances Hunt (2012) in discussing 'global learning' in English primary schools highlights that:

- schools include it into subject knowledge and curriculum content – particularly in subject areas such as Geography, Personal, Social and Health Education (PSHE) and Citizenship;
- schools tend to promote a 'soft', non-threatening global learning, tending to avoid areas perceived to be too complex or difficult (for either or both pupils and teachers), including learning about conflict and the political, economic and social contexts of people in which people live and social justice;
- for most children, active engagement in global learning seems to involve interactions with link-schools overseas, fundraising activities and making small scale lifestyle changes; and
- as children progress through primary school the volume of global learning activities increases.

Such an approach is focused mainly on knowledge about the world and on relatively uncontroversial areas. In discussing education in a world characterised by change and diversity, Hargreaves (2003) calls for more emphasis, for children and teachers, on qualities such as flexibility and teamwork, resilience and empathy. Such a view is supported by Claxton and Carr (2004, p. 87) who write that children from a young age must be 'ready, willing and able to engage profitably with learning', emphasising that they do not just need to learn knowledge and skills, but how and when to apply them, and to be engaged and motivated to learn.

Douglas Bourn (2008) emphasises that for young people to make sense of their identity and develop a sense of belonging, both of which are aspects of children's spirituality (de Souza, 2016), establishing the relationship between global processes and local experiences is critical. One major aspect of educating young children is to enrich their cultural experience and so to extend their cultural horizons. By this, I do not mean only enabling a wider experience of art, music and drama, by hearing different types of music or visiting theatres, museums and places of worship; but helping children, especially, but not only, those from disadvantaged backgrounds, to break free from a culture of low aspirations and expectations. In the context of a world of constant change, children from a young age need to:

- know about, experience and welcome cultural diversity, exploring both similarity and difference – and, where appropriate, question and challenge cultural norms, including their own, which may prove controversial; and
- have opportunities and encouragement to create what Putnam (2000) calls bonding and bridging capital, the former refers to what binds those who are similar and the latter, which is much harder, to what leads to a greater understanding of those who are different.

## Children's wellbeing

Concerns about children's happiness, wellbeing and mental health are prevalent in many industrialised countries, though these pale when compared with countries ravaged by war or the lack of basic necessities. As Abraham Maslow's hierarchy of needs (1998) indicates, wellbeing must involve basic physical and psychological needs being met before other needs or wishes are considered.

Most young children want to be happy and have fun. They enjoy play and activities such as songs, drawing and construction. Most adults say that their children's happiness is a priority. Nel Noddings (2003) argues that happiness should be a major aim of education, as children learn best when they are happy, though they also need and enjoy appropriate challenges. However, children often equate happiness with fun – activities which offer immediate and undemanding enjoyment – and they receive strong messages that happiness can be achieved, relatively quickly, by means of possessions, consumption and looks. Moreover, there is a long tradition in philosophy that the search for happiness, paradoxically, makes it harder to achieve; and that happiness usually comes as a by-product, for instance through challenges overcome or service to other people. (Eaude, 2016, pp. 37–39).

As discussed in Eaude (2009), the idea of achieving happiness as one of the chief motivations for action goes back to the ancient Greeks, for whom the exercise of virtue was fundamentally linked to happiness. One of Aristotle's conceptions of a life truly worth living was that it leads to *eudaimonia*, usually translated as happiness. However, as Anthony Grayling (2001, pp. 72–73) points out, this loses the original 'strong, active connotation of *eudaimonia* as well-doing and wellbeing, as living flourishingly'. This is closely associated with conducting oneself appropriately. The Greeks emphasised that *eudaimonia* should be independent of health, wealth or the ups and downs of everyday life; seeing this as a sustained, rather than episodic, state, distinguishing between immediate and long-term happiness. The former is more like gratification, or feeling good, which may result from a range of stimuli, possibly not linked to, or even militating against, longer-term wellbeing.

I suggest that a view of wellbeing based on *eudaimonia* where children flourish and thrive rather than search for, and expect, instant gratification is more appropriate than one based on happiness as such. As argued in Eaude (2016, especially Chapter 7), the exact qualities deemed necessary may vary between cultures, but interactive, relational qualities such as empathy and thoughtfulness are an essential basis for moral education. A virtue ethics approach (see Eaude, 2016) emphasises qualities such as acting kindly and thoughtfully towards others with these learned primarily through enacting them, so that, for instance, one learns to be generous by being generous. This accords with Nussbaum's view (2010) and Noddings' (2013) work on what she calls the ethic of care, where children – and adults – need not just care *about* others, but more actively care *for* others. Both, but especially the latter, are particularly important in children who otherwise have not been, or are, not well cared for, and who have little experience of caring for others. As a result, they may manifest anti-social rather than empathetic behaviour. For such children, opportunities for play and caring for pets, plants or dolls may help to some degree. To gain further insight as to how *eudaimonia* can be achieved, we now consider children's spirituality.

## Children's spirituality

While exact definitions of what children's spirituality entails are contested, one common feature is an assumption is that there is more to life than the material world. I have argued previously (e.g. Eaude, 2008) for spirituality to be understood as referring to questions which can be explored either within or outside the framework of organised religion; and so must not, in Terence McLaughlin's phrase (see Best, 2014, p. 12), be 'tethered' to organised religion. All children, from a young age, need opportunities to explore existential questions, such as: Who am I?; Where do I fit in?; And why am I here?, associated with the search for meaning, identity and purpose. Such questions inevitably entail difficult and painful issues, not just pleasant and life-enhancing ones. But the search is not just an individual one, re-emphasising the need to belong, in line with Brendan Hyde's (2008) emphasis on meaning and connectedness. Enabling and supporting such a search matters especially for children who find it hard to belong. Thus, they seek a sense of identity through superficial but attractive means such as possessions or being involved in activities or groups which may militate against their longer-term wellbeing.

John Hull writes that 'spirituality exists not inside people, but between them' (1998, p. 66), suggesting that this does not just involve individualistic, interior processes. Qualities such as care and compassion for others are strongly associated with spiritual development, in line with David Hay with Rebecca Nye's (1998) conceptualisation of what they call 'relational consciousness' as central to children's spirituality. They identify four elements of relational consciousness:

- awareness of self;
- awareness of others;
- awareness of the environment; and
- (for some people) awareness of a Transcendent Other.

Thus they recognise how young children often focus initially on themselves and only learn slowly over time how they fit into a 'bigger picture', with an emerging sense of identity and a broader perspective on life.

Hay with Nye (1998) argue that value-sensing (along with awareness- and mystery-sensing) is one of three dimensions of children's spirituality. Hull (1996, 1998) sees spirituality as inevitably value-laden, with it making little sense to talk of spirituality, *per se*, rather than the spirituality of a particular group or society. Consumerist societies represent a form of spirituality, albeit in his view a distorted one. Hull relates the dominant values of modern, Western society, based on money and consumption, to an individualistic, privatised – and consequently depoliticised – view of spirituality. Discussing the curriculum, he writes:

> we need to ask of each subject whether it is exploring its potential to inspire people to live in solidarity with others, rather than offering them a spirituality which will live only too easily with the selfish and individualizing values of the money culture.
>
> (1998, p. 66)

This resonates with Hyde's (2008) identification of two factors which inhibit children's spirituality, namely material pursuit and trivialisation. As a result, one major task of educators is to encourage children to explore values and beliefs, both their own and other people's, and to challenge many current assumptions about the nature of success and wellbeing.

While Religious Education (RE), the humanities and the arts may offer particularly fertile opportunities to explore such questions, chances occur, and can be created, across the whole curriculum. In Eaude (2014), I used the term 'hospitable space' to describe the sort of environment which encourages and enables this. Such space is nurturing, welcoming and not over-competitive, offering opportunities for children to play, to investigate, to question, to reflect and to be heard; and to be quiet, or silent, as well as active; and to participate in a broad range of experiences including that of nature and co-operating with a range of other children.

## Implications of psychological and neuro-educational research

Jerome Bruner (1996) emphasises that from the very beginning children are active meaning-makers, highlighting the centrality of a sense of agency. Carol Dweck (2000) emphasises what she calls a growth mindset in building resilience. A growth mindset entails the belief that when one fails this is not because of inherent qualities which cannot be changed, but that success can be achieved by trying again with greater experience, more support or a different approach, helping to explain why many students' self-esteem and resilience is fragile, despite academic success. Without a sense of agency, and a belief in their ability to overcome challenges, children learn to be vulnerable.

Margaret Donaldson (1992) highlights how relationships, and the context in which young children operate, affect what they are able to do, bringing into question many of Piaget's assumptions about a hierarchy of stages. The importance of relationships which are caring but challenging, when appropriate, in helping to shape children's identities is hard to overstate. As Phyllida Salmon (1995, p. 63) suggests, 'identity . . . is forged out of interaction with others. Who we are is inextricably bound up with who we are known to be.'

Learning involves not only having experiences but re-presenting experience, through one or more modes: enactive; iconic; and symbolic including language (see Bruner, 2006, volume 1, p. 69). For young children, the enactive and iconic modes are especially important, with opportunities to learn actively and in different modes, rather than primarily through listening.

Play helps young children to explore their own understanding, to make meaning and to create a secure sense of identity (Goodliff, 2016). Play is not just an activity, and one which children should abandon as they grow older. It is more like a process, closely linked to imagination and playfulness, which helps one to understand oneself and other people, without the anxiety that often accompanies real interactions. In Donald Winnicott's words (1980, p. 63) 'it is in playing and only in playing that the individual child or adult is able to be creative and to use the whole personality. It is only in being creative that the individual discovers the self.'

In considering what can be learned from research about the brain, one must recognise that 'while neuroscience can provide valuable insights into learning, it is important to recognize its limitations. Educators should be cautious when transferring results from controlled laboratory settings to the complex classroom.' (OECD, 2007, p. 148). As Hall (2005, p. 2) suggests, 'it is a very long journey from a discovery about the physiology or organisation of the brain to a practical application in a classroom'.

Therefore, one should be tentative, and avoid simplistic views claiming to be based on neuroscience, but lessons from neuro-educational research (see TLRP, 2007 for a brief summary) which relate directly to children's global citizenship, wellbeing and spirituality include:

- emotion and cognition are closely linked, but emotion affects young children very strongly;
- much learning takes place without words, for instance by modelling;
- multiple ways of representing experience help to commit these to long-term memory;

- learning important aspects of music and foreign languages is easier before adolescence;
- physical activity leads to the release of chemicals such as endorphins, resulting in a sense of wellbeing;
- while learning must involve some stress, intense and/or constant stress, such as that linked to anxiety, affects brain function adversely.

## Implications for teachers

Before considering what teachers can do, one should recognise that they cannot stop children experiencing poverty, violence and neglect. However, they can help by providing an inclusive, caring environment where children have a sense of belonging, are protected and equipped to deal with difficulties. Rather than adults imposing their views, children need chances to participate, explore and discuss, exercising agency from an early age. Teachers should expect that children will do so rather than being over-protected or just told what to believe or do. For instance, children should learn to keep themselves safe and to be respectful when communicating through the Internet, though young children, especially, may need regular guidance and support.

The foundations of global citizenship have been described not only in terms of knowledge, but of qualities and the disposition to manifest these throughout children's lives. Building these implies an emphasis on embedding the qualities such as respect, empathy, teamwork and adaptability needed for living in a diverse society. Such qualities can, and should, be learned from a young age, mainly through example and enactment, rather than through direct instruction. For instance, teamwork and adaptability may be developed by working in teams and coping with unexpected situations, with support where necessary. Opportunities to exercise such qualities must be regular to make them habitual and to build up the motivation and disposition to manifest them. Moreover, education for global citizenship should involve children questioning many of the values they witness around them. Rowley et al. (2007) suggest that stereotypes about others are already embedded by 9 or 10 years. So, attempts to challenge stereotypes and promote respectful attitudes towards those who are different are particularly important by this age. The interlinked nature of emotion and cognition suggests that this requires not only factual information but a range of experiences to help children understand the world from perspectives other than their own.

Such an analysis calls for a greater emphasis on humanities, which, as Martha Nussbaum (2010) argues, are an essential basis for empathy and the foundation of democracy. The humanities should be understood not just in the sense of history, geography and RE but activities and experiences such as play, drama and literature which help in understanding oneself and other people. For instance, in RE, children must not only learn *about* the beliefs and practices and the centrality of religion in many people's lives, but learn *from* religion, to gain greater insight into their own and other people's beliefs and identities (Grimmitt, 2000). Having some knowledge of languages other than their own is likely to enable children to have a greater understanding of, and empathy for, those from different cultures.

However, to understand education for global citizenship only in terms of the formal curriculum is, in many respects, to miss the point. Young children need opportunities to play and to explore and not be introduced to formal instruction too soon, so that their lives are not prematurely 'scholarised'. Given the accessibility of information, through technology, the ability to assess critically the reliability of information becomes particularly important. Moreover, a greater emphasis is needed on how children and teachers act and interact, across the whole of life, and on creating throughout school life a nurturing and hospitable environment.

## Conclusion

This chapter has argued that preparing young children for a world of change and diversity requires a significant re-thinking of the aims of education and of much current practice; or taking existing aims more seriously and basing provision on a broader, more humane and less competitive vision. The focus has been on schools, but many of the implications apply in other contexts. Maybe, we should aim more explicitly for children not only to be successful and happy but also to be kind and thoughtful. While knowledge about others is necessary for global citizenship, it is not sufficient. In particular, qualities like empathy and compassion, associated with spirituality, and flexibility and resilience, are vital. These can, and should, be learned from a young age, mainly through trusting relationships, example and active experience, rather than instruction. Children should be enabled and encouraged to be questioning and imaginative in a hospitable and inclusive, but challenging, environment where diversity of language, ethnicity, religion and background is not just tolerated but welcomed, so that all children have a sense of belonging, creating bridging as well as bonding capital. Such factors are major sources of children's wellbeing, identity and spirituality in a diverse world.

For children to create a secure sense of identity requires a recognition that this does not rely on superficially attractive aspects, such as possessions. Such a message runs counter to the search for happiness in the sense of immediate gratification, as often encouraged in the powerful messages from advertising and the media.

Children from a young age must be encouraged to ask questions and to explore their own, and others', values and beliefs and to experience and welcome diversity. They need opportunities to be active and to be quiet, or silent, if they are to thrive and have a long-term sense of wellbeing, as captured by the idea of *eudaimonia*. This calls for more emphasis on a broad and balanced range of opportunities and experiences, especially in terms of play, the humanities and the arts. More generally, such an approach involves adults recognising that much of what matters in the long term is not measurable; and that attempting to measure everything threatens to skew educational priorities and to affect young children adversely. If children are to be, and become, confident and compassionate global citizens, capable of adapting to a world of change, a move away from the current obsession with what can be measured is not just desirable, but a necessity.

## Note

1   See http://rootsofempathy.org/

## References

Alexander, R. (ed.). (2010). *Children, their world, their education – final report and recommendations of the Cambridge Primary Review*. Abingdon: Routledge.

Astley, J., Francis, L. J., & Robbins, M. (2007). *Peace or violence: The ends of religion and education?* Cardiff: University of Wales Press.

Ball, S. J. (2003). The teacher's soul and the terrors of performativity. *Journal of Education Policy, 18*(2), 215–228.

Best, R. (2014). Spirituality, faith and education: Some reflections from a UK perspective. In J. Watson, M. de Souza, & A. Trousdale (eds), *Global perspectives on spirituality and education* (pp. 5–20). New York: Routledge.

Bourn, D. (2008). Young people, identity and living in a global society. *Policy & Practice: A Development Education Review*, 7, Autumn, 48–61.

Bourn, D., Hunt, F., Blum, N., & Lawson, H. (2016). *Primary education for global learning and sustainability – A report for the cambridge primary review trust*. Cambridge: CPRT.

Bruner, J. S. (1996). *The culture of education*. Cambridge, MA: Harvard University Press.

Bruner, J. S. (2006). *In search of pedagogy*. Abingdon: Routledge.

Childwise. (2015). *Connected Kids: How the internet affects children's lives now and into the future*. Retrieved from http://childwise.co.uk/special.html (Accessed 31 October 2016).

Claxton, G. (2008). *What's the point of school? Rediscovering the heart of education*. Oxford: Oneworld Publications.

Claxton, G., & Carr, M. (2004). A framework for teaching learning: The dynamics of disposition. *Early Years, 24*(1), 87–97.

de Souza, M. (2016). *Spirituality in education in a global pluralized world*. Abingdon: Routledge.

de Souza, M., & McLean, K. (2012). Bullying and violence: Changing an act of disconnectedness into an act of kindness. *Pastoral Care in Education, 30*(2), 165–180.

Donaldson, M. (1992). *Human minds – an exploration*. London: Allen Lane.

Dorling, D. (2015). *Inequality and the 1%*. London: Verso.

Dweck, C. S. (2000). *Self theories: Their role in motivation, personality and development*. Philadelphia: Psychology Press.

Eaude, T. (2008). *Children's spiritual, moral, social and cultural development – Primary and early years*. Exeter: Learning Matters.

Eaude, T. (2009). Happiness, emotional well-being and mental health – what has children's spirituality to offer? *International Journal of Children's Spirituality, 14*(3), 185–196.

Eaude, T. (2014). Creating hospitable space to nurture children's spirituality: Possibilities and dilemmas associated with power. *International Journal of Children's Spirituality, 19*(3–4), 236–248.

Eaude, T. (2016). *New perspectives on young children's moral education – Developing character through a virtue ethics approach*. London: Bloomsbury.

Ecclestone, K., & Hayes, D. (2009). *The dangerous rise of therapeutic education*. London: Routledge.

Goodliff, G. (2016). Spirituality and early childhood education and care. In M. de Souza, J. Bone & J. Watson (eds), *Spirituality across disciplines: Research and practice* (pp. 67–80). Springer: springerpub.com.

Grayling, A. C. (2001). *The meaning of things*. London: Weidenfeld & Nicholson.

Grimmitt, M. (ed.). (2000). *Pedagogies of religious education: Case studies in the research and development of good pedagogic practice in RE.* Great Wakering: McCrimmons.

Hall, J. (2005). *Neuroscience and education: What can brain science contribute to teaching and learning?* Retrieved from www.scre.ac.uk/spotlight Research report 121/2 (Accessed 31 October 2016)

Hargreaves, A. (2003). *Teaching in the knowledge society – Education in the age of insecurity.* Maidenhead: Open University Press.

Hay, D., with Nye, R. (1998). *The spirit of the child.* London: Fount.

Hull, J. (1996). The ambiguity of spiritual values. In J. M. Halstead & M. J. Taylor (eds), *Values in education and education in values* (pp. 33–44). London: Falmer.

Hull, J. (1998). *Utopian whispers–Moral, religious and spiritual values in schools.* Norwich: Religious and Moral Education Press.

Hunt, F. (2012). *Global learning in primary schools in England: Practices and impacts.* London: Development Education Research Centre, Institute of Education.

Hyde, B. (2008). *Children and spirituality: Searching for meaning and connectedness.* London: Jessica Kingsley.

Lucas, B., & Claxton, G. (2010). *New kinds of smart: How the science of learnable intelligence is changing education.* Maidenhead, UK: Open University Press.

Luther, S. S., & Latendresse, S. J. (2005). *Children of the affluent: Challenges to well-being.* Retrieved from https://ncbi.nlm.nih.gov/pmc/articles/PMC1948879/ (Accessed 31 October 2016)

Maslow, A. (1998). *Toward a psychology of being.* New York: Wiley.

Mayall, B. (2010). Children's lives outside school and their educational impact. In R. Alexander (ed.), *The Cambridge Primary Review Research Surveys* (pp. 49–82). Abingdon: Routledge.

Mercer, J. A. (2006). Capitalizing on children's spirituality: Parental anxiety, children as consumers, and the marketing of spirituality. *International Journal of Children's Spirituality*, *11*(1), 23–34.

Noddings, N. (2003). *Happiness and education.* Cambridge: Cambridge University Press.

Noddings, N. (2013). *Caring – A relational approach to ethics and moral education.* Berkeley: University of California Press.

Nussbaum, M. (2010). *Not for profit: Why democracy needs the humanities.* Princeton: Princeton University Press.

OECD (Organisation for Economic Co-operation and Development) (2007). *Understanding the brain: The birth of a learning science.* OECD Publishing. Retrieved from http://dx.doi.org/10.1787/9789264029132-en (Accessed 31 October 2016)

Palmer, S. (2006). *Toxic childhood.* London: Orion Books.

Putnam, R. D. (2000). *Bowling alone: The collapse and revival of American community.* New York: Simon & Schuster.

Robinson, C. (2014). *Children, their voices and their experiences of school: What does the evidence tell us?* Retrieved from http://cprtrust.org.uk/research/childrens-voice/ (Accessed 31 October 2016)

Rowley, S. J., Kurtz-Costes, B., Mistry, R., & Feagans, L. (2007). Social status as a predictor of race and gender stereotypes in late childhood and early adolescence. *Social Development*, *16*(1), 150–168.

Salmon, P. (1995). *Psychology in the classroom – Reconstructing teachers and learners.* London: Cassell.

Smith, C., & Denton, M. L. (2005). *Soul searching: The religious and spiritual lives of American teenagers.* Oxford: Oxford University Press.

TLRP (2007). *Neuroscience and education: Issues and opportunities.* London: TLRP. Retrieved from http://tlrp.org/pub/commentaries.html (Accessed 31 October 2016)

United Nations Convention on the Rights of the Child (UNCRC) Retrieved from www.unicef.org/crc/files/Rights_overview.pdf (Accessed 31 October 2016)

UNICEF (2007). *Child poverty in perspective: An overview of child well-being in rich countries: A comparative assessment of the lives and well-being of children and adolescents in economically advanced nations.* Florence. Unicef Innocenti Centre (Innocenti Report Card 7). Retrieved from http://unicefirc.org/publications/pdf/rc7_eng.pdf (Accessed 31 October 2016)

Wall, J. (2010). *Ethics in light of childhood.* Washington, DC: Georgetown University Press.

Winnicott, D. (1980). *Playing and reality.* Harmondsworth, UK: Penguin.

# 6

# WORLDVIEW EDUCATION AS A VIABLE PERSPECTIVE FOR EDUCATING GLOBAL CITIZENS

*Dzintra Iliško*

## Welcoming diversity: defining the context

There is hardly a country in Europe and possibly, the world where the population is composed of just one ethnic or religious group. Latvia is not an exception. Latvia is inhabited by people with diverse ethnic backgrounds who engage and encounter one another on a daily basis. The context in which Latvian teachers work today is contextualised by plural worldviews as there is a high number of mixed marriages among people of diverse ethnic and religious backgrounds. According to the statistical data provided by the Justice Ministry, the largest religious groups in Latvia are Roman Catholics (22.7 per cent), Lutherans (19.7 per cent) and Orthodox Christians (16.8 per cent). The largest religious minorities include Baptists, Pentecostals and other evangelical Protestant groups. The Council of Jewish Communities estimates there are 10,000 Jews living in Latvia. Other small religious groups include Muslims, Jehovah's Witnesses, Methodists, Hare Krishna's and Buddhists (International Religious Freedom Report, 2012, p. 1).

The constitution of Latvia protects religious freedom. There is no state religion. The law allows the representatives of Catholic, Evangelical Lutheran, Orthodox Christian, Old Believer, Baptist, Methodist, Adventist and Jewish groups to teach religion in public schools to students who choose to take such classes. The government provides funds for these classes (International Religious Freedom Report, 2012). These classes are carried out on a confessional basis and, therefore, they do not address the spiritual needs of contemporary students who have no religious background at all. Consequently, teaching about religious and spiritual worldviews requires a more inclusive approach in contemporary classrooms.

The issues of intolerance has attracted much attention given the refugee crises in Europe and elsewhere. However, the survey carried out by the Baltic Social Sciences Institute, indicated that the people of Latvia are less tolerant of people with deviant social behaviour (for instance, alcoholics, drug addicts, people with a criminal past) rather than those who are different due to race, ethnicity and religious affiliation. One exception is the level of prejudice towards Gypsies (Roma), as 27.2 per cent of the respondents would not like to have them as neighbours (Baltic Social Sciences Institute, 2003).

The situation in Latvia is witness to a variety of religious expressions and belongings but people do not fit into well-defined boundaries or distinct labels. Instead, attention may be given to the dynamic processes of interpretation, reinterpretation and reconstruction of religious meanings in ever changing historical and social circumstances (Iliško, 2009, p. 43). There are an increasing number of children who have grown up in mixed interfaith families with two different faith traditions so that their identity is formed by 'several interlocking religious cultures' as they grow up in the 'in-between' spaces of different cultures (Hall, 1996, p. 206). To describe this situation many authors use the term 'bricolage' (Dobbelaere, 1998). to indicate the process of blending institutional and popular forms of religion by an individual. As well, there is reference to the multiple 'religious belongings' of an individual when several traditions coexist without 'subsuming one system into another' and where they communicate with one another as separate units (Schreiter, in Suomala, 2012).

As a rule, individuals tend to seek a spirituality that is authentic for each of them by combining diverse sources of religious and non-institutional sources. This includes a search for the answer to moral dilemmas of what is good and evil, and the existential question about the meaning in one's life. Therefore, their search for religion and spirituality is encased in ontological insecurity.

Latvians have also kept alive pre-Christian forms of religion as some sort or inner resistance. Thus, old mythology, folklore and deities are still alive in peoples' spirituality (Astra, 2008). The sanctity of and experiences of solitude in nature, worshipping sacred objects like stones and crosses are all a part of pre-Christian rituals that are popular in the Baltic countries (Astra, 2008). Traditional Christianity, where many may have previously experienced an invitation to a full participation in life, is not always appealing for youth anymore.

I concur with Kathryn Tanner that Christian identity is not constituted by sharp borders but rather Christian identity 'always shares cultural forms with its wider host culture and other religions (notably Judaism)' (Tanner, 1997, p. 114). Christian distinctiveness emerges in the processes occurring at the boundary, processes that construct a distinctive identity for Christians 'through the distinctive use of cultural material shared with others' (Tanner, 1997, p. 114). The situation in Latvia today, consisting of multiple religious belongings, may best be described as syncretistic, eclectic and pluralistic and, to be sure, 'there is a messy and fluid process of cross-permeation among different religions' (Chung, 1996, p. 31).

As well, we can recognise that culture and religious identity is 'elusive and fluid, rather than rigid and determining. . . helps us to understand the multiple strategies and shifting positions that one takes up in these different and shifting positions' (Yon, 2000, p. 122). Thus, it promotes understanding of identity construction in relation, and often in opposition, to the constraints imposed by gender, culture and religion. Belonging to a community of faith means that 'part of the cultural identities one brings into collective configuration would be challenged and changed through (the) community process of mediation and negotiation, relation and opposition' (p. 122). Hence, community of faith becomes 'a new community of interest and identification' requiring 'new forms of subjectivity' (p. 122). Religious and cultural identity is not an unchanging essence handed on from one generation to another, but rather, it is a dynamic process through which religious and spiritual meanings are interpreted, reconstructed and changed over time, in light of new and ever changing historical and social circumstances. Further, it is a relational and constant process of negotiating boundaries requiring fluid and complex interpretations and definitions and subject to multiple understandings. Therefore, it is appropriate to use the term 'translocational positionality' (Anthias, 2002) which refers to the complex nature of one's positionality, since each of us is at the interplay of a range of locations and dislocation in relation to gender, ethnicity, national belonging, class, race and religion. It is important, then, that Christians learn to view themselves as just one among the others in a plural society since Christians, Muslims, Jews and other non-religious traditions and worldviews have a right to their own existence. Nevertheless, the older generation which forms the majority, continue to hold perceptions of a stable religious identity and are fearful of the emergence of a fluid and changing religious identity. As well, religious authorities insist that a unified, stable and organisationally defined set of beliefs and practices of certain religious groups is important for students.

## Negotiating a worldview education

In a world of increasing diversity it becomes ever more difficult to speak about 'one worldview' but pluralism has caused a crisis in moral education and a collapse of a single authority. Worldview education is focused on increasing students' personal awareness, assisting them in a meaning-making process and engaging them in critical decision-making about their own and others' values. Worldview education incorporates students' religious affiliation with one religion and also the spiritual and worldview identities that extend beyond a structured religious denomination for both religious and non-religious students (Mayhew et al., 2014). Accordingly, atheists who may be described as individuals with shifting religious and secular identities and people with no religious experience at all (Putnam & Campbell, 2010) can be included. In addition, there are strongly committed Christians who sincerely believe in divine authority and absolute truth. All these groups have a right to make sense of their lives in an increasingly secular and pluralistic society.

Consequently, schools need to pose questions about whether they can be inclusive in their responses to the needs of students who subscribe to different worldviews. For instance, does the school provide a space for exploration of the religious beliefs of students? Or, does it provide a space and a safe environment for the committed Christians to integrate new epistemologies into existing beliefs or to challenge uncritically accepted existing beliefs? Since the traditional Christian paradigm is gradually being replaced by a variety of worldviews – both religious and secular, multiple worldviews and perspectives, worldview education raises the potential for educators to respond to these challenges.

Students' worldviews are shaped by peers, their culture, denominational heritage and their own search for meaning (Kanitz, 2005), and they compete for space and existence. Therefore, education needs 'to reconcile individuals with different value systems and to redirect their conflicting values towards a life in common that would be good for all' (Gray, 2009, p. 25). Accordingly, worldviews may be seen as the individual's theories about the meaning of life. Each individual strives to organise the 'kaleidoscopic flux of impressions' (Whorf, 1956, p. 213) which comprise their perceptions of their world into the concepts and theories that bring significance to their lives. If schools provide opportunities for students to engage with diverse worldviews they will become proficient with different ways of knowing and experiencing (Cooling, 2010). Moreover, if an open dialogue between students from diverse religious and non-religious backgrounds occurs, students will become more aware of the diversity in their midst and grow in a greater understanding of their world (Jackson, 2014). A close and critical examination of their views as well as the sources and foundations upon which those views are based will lead them to learn 'to live together' in a community of diverse individuals, and allow them to develop a more coherent vision based on aspirations grounded in their particular worldview (Valk, 2007).

The perception of Christianity as a worldview has been the most significant development in the Church (Naugle, 2002). However, there has been a gradual shift in academic writings from grand-scale theorising to a more 'decentered, multi-lateral, and postmodern orientation' (Jacobsens, 2005, p. 1). Oppressive narratives are being challenged, and room is being made for the silenced voices of others. The restrictive thinking in terms of one single model has become improbable. To introduce an integrated worldview education would require a hermeneutics of suspicion. Also, it needs to be acknowledged that worldview education may lead to confusion for young people. However, as some scholars have pointed out, there is always a need to tread cautiously due to the danger that a worldview education may lead to 'inadvertently privileging religious students, particularly Christians, in the absence of careful attention to the language and assumptions woven into educational practice' (Fairchild, 2009, p. 7).

## Developing global citizens via worldview education

Global citizenship is not a separate subject in a school's curriculum but, in Latvia, aspects of citizenship are integrated in civic education and other subject areas. A citizenship dimension is also embedded within particular outcomes and competences which aim to encourage students' awareness of their local and national contexts, including respect for oneself and others, and diversity in a wider context. This has relevance for issues of identity, belonging and therefore, spiritual wellbeing since the intentions are to educate responsible citizens who are respectful of others and, also, to create a sustainable global community. Sustainable community is seen not as a destiny but, rather, as a continuous learning path towards a state that is more desirable.

The notion of global citizenship is a relatively new and evolving concept for Latvia and it is being gradually introduced via international projects and networking. Many initiatives to introduce this concept has come from non-governmental organisations and individual educators. Global education initiatives introduced in line with intercultural and sustainable education have mainly focused on developing an awareness of the interconnectedness of issues, active participation and the ideal of a just and sustainable world. Numerous international projects offer students opportunities to, both, develop their personal identities and explore issues related to the interdependence of social, economic, cultural and environmental concerns. Further, global education fosters an appreciation for cultural diversity, a familiarity with rights and responsibilities, and sustainability and global justice. These issues are introduced by the use of co-operative teaching methods aimed to develop critical awareness, thinking and communication in diverse contexts including issues of bias and stereotypes. They also encourage an ability for action in pursuit of a worthy goal towards some greater good which can lead to a purposeful life for each and every individual.

A global citizen is one who appreciates cultural and religious diversity, responds critically to issues which transcend national boundaries, 'expresses empathy for neighbours' and 'promotes a world view of peace, justice and sustainability for all' (Schattle, 2008, p. 77). She adds that a global citizen is one who is aware of the wider world, respects diversity, 'tackle(s) injustice and inequality, and is willing to act to make the world as a more sustainable place' (p. 78). As Martha Nussbaum (2002) emphasizes, global citizens need to engage in critical self-examination as well as an examination of their own traditions, explore their misconceptions and stereotypes of other beliefs and contexts, exercise their imagination in order to see the world through the eyes of others, and develop empathy and a concern for others and the planet as a whole. This will help them to develop their own worldview and to encounter others as 'spiritually literate' (Woolley, 2008, p. 120).

Alfred North Whitehead (1926) offers the argument that in order to come into the 'inter-counter' with the other, one needs to become aware of others' habits, perspectives and religious and spiritual beliefs. Such awareness is necessary to prepare one for life in a complex and pluralistic society. Thus, a classroom and its wider community needs to become an open communicative space that enables students to engage in a transformative experience with the 'other' that will facilitate a shift in the students' frame of reference (Caruana, 2014; Killick, 2012). As Thomson & Taylor (2005) argue, 'global citizenship is about being proactive, (and) living ethically' simultaneously at both, global and local levels, the distant and proximate, (cited in Caruana, 2014, p. 91). A global citizen is the one who appreciates a sense of interconnectedness with others in the wider world, and shares a spiritual sense of the oneness of humanity. The moral and spiritual vision of a global citizen includes wisdom, courage, a stand against injustice, responding critically to issues which transcend national boundaries by the use of imaginative empathy, and promoting sustainability for all. Thus, worldview education involves a multiple perspectives approach where one is encouraged to step out of one's own cultural and religious location and to develop a habit of 'learning to imagine the other' (Arendt, in Richardson, & Abbott, 2009, p. 387).

Worldview education fights fear, discrimination and intolerance and promotes a development of a competency 'to live together'. Pupils gain greater awareness of their local and global environments, and are encouraged to embrace multiple perspectives that go along with the practice of intercultural understanding and global responsibility. The awareness of the worldviews of others contributes to a holistic notion of the world as well as care for local and global communities. This engenders a re-evaluation of stereotypes, engages in a dialogue with other world-views, both, religious and non-religious, and allows an acceptance of alternative means and strategies to accomplish tasks. In the words of Anthias (2002, p. 61), a dialogue means 'going beyond merely seeing the other persons point of view', and entails going beyond one's own point of view so that both parties shift their position, not in coming closer to each other but developing an alternative vision which is transformative.

Dialogue is a means of finding a balance between one's own values and openness to even contradictory values (Ilisko, 2007). In Latvia, instead of fostering a dialogue, there is a widespread tendency to stereotype other religious and cultural communities, usually focusing on their worst features. Sometimes it becomes problematic for representatives of one religion to believe that representatives of other religions can be authentic, moral and have integrity. A genuine dialogue engaging the worldviews of other Christians and non-Christians can, potentially, correct, deepen and strengthen a student's own commitment and worldview. The notion of dialogue involves being oriented towards the other (Iliško, 2007). By being in a dialogue with the other, one begins to experience a sense of connected-ness with others who are different and their belief systems which may result in a growing conviction that all people are God's creation. This will foster empathy, compassion and appreciation of other worldviews and encourage a sense of global belonging. It may also include the acceptance of cultural diversity and learning how to act in contextual situations. Therefore, fieldwork to sacred places, such as shrines, can foster a deeper understanding of otherness and can lead individuals to develop a practical wisdom or '*phronesesis*' in striving for general wellbeing and for socially and environmentally sustainable communities. Worldview education, thus, can play a role in developing multiple perspectives about the world in its integrative and participative character.

Several other researchers (Richardson & Abbott, 2009) also support the argu-ment that worldview education involves a transformative aspect aimed at developing 'a new sense of word-mindedness' and empowering students to become agents in tackling the issues that impact the global community (p. 386). In general, they agree that students will develop a sense of agency in critically examining their own perspective or worldviews and will formulate an informed response to contemporary issues. Finally, interdependence which involves exploring issues in the local community, national or international organisations, should be seen as an integral part of worldview education. This can be promoted by engaging students in short- and long-term projects that link students to the world beyond the classroom.

## Changing perspective on students as holistic human beings

Within a worldview perspective, students should be seen as holistic human beings with religious, spiritual, physical, ethical, emotional and physiological aspects (modalities). This view of students should be unfolded systematically in the educational process by providing a pedagogically sound approach. Thus, students will crystallise a worldview for themselves since they are not confined to isolated facts of knowledge. Instead, their spiritual wellbeing will be nurtured as they are encouraged to live their lives as meaningful and integrated whole people (Potgieter and van der Walt, 2014.

A holistic vision of RE also goes beyond formation and indoctrination into one particular religion or religious worldview. It calls upon engagement in a dialogue across diverse traditions. It requires adopting contextual approaches that take into account students' worldviews, their understandings of religion, their hopes, fears, anxieties and aspirations that may run counter to their family beliefs with a possibility of causing family conflict.

It is important to consider that abolishing the teaching of religions in public schools may run the risk of educating students into only one worldview, namely, secularism, thereby making them ignorant of the existence of other worldviews. Secularism can be defined as a kind of 'closed worldview' which does have a role of a 'religion' (Cox, 1965, p. 18) because it has the power to erode particular religious traditions. In a society based on the ideals of equality and justice, every person has a right of his/her own way and value system that should be respected (Schneller, 2011). This will help to reduce tensions among religions and will facilitate building a just society.

Some scholars (Searle, 2014) do provide a critique of over-reliance on a 'worldview' that can lead to a reductive representation of the Christian faith as a system of truth claims rather than a comprehensive and holistic mode of being in the world. They argue that worldview education needs to involve students in a formation of hopes and passions, and inspire them to take a stance against injustice, thereby leading them to a transformed life. Therefore, worldview education needs to remain true to its holistic nature and take seriously the role of dreams and visions as 'basic realities governing human volition' (MacQuarrie, 1982, p. 3). A holistic and integral concept of worldview education can be implemented by focusing on those practices that 'shape the imaginative core of our being in the world' (Smith, 2013). Finally, worldview education needs to take into account the personal experience of the learner which was advocated by John Dewey (1908) who criticised confessional religious education which, he felt, acted as an impediment to the moral development of a child.

## Conclusion

This chapter has focused on the significance and relevance of a worldview education for pluralist societies in the contemporary world. While it focused on the Latvian context, the issues discussed have implications for education across the globe. It identified the gradual shift that has been taking place from institutional and rationally bound religion to an increasingly individualised, non-institutional religious and spiritual expression. Since indoctrination may limit the students in making choices, it needs to be avoided in any educational setting, including a classroom of individuals belonging to the same religious group. Instead, religious and spiritual education should help learners to recognise, understand and express their personal choices and values as well as the foundations upon which they are based. There is also a need to engage students in a critical dialogue with the participants from other religious or non-religious groups so as to develop their awareness and understanding of their own and different religious and spiritual commitment. In an increasingly diverse society, a 'one worldview' educational model becomes problematic. The Christian paradigm needs to give way to an emerging variety of traditions and worldviews (Iliško, 2016).

It is important to recognise that no single subject can teach students how to interact with individuals from different cultures and religions. Heterogeneous environments in the classroom will not automatically teach students how to communicate across differences. There needs to be a space for 'an open and respectful exchange of views between individuals and groups from different ethnic, cultural, religious and linguistic backgrounds based on mutual understanding and respect' (CE, 2008, 10–11). It is within such spaces that the spiritual wellbeing of the individual and community may be nurtured.

As outlined earlier, a worldview education model may be considered a viable educational approach in public schools since it welcomes different views and visions of life among the students. The demise of traditional moral authorities suggests that the approaches towards teaching religion in public schools need to be renewed. Worldview education offers a promising alternative since its essence is in engaging the students with complex and interdependent systems so as to investigate their implications for human life. Further, worldview education will foster resilient thinkers who may develop openness to 'in-between spaces', and resist one-sidedness in favour of the constant renegotiation of one's Self in the light of 'other' (Gadamer, 2004). Such practices could lead to deeper self-understanding and the formation of new horizons (Wright & Ashwin, 2011). This would enable schools to provide greater opportunities to develop students as resilient thinkers by helping them reach new levels of personal development.

Additionally, acknowledging a plurality of worldviews may enrich students' understanding and will prevent the indoctrination of one particular view. This does not mean that public schools will become secularist schools but, rather, they should be 'inclusive schools' (Jackson, 2004, p. 167). Inclusivity of worldviews will indicate the relevance of plurality and will teach students the dignity of every human being, care for others, justice, equality and care for the environment. These issues are not restricted to secular culture but are relevant for all religions (Valk, 2007). Worldview education, therefore, will help students to come to a greater understanding of themselves in the world.

Finally, schools need to become welcoming places for all students regardless of their faith or non-faith positions. This would require schools to undertake strategic re-visioning in building inclusive communities which should be reflected as a priority in the school's mission, vision, core values, curriculum and practices. A whole school policy needs to consider a worldview education as a viable perspective in promoting equality and valuing diversity. Indeed, educating students about various worldviews will help the students to develop a moral vision that affirms every human's dignity, equality and justice among people. As well, this will promote spiritual wellbeing for individuals and their communities, and will promote self-knowledge among students, deepen their own beliefs, and embrace the diversity they encounter in the reality of their everyday.

## References

Anthias, F. (2002). Beyond feminism and multiculturalism: Locating difference and politics of location. *Women's Studies International Forum, 25*(3), 275–286.

Astra, L. (2008). The changing of Lithuanian identity in global modernity. *Limes, 1*(1), 55–66.

Caruana, V. (2014). Re-thinking global citizenship in higher education: From cosmopolitanism and international mobility to cosmopolitanisation, resilience and resilient thinking. *Higher Education Quarterly, 68*(1), 85–104.

Chung, H. K. (1996). The wisdom of mothers knows no boundaries. *Women's Perspectives*. WCC Gospel and Cultural Series: Geneva, 31.

Cooling, T. (2010). *Doing god in education*. London: Theos.

Cox, H. (1965). *The secular city: Secularization and urbanization. theological perspective*. New York: Macmillan.

Cultural Diversity and Tolerance in Latvia. Data. Facts. Opinions. (2003). Riga: The Secretariat of the Special Tasks Minister for Social Integration. Retrieved from: http://www.mfa.gov.lv/data/file/e/Cultural_Diversity_and_Tolerance_in_Latvia.pdf

Dewey, J. (1908). Religion and our schools. *Hibbert Journal, 7*, 796–809.

Dobbelaere, K. (1998). Secularization. In W. H. Swatos (ed.), *Encyclopedia of Religion and Society*. Lanham: Altra Mira Press.

Fairchild, E. E. (2009). Christian privilege, history, and trends in U.S. higher education. In S. K. Watt, E. E. Fairchild, & K. M. Goodman (eds), *Intersections of religious privilege: Difficult dialogues and student affairs practice. New directions for student services* (125, pp. 5–11). SanFrancisco: Jossey Bass.

Gadamer, H. G. (2004). *Truth and method*. Translated by Joel Weinsheimer & Donald G. Marshall. New York: Continuum.

Gray, J. (2009). *Gray's anatomy*. London: Allen Lane.

Hall, S. (1996). New cultures for old. In D. Massey & P. Jess (eds), *A Place in the World? Places, culture, and globalization* pp. 175–213. Oxford: Oxford University Press.

Iliško, D. (2007). Pedagogical challenges of educating for authentic responsible pluralism and democratic values. In J. Hytonen (ed.), *Education for democracy as a part of sustainable development* (pp. 337–349). Helsinki: Department of Applied Sciences of Education.

Iliško, D. (2009). Pedagogical challenges for educating an authentic religious identity and responsible pluralism. In W. A. J. Meijer et al. (eds), *Religious Education in a World of Religious Diversity* (pp. 47–60). Berlin: Waxmann.

Iliško, D. (2016). Shifting frames of solidarity of religious education towards greater frames of solidarity. *Theological Journal, 1*(69), 38–49.

International Religious Freedom Report (2012). Retrieved from http://state.gov/docu ments/organization/208544.pdf

Jackson, R. (2004). *Rethinking religious education and plurality: Issues in diversity and pedagogy.* London: Routledge Falmer.

Jacobsens, (2005). Postmodernism, free markets and prophetic margins. *Themelious, 3*(1).

Kanitz, L. (2005). Improving Christian worldview pedagogy: Going beyond mere Christianity. *Christian Higher Education, 4,* 99–108.

Killick, D. (2012). Seeing ourselves-in-the-world: Developing global citizenship through international mobility. *Journal of Studies in International Education, 16*(4), 372–389.

MacQuarrie, J. (1982). *In search of humanity.* London: ACM.

Mayhew, M. J., Bowman, N.A., Rockenbach, A. B. (2014). Silencing whom? Linking campus climates for religious, spiritual, and worldview diversity to student worldviews. *The Journal of Higher Education, 85*(2), 221–245.

Naugle, D.K. (2002). *Worldview: The history of a concept.* Grand Rapids, MI: William B. Eerdmans Publishing Company.

Nussbaum, M. (2002). Educating for citizenship in an era of global connation. *Studies in Philosophy and Education, 21*(4–5), 289–303.

Potgieter, F., & van der Walt, J. (2014). Is religious fundamentalism our default spirituality? implications for teacher education. *Hervormde Theologies Studies.* South Africa: African Online Scientific Information System.

Putnam, R. D., & Campbell, D. E. (2010). *American grace: How religion divides and unites us.* New York: Simon & Schuster.

Richardson, G., & Abbott, L. (2009). Between the national and the global: Exploring tensions in Canadian citizenship education. *Studies in Ethnicity and Nationalism, 9*(3), 377–394.

Schattle, H. (2008). Education for global citizenship: Illustrations of global ideological pluralism and adaptation. *Journal of Political Ideologies, 13*(1), 73–94.

Schneller, P. L. (2011). The creative spirit. In P. L. Schneller & C. C. Wolhuter (eds), *Navigating the C's: An introduction to comparative education* (pp. 169–192). Keurkopie: Potchefstroom.

Searle, J. T. (2014). From Christian worldview to Kingdom formation: Theological education as mission in the former Soviet Union. *European Journal of Theology, 32*(2), 104–115.

Smith, J. K. A. (2013). *Imagining the Kingdom. How worship works.* USA: Baker Academic, 12, 15.

Suomala, K. (2012). Complex religious identity in the context of interfaith dialogue. *Crosscurrents,* Association for Religion and Intellectual Life.

Tanner, K. (1997). *Theories of culture. A new agenda for theology.* Minneapolis: Augsburg Fortress Press.

Valk, J. (2007). Plural public schooling: Religion, worldviews and moral education. *British Journal of Religious Education, 29*(3), 273–285.

Whitehead, A. N. (1926). *Religion in the making.* Cambridge: Cambridge University Press.

Whorf, B. L. (1956). *Language, thought, and reality: Selected writings of Benjamin Lee Whorf.* Cambridge, MA, MIT Press.

Woolley, R. (2008). Development, well-being and attainment. In M. Cole (ed.), *Professional attributes and practice* (pp. 108–27). Routledge: Abingdon.

Wright, H., & Ashwin, P. (2011). Questioning and readiness between biography, theory and power in biographical teaching methods: A dialogue. *Enhancing Learning in the Social Studies, 3*(3), 3–21.

Yon, D. A. (2002). *Elusive culture: Schooling, race, and identity in global times.* New York: Suny Press.

# 7

# BEING SPIRITUALLY EDUCATED

*R. Scott Webster*

## Introduction

For over 2,000 years, the West has inherited many problems since misinterpreting Aristotle's 'substances' and having also 'forgotten' the meaning of *Being* (Heidegger, 1982, p. 207; Dewey, 1929, 1958). This 'misinterpretation' has led to a tendency to essentialise and reify many concepts such as spirit, mind, values and the like. In response, John Dewey (2008a) argued that values, for example, are not 'things' but refer to a disposition for *valuing* something, which then becomes identified as 'a value'. Similarly the notion of 'mind' is often reduced to some 'thing' or some 'part' of the brain but Dewey preferred that we understand it in terms of existence, as *being mindful* of how we relate to elements in our environment. While Dewey's works might appear to be dated his ideas remain largely unknown, yet they offer significant challenges for today's societies and for understanding what it means to be educated. Through his promotion of democracy we can recognise that at the heart of this was the idea of the moral self (Biesta, 2016). Indeed democracy for Dewey referred to both 'a moral and spiritual way of life' (Wang, 2016, p. 170).

'Spirit' is also often conceived as a sort of substance which inhabits the 'machine' of the human body, having an existence of and by itself. In contrast to the noun *spirit* we can explore and clarify how *spirituality* might be understood via *being* as a *way*. Following this argument, we don't *have* a spirit or even *have* a spirituality but we *are* spiritual. We can appreciate then, that drawing upon the Latin *spīritus* and the Greek *pnĕuma*, basically meaning breath of air and vigour of life, that this is not referring to some substance which self-exists as if spirit were a thing, but rather it refers to the *way* or the manner in which people live their lives (Fromm, 1992; May, 1969).

Spirituality thereby pertains to the *being* of persons and is not some *thing* to be acquired or *had*. When one is full of the spirit one is full of vitality, energy and enthusiasm. When one is feeling spiritually empty or spiritless one is usually experiencing apathy, ennui and possibly depression. Indeed Mackay (2016) argues that it is from our lived, existential anxieties that we seek, what De Botton (2012) refers to as the *consolations* offered by becoming a little more spiritual in order to experience ourselves more at peace. Because this is acknowledged as being a universal human need (Comte-Sponville, 2007) it is considered important for the religious, agnostics and atheists. Spirituality tends to direct us purposefully and moves us energetically towards fulfilling aspirations. Therefore, spirituality might be understood to be similar in nature to other phenomena such as life energy, purposefulness, will, interest, desire and even *eros*. Spirituality is quite different to morality and religion. It is more encompassing than these other two and is able to provide the framework which enables people to respond to the questions 'why be moral?' and 'why commit (or not) to a particular religion?' Hence, spirituality addresses the ultimate purposes and meanings upon which one invests one's life, and so it is regarded here to be quite existential in nature (Webster, 2009).

The focus of this chapter will be examining how one's spirit might be understood as an aspect of one's *being*. Rather than *having* spirit, we *are* already spiritual as part of our *being*. Gabriel Marcel (1949) regarded that through the *having* mode persons and their issues are reduced to specific and fragmented 'problems' which require 'solutions'. He argued 'that the realm of the having is identical with the realm of the problematic and, at the same time, with the realm where technics can be used' (p. 172). He contrasted this with the 'mystery' of humankind's *being*. It is through the mystery that desire and love are to be found, as individuals inescapably become involved with others. In regard to education, *being* spiritually educated ought to be the focus rather than what it might mean to *have* a spiritual education because spirituality is not a commodity consisting of particular information, knowledge or skills needed to 'solve problems'. Therefore, the *being* mode more readily allows engagement with the 'mystery' of human persons as individuals *and* as members of communities, responding to existential questions of purpose and meaning. The education of spirituality involves reflecting upon, re-evaluating and possibly redirecting such meanings and purposes. This involves becoming or *being* spiritually educated rather than obtaining or *having* a spiritual education which shall be examined in more detail in the following sections.

## 'Being' rather than 'having'

UNESCO's (2016) four pillars of learning are listed as: *learning to know*; *learning to do*; *learning to be*; and *learning to live together*. They argue that the most important pillar is *learning how to live well with one another*. To achieve this, people *first* ought to attain the third pillar of *learning to be*. UNESCO affirms the importance of the spiritual dimension, arguing that 'the survival of humanity depends' on overcoming the tension between the spiritual and material, and that this 'should serve to make human beings not the means but the justification of development' (Delors, 1998, pp. 18 & 80). Clear links are made to UNESCO's earlier report *Learning to Be*

(Faure et al., 1972, pp, xxxi, 66) in which it was argued that humankind ought to be educated 'to become himself [sic]' through learning 'the art of living, loving and working in a society which they must create as an embodiment of their ideal'. The recommended ideal throughout UNESCO's publications is democracy, where recognising 'others' involves acknowledging the common humanity among all individuals.

UNESCO have identified that *learning to be* involves spiritual values and they argue that '[e]ducation cannot be satisfied with bringing individuals together by getting them to accept common values shaped in the past. It must also answer as to *what for and why we live together*' [original emphasis] (Delors, 1998, p. 61). From the perspective of *being* and by making reference to Dewey's notion of *valuing* as mentioned above, we might understand this better if it was worded that individuals ought to be brought *to value* important understandings which are crucial for attaining a socially just and peaceful world. In order for this valuing to occur people must be encouraged to engage with the *why* dimension. In education the *what* and the *how* of knowledge and skills are often emphasised, but in order for people to *value* certain aspects of life, they need to appreciate the reasons and purposes – the *whys* – for certain valuing. This is always more than simply a rational comprehension of *whys*, as these become embedded in our valuing to form our very passion or *eros* for living (Alexander, 2013). Consequently, UNESCO's most important pillar of *learning to live together*, ought to be recognised through including *why* such a pillar is significant. This is important because it provides an 'ultimate goal' to give sense and purpose to all other activities including the learning associated with the other three pillars.

To engage with the *why* of things requires engaging with worldviews, ideologies and religions. These provide the 'horizon of understanding' for making interpretations and giving sense and meaning to all of one's encounters and experiences. They provide 'frameworks' (Taylor, 1989) which are important sources for providing a sense of identity, meaning and purpose. Not only do such frameworks provide responses to the *why* of things, but they also provide the criteria by which we understand significant norms of life such as what is good, evil, right, wrong, etc. As such they give sense to all of our activities, attitudes and interests – in short, to our *being*.

With a similar concern to UNESCO's publications referenced above, social psychologist and psychoanalyst Erich Fromm (1976, p. 8) claimed that 'the *physical survival of the human race depends on a radical change of the human heart*' [original emphasis], which he argued could be achieved by focusing on the mode of *being* over and above the mode of *having*. His analysis of our failure to change the human heart has been due to understanding ourselves by what we have 'acquired' and accumulated such that 'I am = what I have and what I consume' (p. 23). This is very similar to Dewey's (1988a, p. 82) criticism of the philosophy of 'I own, therefore I am'. In contrast the *being* mode of existence is activity-based interest in which one *becomes* what one *values* through habitual activity. Hence the *being* mode can be likened to the virtues – what one is *becoming*. Having all of our activities based upon what we value led Fromm to identify the importance of the religious *attitude* – not religion as a framework per se, but the attitude of one's being that is developed through what one regards to be most meaningful in terms of life itself. He describes this religious attitude as being made evident through our character where 'we are what we are devoted to, and what we are devoted to is what motivates our conduct' (Fromm, 1976, p. 111).

Understanding humankind's potential through the *being* mode clarifies for Fromm the importance that education can play in terms of enabling individuals and societies to become devoted to what they ought to be devoted to, for example *learning to live peacefully together*, in order not only to survive but also to lead to good and fulfilling lives. He argues that: 'If spiritual culture, the culture of the inner Man, is neglected, then selfishness remains the dominating power in Man and a system of selfishness, like capitalism, fits this orientation better than a system of love for one's fellow beings' (Fromm, 1976, pp. 134–135). He describes the goals of education most suitable for developing the *being* mode of persons as 'essentially a matter of character; more specifically, of the degree of personal independence from irrational authorities and idols of all kinds that one has achieved' (Fromm, 1992, p. 43). Similarly to UNESCO, Fromm does not call for information *about* spirituality to be taught and delivered to students but he argues for an education of the spiritual culture of the inner person – one's being – in order to enable people to become different to their often short-sighted and selfish orientation.

The psychologist May, like Fromm, also draws upon similar existential ideas. He describes our being as the 'pattern of potentialities' to argue that respecting and loving others is not something innate to our inner selves, but these are potential characteristics that might grow in one's character through educative experiences, most usually involving encounters with other beings (May, 1983, p. 17). Interestingly such encounters with others are considered important for enabling one's spiritual 'inner culture' to grow and become more accepting, tolerant and loving. Simultaneously it involves *willing* and being interested in extending oneself genuinely to interact with others in this way. Here we see that the characteristics of being spiritually educated pertain to be moved by one's *will* to take an interest in others and the public world. This is why May (1969) considered that the greatest threat preventing the growth of one's will and love is apathy. Apathy, therefore can be understood as being spiritless as discussed briefly in the Introduction.

Victor Frankl (1988, p. 63), another existential psychiatrist, has identified that education as well as psychiatry, are challenged by both apathy and a tendency to conform. Frankl refers to the triad of 'freedom of will, will to meaning, and meaning of life' as being worth pursuing as a way for emancipating one's *being* from the clutches of apathy and the tendency of passive compliance. Like Fromm and May, Frankl (p. 30) argues that the growth of 'a strong meaning orientation is a health-promoting and a life-prolonging . . . agent'. Consequently, through his Logotherapy (where *logos* means 'spirit') he argues that if the will to meaning can grow it can 'bring out the human potential [to be] at its best' (Frankl, 2000, p. 88). This is recognised by some educators (e.g. Barnett, 2007, p. 15) who states that ' "will" is the most important concept in education'. To refer to one's being consisting of one's will, desiring and valuing, is to focus on ontology and therefore we can appreciate that education in general, and spiritual education in particular, are primarily ontological affairs rather than epistemological.

## Education promotes ontology over epistemology

The word curriculum originates from the Latin meaning 'running a course' or a 'race chariot'. It can be conceptualised via the noun *curro* which refers to the course to be run. It can also be conceptualised via the verb *currere* which refers to *how* the race is run or ought to be run (Webster & Ryan, 2014, p. 10). Such etymological referencing draws attention to the way that a curriculum is understood, which is mainly as per the Latin *curro* indicating the course of subjects to be studied, and often involves essential knowledge to be acquired. This is sometimes referred to as the epistemological concern. The other aspect which we gain from *currere* is the ontological concern regarding what sort of people students are becoming. Rather than simply being 'filled' with information, lessons are focussed on the character and virtues of students in addition to what content they might be learning. A person who *wants* to learn is more important than the content to be taught because a student's desire to search is recognised as a prerequisite for further learning. This is reflected in Biesta's (2017, p. 7) argument that education is to enable persons to want and to desire what they ought to desire in terms of existing 'in and with the world in a grown-up way'.

Dewey (1985, p. 165) prioritised the ontological over the epistemological by arguing that:

> '"Knowledge" . . . Frequently it is treated as an end in itself, and then the goal becomes to heap it up and display it when called for. This static, cold-storage ideal of knowledge is inimical to educative development. It . . . swamps thinking'. He was keenly aware that people tend to avoid thinking – dealing with the contingency and contestability of knowledge – and would much prefer the easier way of delivering and receiving inert 'objective' knowledge. He observed that '[m]en [sic] still want the crutch of dogma, of beliefs fixed by authority, to relieve them of the trouble of thinking'.
> (Dewey, 1985, pp. 348–349).

While this might seem understandable – especially for curriculum designers who simply want to attend to various demands on the curriculum such as spiritual education, by defining what content ought to be delivered, there is a profound consequence that may occur. This has been recognised by Dewey (2008b, p. 29) who warned that an individual ought not to lose one's 'own soul' through acquiring prescribed information.

Dewey (p. 29) identifies the importance of 'collateral learning' which refers to the 'enduring attitudes, of likes and dislikes' where 'the most important attitude

. . . is that of desire to go on learning'. The implication of this is that rather than attempt to get students 'to learn' educators ought to focus upon enabling students to '*want* to learn'. If there is an interest, will and want as per the spiritual dimension, then a more profound sort of educational learning can occur. However Ronald Barnett (2007, p. 6) adds that the student's being in the world is more important for her learning and concludes, that for *education*, 'ontology trumps epistemology'. Central to the ontology of students is the notion of their *will*. According to Barnett (pp. 18–19) '[w]ill is the state of the person's being. It provides internal energy; spirit even. . . . It indicates that a student is committed, is energized, is giving of herself in a firsthand way'. Barnett relates what is understood as one's *will* with Heidegger's notion of 'care'. Heidegger (1996, p. 114) did not argue that 'care' is some reified 'thing' that must be *added* to one's being, but it is simply an attribute of one's being in the sense of 'taking care' through being concerned. Consequently, we can appreciate that through its forward-looking orientation, it is also teleological in nature – in the sense that there is a purposeful goal to which one invests one's will and activities. Barnett recognises that one's *will*, or one's *care*, is a major constituent of one's identity. While it provides the source for meaning-making and is the 'horizon' upon which interpretations are made, it also can lend itself to a certain closed-mindedness through establishing a taken-for-grantedness attitude that is considered to be mere common sense to the individual and hence is beyond doubt and critique. Consequently Barnett (2007, p. 24) contends that this 'taken-for-grantedness character of the student's will bedevils higher education' and ought to be 'the supreme element' that educators should be working with and challenging.

A similar focus is found in the work of William Perry (1999) who constructed a scheme for intellectual and ethical development which basically consists of three stages. The first involves dualistic thinking where people at this level see knowledge as discrete and absolute. Therefore they approach phenomena and knowledge as being either right/wrong, good/bad, us/them, etc. The second stage is typically experienced at university and colleges where students are exposed to multiple viewpoints and theories. Students who are at this second stage understand that there is multiplicity or plurality to knowing. It is possible that if students remain within this stage they simply resign themselves to the view that everything is 'relative'. However, Perry argues that the third stage described as 'commitment' becomes very important because people take personal responsibility for having a particular view, knowing that their view is only one of many, and yet they can provide a justification for why their stance might have more value for them in their particular context. Being familiar with the works of the existentialists and Dewey, Perry (1999, p. 170) recognised persons in this stage are 'faced with the responsibility for choice and affirmation' in their lives – what the existentialists refer to as *authenticity*. He draws on Michael Polanyi to explain that this third stage represents 'the ultimate welding of epistemological and moral issues in the act of Commitment', where within this act of commitment is 'integrity of purpose' (Perry, 1999 pp. 181, 226). It is this sense of 'purpose' and 'meaning' which has great relevance for spirituality, and being spiritually educated, as explored in more detail below.

## The ontological and existential nature of being spiritual

It follows from the discussion presented above that *all* people are spiritual – irrespective of whether they might also be religious or even educated. The educational concern is not to impart a certain spirituality which ought to be received as if it were a commodity as per the *having* mode, but rather the task is to discipline and even redirect the existing spirituality of students so that their lives are benefited in some way. Through adopting an ontological approach which emphasises the *being* mode of existence, this reduces the role that knowledge and doctrine might have – but it doesn't remove them. Irvin Yalom (1980) has described the concern 'what is *the* meaning of life?' as Cosmological as it often addresses the knowledge, creeds and doctrine of various religions, ideologies and worldviews, and this is often contrasted with the specifically existential concern which is 'what is the meaning of *my* life?' which he terms as the Terrestrial. What is important to recognise is that these two concerns do not exist separately from each other. When an individual is confronted with a sense of existential anxiety she struggles to give sense, meaning and purpose to her own particular life. However, this existential struggle occurs in a world in which she is already familiar with its cultural traditions and religious understandings. Therefore, the issue of spirituality for the *being* mode of existence is *how* one relates to all that one encounters, knows and believes.

The importance for *how* one relates to all other entities in one's world, including one's beliefs, is best represented through Søren Kierkegaard's concept of 'subjective truth'. Objective truth, for Kierkegaard, refers to the *what* of things, and he quite correctly acknowledges that we, as humans, can never completely know the 'whatness' or true essence of various phenomena in an objective manner. From his Christian perspective, he argued that what is most important therefore is *how* we relate to and believe certain phenomena – for example whether God exists. He argued that 'all ethical-religious knowing is essentially a relating to the existing of the knower' and much like Perry's third stage, Kierkegaard argues for the importance of the individual taking a committed stance – a leap – in an uncertain world (Kierkegaard, 1992, p. 196).

The position adopted in this chapter is that spirituality is best understood existentially. That is, spirituality provides the meaning and purposefulness that gives direction and energy for all of a person's activities. If one's spirituality is 'weak' or uneducated then one can end up believing in things that one has been seduced into believing or that one's base appetites have drifted one to adopt quite unconsciously. From this we can appreciate that an emphasis for education is not necessarily to prove the objective truth of particular spiritual beliefs, but rather to draw attention to the basis for one's beliefs. This takes effort and is recognised through John Macquarrie's (1972, p. 107) explanation that ' "[s]pirituality" is the disciplined path along which "existence" is enhanced'.

Spirituality, then, is not knowledge-based. According to Dewey (1988b, p. 196) 'knowledge of spiritual truth is always more than theoretical and intellectual. It was the product of activity as well as its cause. It has to be lived in order to be known'. Spirituality is existential in nature, referring to how one relates and is the way that individuals relate to such things as death; the meaning of existence; who one is; what one should do; and how one ought to live. Spirituality does not predominantly comprise of the content of one's beliefs but is found in the way that one relates to these. This is why David Carr (1996, p. 462) acknowledges that 'spiritual development is not infrequently about struggle, anxiety, temptation, loss, alienation, defeat, and even despair – about precisely, the dark night of the soul'.

In this chapter the case has been made to understand human persons primarily through the *being* mode of existing, rather than via the *having* mode which currently predominates through much of Western society. Such an approach assists educators and policy makers to recognise that education ought to mainly address the ontology – the *being* mode – of students rather than through epistemology which pertains to *what* and *how* they are to know. By continuing with this perspective we can now articulate a particular understanding of spiritualty which is argued to be more suitable for *education*.

## Being spirituality educated

According to Gert Biesta (2010, 2013) education can be understood to have three broad functions. First, it offers qualifications which can be understood via Richard Peters' (1966) notion of 'training'. Second, it offers socialisation, or initiation according to Peters, where the younger generation are inducted into the status quo of cultural and institutional life. Each of these first two aspects could also pertain to learning which is not specifically 'educational', so for Biesta the third function – subjectification – is essential if the learning is to be regarded as having *educational* value. Subjectification, according to Biesta, seeks to enable the uniqueness of individuals to flourish within a social environment. He locates this to Immanuel Kant and the ideas of the Enlightenment which mark the beginning of modern education through notions 'such as autonomy, rationality and criticality', where persons 'become self-motivated and self-directing' (Biesta, 2010, p. 76). Education thus has an inescapable moral dimension dealing with the personhood of the people involved. This is why Dewey (2008c, p. 274) recognised that through this moral aspect of teaching the focus is 'making a difference in the self, as determining what one will *be*, instead of merely what one will *have*' [my emphasis]. Peters (1966, p. 91) has pointed out that because education involves 'notions such as "improvement", "betterment", and "the passing on of what is worthwhile"' there is, inescapably, an ethical dimension pertaining both to 'its matter and its manner'. This third aspect of subjectification provides some useful criteria to ensure that becoming spiritual is indeed an *educational* activity and not one of indoctrination.

From this conception of education, a clearer understanding can now be formulated regarding what it means to *be* spiritually educated in contrast to only acquiring or receiving information about spirituality. *Being* spiritually *educated* is quite different to being spiritually informed or even *having* a spiritual education. It consists of the existential dimension in which one evaluates and responsibly chooses *how* to relate to ultimate meanings and purposes. It means maturing beyond the stages of Perry's dualistic thinking and multiplicity, to responsibly determine how one ought to invest oneself. This demonstrates one's authenticity and does not simply involve doing and believing 'what one has been told'.

Engaging with spiritual education which is existential in nature, is difficult as it requires a serious engagement with students and is quite different to the traditional approaches of 'delivering' information in the guise of knowledge and values to students who are expected to 'accept' them as if they were 'things'. In order to assist providing educative experiences which might encourage the spirituality of students to become authentic in this regard, an engagement with the following queries can be helpful:

- Who am I?
- What things do I value most and why?
- What does it mean to live a good life and to die a good death?
- What criteria can be used to distinguish good from evil?
- What criteria can be used to distinguish truth from untruth?
- Who should I trust?
- How are freedom and responsibility to be balanced?
- What sort of impact upon the world would I like to have?
- On my epitaph, what would I like to be remembered for achieving and for the sort of adult I might become?
- How might I know whether a God exists and why might this matter – or not?
- What is the meaning and purposes of life – and in particular – of *my* life?

However, while engaging with these existential questions is regarded as essential it remains inadequate to ensure that one's spirituality is *educated*. Individuals could provide their own personal responses to these questions but the rest of society might find some of these to be inappropriate, disturbing or even evil. Therefore, education ought to provide opportunity to have responses 'disciplined' through rigorous thought and 'testing' regarding their actual or potential impact on others. In addition to being spiritual in an authentic sense, it must be recognised that not *any* kind of spirituality can be considered as being beneficial to the individual and/or others around them. Therefore, in addition to individual authenticity, consideration also needs to be given to how this might contribute to the good of the public. This can be demonstrated through some sustained and disciplined foresight into the anticipated consequences for living one's life according to what one currently values, desires and aspires towards. As Dewey (1988c, p. 132–133) concludes, being educated 'requires a cultivated mind to have significant conscious desires, to know what one really wants'.

This is also recognised by Charles Taylor (1991, p. 82) who acknowledges that '[a]uthenticity is clearly self-referential: this has to be *my* orientation' but he also argues that 'this doesn't mean that on another level the content must be self-referential'. Here we can appreciate that an existential spirituality is not solipsistic nor self-indulgent but rather it is a responsible engagement with the world at large. This is why Taylor (1991, pp. 8 & 44) identifies that 'authenticity incorporates some notions of society' and therefore recommends that it is valuable to publically deliberate 'what ought to be our ends' and our purposes in life. This then offers educators a significant insight into ensuring that the spirituality of our students becomes educated. Spirituality does not only consist of inward existential introspection but there is also the social responsibility for providing an account regarding what justifies one's spirituality as being 'good' for the shared world in which we coexist. As Taylor (1989, p. 36) has argued elsewhere, 'someone's identity thus usually involves not only his stand on moral and spiritual matters but also some reference to a defining community'.

Education, including spiritual education, thereby is not only to be of benefit for the individual, but it must also advance the interests of society. Here we can appreciate Dewey's approach regarding how education ought to contribute towards a greater sense of democracy, as this directly benefits the public good, and is also the preferred approach recommended by UNESCO as noted at the beginning of this chapter. *Being* spiritually educated is, therefore, both an individual and a social activity. This can be recognised through three major shared characteristics for what it means to be spiritually educated as will now be explained further.

First, because spirituality can be contrasted with apathy, ennui and even a sense of nihilism, persons and society ought to be able to articulate some meanings and purposes for a shared life together. For education, the implications of this is that all curricula ought to be justified in terms of some aims, some rationale, which is made public and is open to further debate and discussion.

The second characteristic of being spiritually educated is to authentically give an account of *how* individuals and society relate to their spiritual understanding. Spiritual understandings need to be meaningful *for them* and should not simply consist of rote memorisation of an authoritative creed – even if it is considered to be a sacred doctrine. People ought to be able to give an account to indicate they are not just simply passively complying in obedience but rather they are actively choosing to relate to such spiritual sources in a responsible manner. This is likened to Peters' notion of having personal 'reasons why' which are not to be found as someone else's reasons or an appeal to abstract rationality, but they must be internalised as being believed and cared for by committed persons – individually and collectively. Importantly, because there is a rejection of absolutes as per Perry's basic dualistic thinking, represented by blind trust and obedience to traditional and cultural authorities, persons and society acknowledge that they are *living the questions* rather than that they are standing on the static high-ground of 'answers'. Life itself is understood as uncertain and so all knowledge is considered to be contingent. As such, this would confront tendencies of intolerance, arrogance, racism, bigotry etc. which lead to sectarianism and segregation.

The third characteristic follows on from these first two and involves being empathetically aware of others and to recognise and listen to their different spiritualities. Being educated is a state of being constantly open to learning more and re-evaluating one's own understandings. Such re-evaluation can sometimes be confrontational through deep reflection. Peters (1966, p. 38) has argued 'all education is self-education' and so confronting through critical reflection is considered to be an important aspect for educating spirituality. Educators must enable students to confront their own spirituality which is usually not an aggressive event. As explained by Shapiro (2016) when working with an existential perspective in psychotherapy, 'confrontation is common' – but this sort of confrontation 'usually involves holding up a mirror to a client' who might feel 'confronted' acknowledging some aspect of belief. Kierkegaard often refers to the importance of looking into a mirror for self-examination.

Being educated to 'travel with a different point of view' means being sensitive to other points of view. However, this does not simply require tolerating or accepting all views as if tolerance is a virtue. Therefore in addition to being empathetic towards others, an educated person must also be willing to confront others and their views. This is because one cares about the potentially adverse consequences for the public good that certain spiritual views may provide. This is echoed by Dewey who argued that conducting disputes and conflicts is necessary in the pursuit of democratic peace. While he and Biesta (2010) acknowledge the important role education has for 'interrupting' or confronting individuals, it is through Dewey (1985, 1988a) that we appreciate that education involves confronting society in general by having one's spiritual faith tempered by 'intellectual thoroughness' and even some militancy so that various evils are addressed.

This reflective and confrontational approach to spiritual education has been conducted for some students in senior secondary school in Australia. Students reported that the sessions 'probably changed my outlook on life more than all my other schooling combined', 'helped me think deeper and clearer about life and what I want out of it' and one recounted that 'I feel it is more than just a knowledge-based subject . . . the benefits from such a course could lead to a friendlier more closely knit school-based community' (Webster, 1999, p. 29).

The implications for prioritising the mode of *being* over the mode of *having* has significant importance for spirituality and for education – and, indeed, more importantly for enabling humankind to tackle the many challenges of our globalised era. It can, potentially, redirect our attention from 'what' might be considered important information, content or knowledge to be 'delivered', to instead, focus upon the character of people in terms of what their interests, *will* and aspirations lead them to value and be devoted and committed towards. This latter approach directly addresses what it means to *be* spiritually educated, and how this can assist students to enhance their own wellbeing and to make a meaningful and beneficial contribution to society.

# References

Alexander, T. M. (2013). *The human eros*. New York: Fordham University Press.

Barnett, R. (2007). *A will to learn*. Maidenhead: SRHE & Open University Press.

Biesta, G. J. J. (2010). *Good education in an age of measurement.* London: Paradigm.

Biesta, G. J. J. (2013). *The beautiful risk of education.* Boulder & London: Paradigm.

Biesta, G. J. J. (2016). Education and democracy revisited: Dewey's democratic deficit. In S. Higgins & F. Coffield (eds), *John Dewey's Democracy and Education: A British Tribute.* (pp. 149–169) London: OIE Press.

Biesta, G. J. J. (2017). *The rediscovery of teaching.* New York: Routledge.

Carr, D. (1996). Songs of immanence and transcendence: A rejoinder to Blake. *Oxford Review of Education, 22*(4), 457–463.

Comte-Sponville, A. (2007). *The little book of atheist spirituality.* (Tr. N. Huston). New York: Penguin.

De Botton, A. (2012). *Religion for atheists.* London: Penguin.

Delors, J. (1998). *Learning: The treasure within.* Paris: UNESCO.

Dewey, J. (1929). *The quest for certainty.* New York: Minton, Balch & Co.

Dewey, J. (1958). *Experience and nature.* New York: Dover Publications Inc.

Dewey, J. (1985). Democracy and education. In J. Boydston (ed.), *John Dewey the middle works, Vol 9: 1899–1924* (pp. 1–384). Carbondale & Edwardsville: Southern Illinois University Press.

Dewey, J. (1988a). Human nature and conduct. In J. Boydston (ed.), *John Dewey the middle works, Vol 14: 1899–1924* (pp. 1–236). Carbondale & Edwardsville: Southern Illinois University Press.

Dewey, J. (1988b). James Marsh and American philosophy. In J. Boydston (ed.), *John Dewey the middle works, Vol 5: 1929–1930* (pp. 178–196). Carbondale & Edwardsville: Southern Illinois University Press.

Dewey, J. (1988c). Construction and criticism. In J. Boydston (ed.), *John Dewey the middle works, Vol 5: 1929–1930* (pp. 125–143). Carbondale & Edwardsville: Southern Illinois University Press.

Dewey, J. (2008a). Theory of valuation. In J. Boydston (ed.), *John Dewey the later works, Vol 13: 1938–1939* (pp. 189–251). Carbondale: Southern Illinois University Press.

Dewey, J. (2008b). Experience and education. In J. Boydston (ed.), *John Dewey the later works, Vol 13: 1938–1939* (pp. 1–62). Carbondale: Southern Illinois University Press.

Dewey, J. (2008c). Ethics. In J. Boydston (ed.), *John Dewey the later works, Vol 7: 1938–1939* (pp. 1–462). Carbondale: Southern Illinois University Press.

Faure, E. et al. (1972). *Learning to be.* Paris & London: UNESCO & Harrap.

Frankl, V. E. (1988). *The will to meaning.* New York: Penguin Group.

Frankl, V. E. (2000). *Man's search for ultimate meaning.* Cambridge, MA: Perseus.

Fromm, E. (1976). *To have or to be?* London & New York: Continuum.

Fromm, E. (1992). *The art of being.* New York & London: Continuum.

Heidegger, M. (1982). *The basic problems of phenomenology.* Bloomington & Indianapolis: Indiana University Press.

Heidegger, M. (1996). *Being and time.* (Tr. J. Stambaugh). Albany: State University of New York Press.

Kierkegaard, S. (1992). *Concluding unscientific postscript to philosophical fragments* (Tr. H. V. Hong & E. H. Hong). Princeton, NJ: Princeton University Press.

Mackay, H. (2016). *Beyond belief.* Sydney: Macmillan.

Macquarrie, J. (1972). *Existentialism.* London: Penguin Books.

Marcel, G. (1949). *Being and having.* New York: Harper & Row.

May, R. (1969). *Love and will.* New York & London: W. W. Norton & Co.

May, R. (1983). *The discovery of being.* New York: W. W. Norton & Co.

Perry, W. G. (1999). *Forms of ethical and intellectual development in the college years.* San Francisco: Jossey-Bass Publishers.

Peters, R. S. (1966). *Ethics and education*. London: George Allen & Unwin.

Shapiro, J. L. (2016). *Pragmatic Existential Counseling and Psychotherapy*. Los Angeles, CA: SAGE.

Taylor, C. (1989). *Sources of the self*. Cambridge, MA: Harvard University Press.

Taylor, C. (1991). *The ethics of authenticity*. Cambridge, MA: Harvard University Press.

UNESCO (2016). *The four pillars of learning*. Retrieved 4 April, 2016 from: http://unesco. org/new/en/education/networks/global-networks/aspnet/about-us/strategy/the-four-pillars-of-learning/

Wang, J. C-S. (2016). Reconstructing Deweyan democratic education for a globalising world. In P. Cunningham & R. Heibronn (eds), *Dewey in our time* (pp. 158–176). London: IOE Press.

Webster, R. S. (1999). Education and the meaning of life. In K. Chalmers, S. Bogitini & P. Renshaw (eds), *Educational research in new times* (pp. 23–30). Flaxton, Qld: Post Pressed.

Webster, S. (2009). *Educating for meaningful lives*. Rotterdam: Sense Publishers.

Webster, S., & Ryan, A. (2014). *Understanding curriculum: The Australian context*. Melbourne: Cambridge University Press.

Yalom, I. D. (1980). *Existential psychotherapy*. New York: Basic Books.

# 8

# LIFE-EDUCATION AND RELIGIOUS EDUCATION IN NATIONAL, PREFECTURAL AND OTHER PUBLIC SCHOOLS IN JAPAN

*Fumiaki Iwata*[1]

## Acceptance and application of the concept of religious sentiment in the west

In Japan, discussions on religious education generally divide the subject into three parts, namely, imparting knowledge about religion, providing religious sentiment education and delivering education on a specific denomination. Among the three, education on a specific denomination based on faith in that particular denomination can be practised by private schools, but not by national, prefectural and other public schools. It is generally accepted that provision of academic knowledge, in this case about religion, is the purpose of education at private or national, prefectural and other public schools. The topic of ongoing controversy has been education aimed to develop religious sentiment. At the time of revising the Fundamental Law of Education, wide deliberations were carried out regarding the appropriateness of developing religious sentiment in school education.

'Religious Sentiment' is translated as *Shūkyōteki-jōsō* or *Shūkyō-jōsō* in Japan. These Japanese terms did not exist until the Meiji period when the term 'religious sentiment' first needed to be translated into Japanese. The example of using the term 'jōsō' (情操) cannot be found in Chinese classic texts. However, as indicated in *Nihon Kokugo Dai Jiten (Great Dictionary of the Japanese Language)* (1973), an example of the word used to express an emotionally rich mind and the activity of the mind is found in literature written in the Heian period (794–1192). This word 'jōsō' began to be applied as a Japanese translation for 'sentiment' in the Meiji (1868) period and onward. An example of its use is found in *Tetsugakujii (Philosophical Terminology)* compiled by Tetsurō Inoue and William Fleming in 1881. Later, the word 'jōsō' came into wider use in academic fields such as philosophy, psychology, pedagogy and so on, implying feelings of a higher order covering values and meaning-making in the realms of morality, art and religion, more complicated than emotions. Religious sentiment is understood as the system of emotions accompanying religious beliefs, and is distinguished by the understanding that these values have ultimate or absolute meanings.

William McDougal, Gordon W. Allport and other socio-psychologists exerted influence on Japanese researchers in the formation of the concept of religious sentiment. McDougal's (1960) *An Introduction to Social Psychology* discusses the concept of sentiment in a systematic manner, which became a model for the formation of concepts of religious sentiment in Japan. McDougal defines sentiment to be composed of various kinds of 'emotions' and emotional dispositions. There are primary emotions directly linked with instincts, which are then combined with different strengths to form complex emotions. 'Reverence' which McDougal refers to as the typical religious emotion comprises complex emotions such as 'awe' and 'gratitude'. When the structure of religious emotions is analysed in greater detail, 'awe' consists of a primary emotion of 'fear' and a complex emotion of 'admiration'. The complex emotion of 'admiration' consists of two kinds of primary emotions, 'wonder' and 'subjection', while 'gratitude' consists of a 'tender emotion' and 'negative self-feeling' evoked by the sense of the superior power of another person (McDougal, 1960, p. 113). Religious sentiment is thereby of a higher order than religious emotions. Sentiment is an organised system of emotional dispositions centring on a particular object, and a feature specific to the complexly organised structure of the mind that underlines all our mental activities, and not a fact or a mode of experience (McDougal, 1960). As such, McDougal's theory is noted for stressing that sentiment is organised by various emotions.

Allport (1950) deals with the concept of religious sentiment as a subject in *The Individual and His Religion*. In this book, he defines religious sentiment as 'a disposition built up through experience', and that 'the disposition responds favorably and, in certain habitual ways, to conceptual objects and principles that the individual regards as being of ultimate importance as permanent or central in the nature of things' (Allport, 1950, p. 64). What should be noted is that although Allport emphasises religious sentiment as being an organised systematic disposition, he does not say that the essence of religion can be captured univocally. He says that the roots of religion are too numerous, and denies the existence of a source of universal religious sentiment common to peoples (Allport, 1950, p. 29).

Prior to Allport, William James (1985, p. 31) negated the presence of a single and abstract 'religious sentiment', attaching importance to subjective feelings in religious experience. In his book *The Varieties of Religious Experience*, James says that there is no ground to assume that religious sentiment exists as a unique state of mind universally found in all religious experiences. Neither Allport nor James considers that the concept of religious sentiment is able to provide the essence of religion, and both admit a diversity of religious experiences of individuals.

The fact that Allport and others do not recognise a singular specific religious sentiment has had a significant impact on the discussion on development of religious sentiment in Japan. Japanese advocates calling for religious sentiment education often refer to theories by McDougal and Allport. Takashi Ietsuka (1980, pp. 26–27), an avid promoter of religious sentiment education, summarises the four features of 'sentiment' based on their theories as follows:

'(1) It is the state of readiness, or an attitude of readiness that sustains; (2) it seeks a value; (3) it is a complex of emotions and thoughts, and not simply an emotion; It is expressed as an intellectual emotion; (4) It is formed through experience. Therefore, it can be considered as an element of education'. He further understands religious sentiment, as 'for those who seek the value with the ultimate and absolute meaning, sentiment that relates to the value'.

This doesn't contradict what Allport and others say, but Ietsuka has developed his own theory. He considers that 'education on religious sentiment in the meaning as mentioned here is not associated with particular denominations, therefore, it should be applied seriously at national, prefectural and other public schools' (Ietsuka, 1980, p. 35). As Ietsuka himself shows in the quotation above, religious sentiment is developed through 'experience'. If so, is it possible to foster religious sentiment without engaging with a specific religious denomination or tradition?

Many Japanese researchers have already noted the impossibility of this education. Here, an explanation on its difficulty is provided through comparing it to education in music. Although knowledge of musical scale and chord can be taught, musical sentiment can only be obtained through hearing music. Likewise, it is difficult to foster religious sentiment without referring to or having religious experiences (Inoue, 2002, p. 32). Despite this difficulty, debates on religious sentiment and education have long persisted in Japan.

## History of religious sentiment and education in Japan

The theme of religious sentiment is a much discussed topic among religious scholars in Japan. By contrast, this subject is rarely discussed in contemporary academic discourses focusing on religion in the West. The closest term that does feature in Western scholarship is religious experience. This is due to the special position that religious sentiment has occupied historically in Japanese politics and religion, specifically in regards to religious education.

The Meiji government, in the process of building Japan into a modern nation state with the emperor system as its central axis, conferred a privileged position to what would be later called State Shinto. State Shinto was defined as a 'non-religious' entity beyond the borders and differences of religious denominations. The Constitution of the Empire of Japan allowed freedom of belief by individuals, but the range of freedom was limited within the specified framework which would not threaten the framework of the emperor system and State Shinto. The Imperial Rescript on Education was read aloud and national ethics and morality were taught at schools, but teaching religions at school was prohibited not only in class but also as an extra-curricular activity (1899, Ministry of Education Instruction No. 12 cited in Yamaguchi, 1993).

However, after World War I, the Ministry of Education issued a notification in 1932 recognising the need for education to develop religious sentiment, and further a notification in 1935 forbidding education from particular religious denominational points of view, but advocating the promotion of religious sentiment as it is necessary for character building of children compatible with developing national morality and 'Japanese spirit'.[2]

The potential positive contribution of religion in cultural formation came to be recognised around this time. In addition, the government was concerned by the spread of socialist ideology and the expansion of labour movements after the so-called Taisho Democracy period (1912–1926) and it intended to suppress these movements (Suzuki, 1986). However, there were some pedagogical scholars who were opposed to the introduction of religious sentiment education. Kumaji Yoshida, Professor Emeritus of Tokyo Imperial University was a typical oppositionist. Yoshida said that religious sentiment could not develop without having faith in a particular religion. This reason is still considered today. It should be noted that behind this has been a notion that the foundation of education should be placed on national morality instead of religion (Takahashi, 1998). The notice in 1935 emphatically articulated that school education should be centred on the Imperial Rescript on Education. In other words, religious sentiment itself cannot be identified with 'Japanese spirit' or a 'national moral system', rather, it was considered to contain elements which might evolve into religious sentiments that could oppose what was provided in the Imperial Rescript (Takahashi, 1998, p. 34). In fact, such opposing tendencies never came into reality.

The promotion of religious sentiment education was emphasised as a foundation stone in postwar reconstruction in education, supplementing and reinforcing the national moral system and Japanese spirit in education. However, there was little discussion on the content of religious sentiment education during this period. In fact, religious sentiment education has been provided to date without having in-depth discussions on its definition and substance, in effect, leaving the contents 'blank' and at the discretion of the schools and teachers themselves (Kaizuka, 2006).

In the 'Image of Ideal Japanese', a report published by Central Council for Education in 1966, the development of 'the sense of awe' was considered to be the focus of religious sentiment education. This understanding has had continued influence on the Courses of Study issued in later years. Preparation of the report, 'Image of Ideal Japanese', was led by philosophical historian Masaaki Kosaka. In this paper, religious sentiment is explained as below:

> Any religious sentiment has its source in the sense of awe toward the origin of life. We do not give birth to our own life. Behind our lives are the lives of our parents, ethnic groups and humankind. 'Life' here does not simply imply physical life. We have spiritual life. The sense of awe that we have toward the source of our life, or something holy is real religious sentiment. The dignity and love of humans are based on this sentiment, the deep sense of gratitude emerges from it and real happiness is based on it.
>
> (Kosaka, 1966)

Following this report, the Course of Study (1977) on moral and ethical education that were issued contained instructions that contents similar to 'the sense of awe' as the source of religious sentiment, as described in the report of 'Image of Ideal Japanese', should be taught to students. However, there was a delicate yet significant difference in wording between the 'Image of Ideal Japanese' and the instruction in the Course of Study. This difference has been overlooked so far, but deserves greater attention.

First, the term 'the sense of awe' is used in the Course of Study, but the object of awe has been changed to 'something beyond human power', instead of 'source of life, or something holy'. When Kosaka used the term 'the source of life', he conceived of 'life' as the bases of all thinking and reasoning as a fundamental fact. In other words, he considered life as the source from which human activities endlessly emerge, and at the same time, as something that humans can never fully comprehend. But by defining the object of awe to be 'something beyond human power', it can be interpreted that the sense of awe is a sentiment which is directed to a specific object.

Second, in the Course of Study, 'nature' and 'beauty' are placed as representative objects for the sense of awe. In school education, it is not permitted to refer to specific religions, so teaching about Gods and the Buddha without religious references is impossible in relation to 'something beyond human power'. Thus, it makes sense that 'nature' and 'beauty' are used as substitutions. As a matter of fact, magnificent nature and beautiful landscapes, or art works are introduced as 'things beyond human power' in textbooks. In this way, 'nature' and 'beauty' are stressed as objects to which the sense of awe should be oriented.

Third, regarding life, the expression 'source of life' has disappeared and been replaced by the clause 'respecting the life of oneself and others'. This means that the focus is placed on cherishing the life of humans, animals and plants. From Kosaka's philosophical standpoint, the above difference reveals that the religious quality originally contained in 'the sense of awe' was transformed into something flat and superficial. On the other hand, it can be said that a more concrete and realistic shape was given to Kosaka's abstract and difficult-to-understand concepts in the Course of Study. Even so, such a change is hardly noticeable. At a glance, 'religious sentiment education' advocated in the 'Image of Ideal Japanese' seems to be put into practice as it is, within moral and ethical education. Thus, there is no wonder that a tacit assumption has persisted that religious sentiment education has been promoted since the publication of the 'Image of Ideal Japanese'. However, as indicated before, religious sentiment education advocated in the 'Image of Ideal Japanese' and the framework for actual moral education textbooks are quite different.

Further, and more importantly although there is a historic connection between 'religious sentiment' in the Course of Study and in the 'Image of Ideal Japanese', the contents of the Course of Study have ceased to use the title of 'religion'. The author collected more than 300 supplementary teaching materials and teachers' manuals from 2005 to 2007 for research purposes, and found no reference 'to foster religious sentiments'. They are so strictly structured that the idea of 'religion' cannot occur in the mind of teachers. Therefore, it is questionable if education to foster 'the sense of awe' in the Course of Study can be considered to be an example of 'religious sentiment education'.

## Promotion of religion sentiment education

At the time of revising the Fundamental Law of Education in 2006, controversies over religious sentiment education were provoked anew. Shigeki Kaizuka (2009a, b) has stated that there are two different positions on religious sentiment in postwar policies, but the difference has not been clearly presented, which is one reason that discussions on religious sentiment education have not been productive thus far. One position is to understand religious sentiment based on the assumption of a religious entity as an 'eternally absolute being', as discussed above, while the other is to understand religious sentiment from a broader perspective of general sentiment education. Immediately after World War II, the Ministry of Education put forth the first stance, but when making the recommendation of the Curriculum Council in 1963, 'measures to enrich moral education at schools' as a turning point 'to cultivate rich sentiment as humans, and to enhance human nature' were also presented. In this recommendation, religious sentiment was considered as an element of the cultivation of sentiment alongside aesthetic sentiment. The education policies issued after the 1963 recommendation contained both of these positions in parallel. The problem was that by reflecting the two positions, the education policies had a 'dual structure', and as a result, actual class teaching became hollow and lacking in substance. To this day, if teachers want to teach 'the sense of awe' at schools, they do not know what to teach or how to teach the subject as the meaning in the description is ambiguous. They feel that they are not well versed in it, and tend to avoid teaching this subject altogether (National Institute for Education Research, 1997).

Religious sentiment education based on an 'eternally absolute being', is essentially flawed as it is difficult to cultivate such sentiment without reference to a specific religion. In contrast to this, it was more realistic to foster religious sentiment from the stance of promoting a broader sentiment education, focused on respect for life and nature. Indeed, the emphasis by the Ministry of Education (now the Ministry of Education, Culture, Sports, Science and Technology, MEXT) has shifted to this direction. A symbolic manifestation of this is Article 2 of the revised Fundamental Law of Education. As the purpose of education, it provides for fostering 'rich sentiment and morality' and developing attitudes 'to respect life and cherish nature' which were not included in the original Law.[3] School education in Japan is heading towards entrusting the spiritual development of pupils and students to this broader sentiment education rather than seeking to link the development of spiritual wellbeing directly to religion.

## Sentiment education in Japanese language and literature

The direct aim for Japanese language and literature is to enhance children's Japanese ability, but it can also be a vehicle for values and sentiment education. The Course of Study provides criteria to select textbooks that would help, for example, 'develop respect for life, foster an attitude to be thoughtful to others', nurture 'love for nature, and the sensitivity to be moved by beauty', and 'deepen thought on life, develop rich personality and will to live courageously'. The cultivation of these sentiments is practised by using these kinds of textbooks in Japanese language and literature classes.

Kenji Miyazawa's works present an easy-to-understand example of this. Literary works of Japan's leading writer of stories for children frequently appear in Japanese textbooks. His works are not only of high quality as literature but also contain valuable hints to help readers contemplate the meaning of life and human life on the emotional level. However, it is well known that Miyazawa's belief in the Lotus Sutra in Buddhism is reflected in his writing. He was a pious follower of the Lotus Sutra and his intention to exalt the Lotus Sutra can be frequently observed in his work, which is known as Lotus Sutra literature.[4]

It would be possible to insist that Kenji's writing, inspired by the Lotus Sutra, and his life as a religious ascetic should not be introduced in school textbooks. If such an assertion were fully applied, school textbooks and tasks could only include contents which maintain a certain distance from religion. Yet, visiting religious institutions such as Shinto shrines, Buddhist temples and Christian churches is included in social visits and school excursions carried out as regular events in school calendars in Japan, although the main purpose of these visits is to study Japanese culture and history. The document Primary Education, General Affairs Section No. 152, issued by the Ministry of Education in 1949 to the Board of Education in all prefectures says: 'In literature and language textbooks, religious teaching materials may be included as long as they are chosen for their linguistic value', and 'for teaching music, art and architecture, religiously inspired works can be used as teaching materials. It is desirable to study religious influences on artistic expressions'. These concepts have been basically maintained in current times.

On 6 April, 2011, after the Great East Japan Earthquake on 11 March, 2011, an impressive official message was published, under the names of the Prime Minister and the Minister of MEXT, to be read by all students in primary, lower and upper secondary schools across the country. In the message for lower and upper secondary students, Kenji Miyazawa was mentioned:

> Kenji Miyazawa, a poet born in the Tohoku region, devoted his life to help farmers in the region who had often suffered from cool weather damage and bad crops become happy with the help of science, religion and art.

> Please acquire the calm intelligence to be able to make rational decisions, while listening to others. Also, develop warm heartedness to pray for others and shed tears for others. Further, do not forget to enjoy your life through art and sports.

Kenji Miyazawa's *Night on the Galactic Railroad* contains the following description:

'I am no longer scared of going into that darkness. I will surely go to look for true happiness for all. Let us go forward together to the end of the world'.

What does 'true happiness' mean in Kenji's story? We would like you to think about this through the experience of this disaster and chaos.[5]

What Kenji means by 'real happiness' may be living as an ascetic follower of the Lotus Sutra. Or, it may be something else based on other principles. The outcome of this inquiry can engage with religious, non-religious or anti-religious values and sentiments.

## From religious sentiment education to life-education

Along with the promotion of broader sentiment education, another type of education is conducted at schools all over Japan. This education is given various names, including 'education of life', 'life and death education', and others. For the sake of this paper, this will be called 'Life-Education'. Life-Education currently plays a central role in spiritual development in Japanese school education. The contents of the education will be considered below.

Considering Life-Education narrowly, the term is used only for classes dealing directly with life and death, and activities include meetings with expecting mothers and hospice-related personnel. In some cases, sexuality education is called Life-Education. Other than these cases of narrowly defined Life-Education, Life-Education can be and is actually provided in a wide variety of class and subject activities.[6] Taku Kondo (2003, p. 14), an advocate of Life-Education grasps it in a broad sense, and defines it as 'an educational activity to help children realise and share that life is irreplaceable, precious, and wonderful, and through which to help them develop the sense of self-efficacy'. The key to understanding this education is found in the meaning of Japanese word *inochi*. Terms such as *Inochi no Kyōiku* or *Inochi no Jugyō* and others are applied for Life-Education, and every term contains *inochi*.

The Japanese word *inochi* embraces a wide range of meanings. First, it means physical life, and appears as a subject in science and health in Japanese school education. Second, it is human life and a subject in social studies, Japanese language and literature, morals and ethics classes, and further in music and art classes. Further, while containing the above meanings, *inochi* has a connotation that is close to religious sentiment and spirituality (Ueda, 2002). Most Japanese may hold a sense of caution or discomfort towards such terms as religion and spirituality, but accept the term *inochi* with more ease.

Life-Education occupies a key position in general sentiment education, and the fields covered by Life-Education are wider than sentiment education, because *inochi* covers what is taught in science and social studies. Life-Education in a broad sense as defined by Kondo can be provided in academic education beside sentiment education. When nature and the human body structure are taught in the classes of science and health, the direct purpose is to transfer natural scientific knowledge, but the preciousness of life and exquisiteness of nature can also be conveyed. While obtaining scientific knowledge, pupils and students can find the wonder of life, and may come to consider problems of life. Based on this observation, Kondo (2003, p. 15) rephrases Life-Education to be 'education dealing with the experiences of encountering, relating with and departing from the social, cultural, and natural environments surrounding children'. Therefore, Life-Education is not limited within a specific field, but is delivered across the curriculum.

Life-Education often aims to inculcate a respect for the life of oneself and others, and at this point, it is in concert with the provision of Article 2 of the Revised Fundamental Law of Education. Despite some problems, Life-Education is approved and carried out in the Japanese school community.[7] Both Life-Education and religious sentiment education, without association with any specific denominations, share the same fundamental respect for and value of life. As introduced in the first section, Ietsuka, a leading promoter of religious sentiment education argued that religious sentiment education is possible without requiring belonging to a denomination, and understands it as 'sentiment education seeking the value with ultimate meaning' with the respect for *inochi* (life) in his mind. Ietsuka contends that although *inochi*, or life belongs to humans, it has aspects that cannot be controlled freely by humans. He says:

> With an understanding that this kind of mystic quality exists at the source of *inochi* (life), the concept of respecting *inochi* emerges. This is a philosophical concept. Moreover, when an impressive feeling is added moved by its mystic quality, a sentiment of awe toward *inochi* develops in human mind. This is religious sentiment.
>
> (Ietsuka, 1980, p. 29)

As long as respect for life is placed at the base of values education, Ietsuka's view and Life-Education can be seen as being the same. As Ietsuka defines it as a sentiment called awe, and understands it as a 'religious' sentiment, there arises an aspect that is different from Life-Education. As Life-Education does not have 'religion' in its title, it can include many fields of education which are not directly related to religion. Under the purpose of cultivating sentiments such as awe, and respecting the life of oneself and others, Life-Education can be grounded on various ideological principles, which can be religious, non-religious or anti-religious.

It is this type of Life-Education that plays the main role in spiritual development in national, prefectural and other public schools in Japan. It can be said that Life-Education has replaced religious sentiment education both in concept and reality. It is necessary to recognise this situation. In order to promote Life-Education, sentiment education within a broad sense should be re-organised and improved for practical application. For educators, appropriate teaching materials should be developed for Life-Education, and teachers should be well trained in instruction methods. As Life-Education aims to enhance children's sense of self-efficacy, and to respect their own and others' lives, educational activities should include elements to enable children to live in harmony with nature, and to improve their physical as well as mental health. And finally, Life-Education can further contribute to world peace, by expanding its contents to help children develop a sense of solidarity with the myriad of peoples and ethnic groups on the earth, as well as the natural world.

## Notes

1 This paper is a further development of the author's previous paper: Iwata, F. (2011). Kokkōritsu gakkō ni okeru shūkyō kyōiku no genjō to kadai (Religious education in national or state schools in Japan: Circumstances and tasks of religious sentiment). *Journal of Religious Studies, 85*(2), 375–399.

2 The editors note, following Iwata's description provided in this chapter, that 'religious sentiment' can be both a view and a feeling. In this sense it encompasses values, morals and convictions that are often strongly held and are emotive. It also shares qualities with what some authors in this volume call spirit or spirituality, and religious sentiment education therefore can be considered in a discussion of spiritual wellbeing education, alongside Life-Education in the Japanese context.

3 The meaning of this description was inspired by Keta, M. (2008). Shūkyōgaku no tachiba kara shūkyōteki jōsō kyōiku wo kangaeru (Consideration on religious sentiment education from the standpoint of religious studies). *Gakujutsu no Dōkō, 13*(12), 46–48.

4 To understand Miyazawa and his concerns with various religions, see Oshima, H. (ed.) (1992). *Miyazawa Kenji no shūkyō sekai (Kenji Miyazawa and his religious world)*.Tokyo: Keisuisha; and Iwata, F. (2014). *Kindai Bukkyō to seinen: Chikazumi Jōkan to sono jidai (Modern Buddhism and youth: Chikazumi Jōkan and his age)*, Tokyo: Iwanami Shoten.

5 The message for lower and upper secondary students from the Prime Minister and the Minister of MEXT, 6 April, 2011 can be retrieved from: http://mext.go.jp/b_menu/daijin/detail/1304684.htm

6 See the following four works on the present status of Life-Education in Japan: Shimazono, S. (2008). Shiseigaku to wa nanika (What is thanatology?). In S. Shimazono & S. Takeuchi (eds), *Shiseigaku I (Thanatology I)* (pp. 9–30). Tokyo: Tokyo University Press; Kondo, T. (2009). Inochi no kyōiku gaisetsu (Outline of life education), *Gendai no Espri (Contemporary Esprit), 499*, 5–19; Sugano, S. (2013). *'Inochi' no Manabikata (Guide to 'Life'-Education)*. Tokyo: Kanekoshobō; Tanaka, C. (2015). 'Ningenkyōiku' no Kongendearu 'Inochi no kyōiku' nikansuru ichikōsatu (A study on 'Life Education' that is the root of 'Humanistic Education'). *Ningenkyōikugaku kenkyū (Journal for Humanistic Education), 3*, 133–143.

7 The author's detailed views on Life-Education can be found in the following articles: Iwata, F. (2002). Inochi kyōiku no genri to kadai josetsu (Principle and tasks of life-education), *Osaka Kyōiku University Bulletin IV Sector, 51*(1), 37–49; Iwata, F. (2005). Shisei ni kansuru kyōiku no han-i to genri (Range and principle of death and life). *Shiseigaku kenkyū (Thanatological Studies), Spring*, 228–235; Iwata, F. (2009). Kyōin yōsei no kanten kara mita inochi no kyōiku (Life-education seen from the viewpoint of teacher training) *Gendai no Espri (Contemporary Esprit), 499*, 166–173.

## References

Allport, G.W. (1950). *The individual and his religion*. New York: Macmillan.

Fundamental Law of Education (n.d.) Retrieved 5 December, from http://mext.go.jp/b_menu/houan/kakutei/06121913/06121913/001.pdf

Ietsuka, T. (1980) Ningen keisei ni okeru shūkyōteki jōsō kyōiku no igi (Significance of religious sentiment education for character building). In Committee on Religion and Education of the Japanese Association for Religious Studies (ed.), *Shūkyō kyōiku no riron to jissai (Theory and practice of religious education)* (pp. 22–36). Tokyo: Suzuki Shuppan.

Inoue, N. (2002). Chūtōkyōiku Kōtōkyōiku niokeru Syūkyō no atsukai (Treatment of religion in middle and higher education – what teachers can/cannot do). *Theological Studies in Japan, 63*(2), 16–39.

Inoue, T., & Fleming, W. (1881) *Tetsugakujii (Philosophical terminology)*. Tokyo: Tōyōsōkan.

James, W. (1985). *The varieties of religious experience.* Cambridge: Harvard University Press.

Kaizuka, S. (2006). *Sengo kyōiku no nakano dōtoku Kyōiku, (zōhoban) (Moral education in postwar education,* (2nd ed.). Tokyo: Bunka Shobō Hakubunsha.

Kaizuka, S. (2009a). Sengo no dōtoku kyōiku ni okeru shōkyōteki jōsō no kyōikushiteki kentō – kyōiku seisaku no kanten wo chūshin-ni ('Religious sentiment' in postwar moral education from the point of view of educational history: Focusing on the view of the educational policy). *Kiristokyō Kyōiku Ron Shū (Christian Education Theories), 17,* 1–14.

Kaizuka, S. (2009b). Sengo no dōtoku kyōiku ni okeru shūkyōteki jōsō to seimei ni taisuru ikei – shūkyō teki jōsō wo meguru futatsu no tachiba (Differences in connotation between 'religious sentiment' and 'veneration for human life' in postwar moral education). *Sengo Kyōikushi Kenkyū (Studies on Postwar Educational History), 23,* 39–55.

Kondo, T. (2003). Inochi no kyōiku to wa nanika (What is life-education?) In T. Kondo (ed.), *Inochi no Kyōiku (Life-Education)* (pp. 8–16). Tokyo: Jitsugyōno Nippon-sha.

Kosaka, M. (1966). *Image of ideal Japanese.* Retrieved 5 December, from: http://mext.go.jp/b_menu/hakusho/html/others/detail/1318178.htm

McDougal, W. (1960 [1908]). *An introduction to social psychology.* London: Methuen (University paperbacks).

Ministry of Education (1949). Primary Education, General Affairs. Retrieved 5 December, from http://mext.go.jp/b_menu/hakusho/nc/t19491025001/t19491025001.html

National Institute for Education Research (1997). *Dōtoku kyōiku curriculum no kaizen ni kansuru chōsa kenkyū – shogakkō & chūgakkō chōsa hōkokusho (Report of research on moral education curricula for primary and lower secondary schools FY1994/95).* Tokyo: National Institute for Education Research.

Suzuki, M. (1986). Tennōsei-ka no kokumin kyōiku to shūkyō – Taishō – Shōwa ki wo chūshin ni shite (People's education and religion under the emperor system – Focusing on the Taishō–Shōwa periods). In Y. Ito (ed.), *Nihon Kindai Kyōikushi Saikō (Reviewing the history of Japan's modern education)* (pp. 220–256). Kyoto: Shōwa-dō.

Takahashi, Y. (1998). Shūkyōtekijoso no Kan-yō ni kansuru Monbu Jikan Tsuchō wo megutte – Yoshida Kumaji no Hihan to Kan-yo wo jiku toshite (On the botification of the Vice-Minister of Education for the cultivation of religious sentiments: How Yoshida Kumaji criticized and participated in it). *Musashino Art University Journal, 29,* 27–36.

Ueda, S. (2002). 'Seimei, sei, inochi' Ron (Theories on scientific life, human life, spiritual life). *Ueda Shizuteru Shū (Shizuteru Ueda Collection), 10,* Tokyo: Iwanami Shoten.

Yamaguchi, K. (1993). *Shin kyōiku katei to dōtoku kyōiku (New curriculum and moral education).* Tokyo: Eidel Institute.

# 9

# MUSIC AND SPIRIT

## Exploring a creative spiritual pedagogy

*Ruth Wills*

## Introduction

Education in England is changing. Since a new National Curriculum for schools became statutory in 2014, school leaders and teachers have been required to develop a new set of information and skills in order to meet Government criteria and most notably prepare Primary School leavers for more rigorous tests. This chapter claims that such educational priorities, not least in the more creative subject areas such as music, minimise the opportunity for the spiritual aspects of belonging, identity and meaning-making that are essential to inspiring a sense of global responsibility and harmony as well as effecting personal growth. It is proposed here that the music classroom can become and remain a safe space in which children and young people might consider the wider questions of existence as well as critique a range of world views. Therefore, the existential value of both the spiritual and creative dimensions of life is explored and philosophical concepts such as Being, potentiality and transformation are highlighted. Furthermore, a pedagogical process is proposed. This process recognises how creative learning experiences need not only concern gaining knowledge or developing skills but can also contribute to the transformation of all.

## Spirituality

It is now widely acknowledged through research in social sciences, education and theology that spirituality is an innate phenomenon and a human predisposition. Beginning with scholars such as William James (1982), whose work documents how religious or spiritual experience is prior to religious belief and activity, and zoologist Alister Hardy (1979) who maintains that spirituality is biological therefore innate and universal, an understanding of the *a priori* nature of spirituality is gained. Through the work of psychologist Robert Coles (1990), whose use of children's drawings and conversations gained extensive illustrations of how the spiritual can be experienced through the everyday, and David Hay (2006) who believes that spirituality begins within but goes beyond the ordinary, it is also argued that spiritual experience is a necessary dimension of life.

Pertaining to the idea of Being, spirituality concerns the primordial dimension of humanity. This dimension exists ahead of the construction or inheritance of any systems of knowledge, belief or values and thus allows for potentiality in terms of how learning individuals experience the world. In turn it is a priority in the formation of identity and as an essential factor in learning, it influences the ways in which individuals reflect on their experiences in order to make meaning.

In *The Spirit of the Child*, David Hay and Rebecca Nye (2006) conclude from their research with 38 children aged between 6 and 11 (2006, pp. 86–87) that spirituality is a vital aspect of existence. They identify 'relational consciousness' (2006, p. 109) as 'an unusual plane of consciousness or perceptiveness' (2006, p. 109) that allows individuals to gain a heightened awareness of their own spiritual existence. The authors also describe categories of 'spiritual sensitivity' such as the here and now, wonder and awe, imagination and meaning (see 2006, pp. 65–77), when individuals become aware of a 'new dimension of understanding, meaning and experience' (2006, p. 109) within which spiritual learning takes place. This learning which cannot necessarily be described or defined, concerns an individual's Being (2006, p. 134).

Relational consciousness also has a dialogic dimension, illustrated in an individual's ontological connection with the transcendent (sometimes referred to as 'God') as well as others, the world and the self (2006, p. 109). These relations are described as foundations of spirituality. Through the *a priori* relation of self and other, which provides the potentiality for mutual relationship, it is proposed that individuals come to understand about themselves, their place in the world, and God through their personal experiences. Such understanding is not knowledge applied from an external source; rather it concerns the potentiality of what individuals might learn and who they can become.

The significance of relational consciousness is that learning does not take place in isolation. Each context acknowledges the 'other'. While recognising the difference of 'other', potentiality within relational consciousness allows for expression and representation that is rooted within each individual. Through their reflections on learning experiences, children and young people are able to create meanings that are authentic to their own experiences of life. As Marian de Souza states,

> 'if a person is deeply connected to their deepest self and others, they develop self-knowledge, a sense of their place in the social order and in turn this connectedness helps them to make meaning of their lived experiences and provides them with a sense of purpose'.
>
> (2010, p. 3)

In the light of this, it is possible to acknowledge spirituality as an existential dimension of pedagogy. As a fundamental aspect of existence, it is not only prior to but also present throughout the process of learning. It is vital then, that teachers acknowledge the spiritual element of learning that pertains to individuals in their Being. The outcome of spiritual learning thus cannot be pre-defined. In existential pedagogy, learners have agency (Hyde, 2008, p. 117) and are free to explore their own potentiality. This involves not only developing knowledge and skills but also includes the promotion of identity formation and meaning-making. In some instances, as will be highlighted in due course, it might even involve inquiry into the purpose of one's life.

Without negating the concept of 'God', Hay and Nye (2006) propose that a child's innate spiritual state has the potentiality to inspire religious enlightenment (2006, pp. 109–11). However, it is important to note that spirituality is the precursor to and present throughout religious activity. Learning in this context, again, pertains to potentiality and the end result is not fixed. Therefore, religious engagement, as with any paradigm that concerns fixed doctrines or ideas, might be considered a tool that can inspire spiritual development. Ideally, it should not control or determine the direction that spirituality might take.

In summary, spirituality as relational consciousness allows the learner to gain a heightened awareness of his or her own spirituality as well as the *a priori* union of self and other, and this in turn forms the basis for belonging, meaning-making and identity. It might also include the search for something beyond the self. Therefore, in identifying the significance of the spiritual in education, it is suggested here that the starting point is the learner's existential spiritual life.

The notion of Being that is the condition for all ontologies, is outlined by German philosopher Martin Heidegger in his major publication *Being and Time* (1962). The idea of potentiality in learning is also explored in this text. Therefore, a brief consideration of Heidegger's ideas is presented now in order to underpin the proposal of an existential pedagogy, and to locate the current discussion in a philosophical framework.

## Existential philosophy

Heideggerian philosophy is existential and concerned with the primordial and ever present state of human life. Heidegger's thesis includes a complex analysis of human existence and concerns the self as an authentic learner. He describes the *a priori* dimension of all human experience as the basic state of Being-in-the-world and it is from this state of Being that authentic learning issues forth. In acknowledging existence, potentiality and possibility, existential learning concerns who the learning individual can be instead of what information she can gain (Heidegger, 1962, p. 236).

In the first place, Being is acknowledged as essence. This is an uncontingent state (Heidegger, 1978, p. 224) that represents humanity 'as it is' (1978, p. 226). It is a universal phenomenon and has no definition; the learner 'is'. From this essential state, the individual possesses a manner of Being. This is termed *Dasein* (Heidegger, 1962, p. 32). *Dasein* reveals 'how' essence 'is'. Yet, being primordial, it is still prior to the understanding of oneself as an entity. As such *Dasein* pertains to the potentiality of what one can become in one's Being (1962, p. 68). In colloquial terms, the child's essence is a blank canvas from which *Dasein* issues forth its potentialities. Thus, creative spiritual learning, for example, involves the issuing forth of the individual's potentiality into what he or she creates.

From its essential state and acknowledging *Dasein's* potentiality-for-Being, learning is revealed authentically through 'care'. This state of Being is self-projective and when *Dasein* is described as being 'ahead of itself in care', the learner becomes Being towards his or her own potentiality (1962, p. 236). This represents the continuation of the learner's own potentiality, ahead of itself and embracing an awareness of what is being learnt. Again using creative learning as an example, the child's potentiality becomes manifest through the art work expressed. Being inextricably present in the whole process, an awareness of his or her sense of self is also established and affirmed. This awareness 'stands out' in what Heidegger calls the 'ecstatic'. From this standing out, the self is able to make meaning drawn from reflections on his or her own potentiality and thus make a response (Heidegger, 1978, p. 241).

Existential philosophy provides a reminder that from the basic state of Being-in-the-world, the innate spiritual Being of the individual is present throughout the learning process and, as a result, learning is drawn out from the inner child. As well as issuing forth from the child, the element of 'standing out' can also encourage a personal impact on the child. For Heidegger, 'standing out' allows learners to draw on their own pre-ontological way of interpreting Being (1962, p. 168). Thus the disclosure represents an authentic expression of *Dasein*, or the learner's potentiality, which is the truth of *Dasein* (1962, p. 343). In this respect it equates with freedom. *Dasein* 'frees itself for its world' and so is allowed to become its own potentiality-for-Being (1962, p. 344). What is created and thus learnt is personal and never separated from the self.

Heideggerian ideas such as those outlined here provide a philosophical basis for an existential spiritual pedagogical process. It is argued, here, that when the potentiality-for-Being of each learner is acknowledged and considered as integral to the learning process, meaning-making that is authentic to each individual and that inspires questioning, growth and change, might take place. This meaning-making transcends any formal learning objective or measurable target but has ongoing significance for the life of each learner.

## Music and creativity

Creative music education might be noted as one example of such a process. Akin to spirituality, which as an ontological expression of Being purported to be universal, innate and located within everyday human experience, creativity might be similarly considered. For example, British Music Professor Jeremy Begbie describes music as 'an intrinsic dimension of the physical world' (2008, p. 220). Arguing that musical elements are embedded in time (e.g. the vibration of strings, the natural rhythms of lived experience or sound waves), Begbie proposes that 'music can be one of the most powerful and wonderful ways we have of enjoying, discovering, exploring and interacting with time' (2008, p. 221) and so the world.

Furthermore, music is an aspect of the spiritual dimension of being human and Begbie discusses how music's association with imagination, intuition and feeling corresponds with the spiritual dimension of life. This resonates with Rudolph Otto's notion of 'creature consciousness' (1950) in which consciousness is aroused through external stimuli such as natural objects, a sense of awe and wonder, a feeling or an idea (see 1950, pp. 27–49). Begbie describes how music and the arts inspire an affective level of human experience, which is deeper than knowledge or thought, and leads to an awareness of being in relation to something infinite (2008, p. 146) thus inspiring transcendence. For the religious learner this might be equivalent to a sense of 'God-consciousness' but, equally, it might concern a non-religious transcendence. As a means of taking the individual beyond present reality into a realm beyond the self, it might be suggested that transcendence allows for the re-evaluation and transformation of that self and reality.

Additionally, potentiality provides the starting point for a creative spiritual pedagogy. Potentiality acknowledges the innate creativity of the learner as the genesis of all creative activity, allowing for agency and the possibility of any outcome. Writing in 1987, Malcolm Carlton suggests that all musical activity should stem from the child, providing him or her with the possibility of creating 'something from nothing' as opposed to re-creating something predetermined or playing from notes. As the potentiality of each sound is explored, the potentiality of the child as a musical learner is illuminated (1987, p. 32).

Commenting on the value of collaborative creative activities, Tobin Hart suggests that children develop an empathetic resonance which is a 'feeling into'. This is done through the system of flesh, chemicals and neurones mixed with the 'magic of consciousness'. Hart's idea is that children start out knowing through their bodies more than their heads and may have more sensitivity to bodily signals than facts. This 'feeling into' inspires a connection with emotion and as awareness brings images and feelings to consciousness, children are able to make a response (2003, p. 80).

This is illustrated in two articles that outline research into the role of music in the Primary school. For example, Nortje and Van der Merwe note how a sense of co-operative play that takes place when children make music together engenders a sense of belonging within a 'safe space' (2016, p. 6). This in turn allows children to take risks and gain responsibility, as well as reaching out to others (2016, p. 7). Furthermore, they highlight how the physicality involved in music-making, which includes interpersonal touch and connection, inspires the overcoming of separation.[1] Again this promotes a deep connection with others that encourages unity in children's working and social relationships. Brendan Hyde (2008, p. 86) as well as Hay and Nye (2006, p. 70) suggest that physicality, or corporeality, is a primary source of knowledge that 'opens up our holistic awareness' and takes learning away from the cognitive to embody the whole person.

Moreover, Wills (2011) highlights how children's participation in the school choir contributed to their spiritual awareness, where one child found that singing made her happy, evidenced by the feeling of butterflies in her tummy, and another felt some pride when singing, especially in performances. The transcendent nature of music was also highlighted through one response where singing took the child to a 'different place', and another where singing allowed her to forget the difficulties of school and home so that she was able to express emotion in the present moment (2011, p. 43).

Arguably, then, music-making and participation in musical activity may be seen as a spiritual experience since it provides a 'space' in which children and young people are able to not only express their feelings, but also consider the value of others and evaluate different aspects of their own lives. Later in this chapter, the significance of the notions of Being and potentiality as pertaining to the spiritual development in Music Education will be considered in order to point towards a model of teaching and learning that is authentic to learners' lives.

## Policy pertaining to spiritual development and music education

The theoretical ideas presented above provide a starting point for a process of spiritual learning that transcends knowledge and skills. It is proposed that a pedagogy of potentiality might be applied across the curriculum, allowing for personal engagement with learning and outcomes that are particular to each child's own potentiality-for-Being. However, at this point it is necessary to outline the current context for spiritual and music education in an English context in order to highlight how ideas presented here might provide not a subversive methodology, but a nuanced perspective for the existential spiritual development of learners.

Schools in England and Wales are legally obliged to promote the spiritual, moral, social and cultural (SMSC) development of children. In England, these themes are intended to be cross-curricular and schools' provision of them is also reported on by the Government's school inspection body, the Office for Standards in Education Children's Services and Skills (Ofsted). Each theme is discretely described in Government-produced documentation and this provides teachers and inspectors with guidance for implementation. Published in August 2016, the latest *School Inspection Handbook* from Ofsted outlines spiritual development as:

- the ability to be reflective about their own beliefs, religious or otherwise, that inform their perspective on life and their interest in and respect for different people's faiths, feelings and values;
- a sense of enjoyment and fascination in learning about themselves, others and the world around them;
- use of imagination and creativity in their learning;
- willingness to reflect on their experiences.

(2016, p. 35)

It is not difficult to identify aspects of identity, belonging and meaning-making in these short statements. Presenting as succinct and user-friendly guidelines, they allow teachers to provide learning experiences for students that are existential in nature, inspire experiences of connectedness and transcendence and consider the value of the 'other'. There is also an inherent sense of creative potentiality and it seems that learners are able to draw on their lives and experiences for the required spiritual development. While no theoretical rationale is given for these statements, and it is unclear who in Government authored them, nonetheless, they provide a tangible expression of the elements of spirituality highlighted in the present discussion, and in practice each might easily be embedded within the curriculum and indeed the whole life of the school.

On the other hand, when it comes to considering the spiritual dimension of music education, Government policy is less helpful. Written in 2013, a new framework for music education in England was published as part of a new National Curriculum for schools. The opening rhetoric of the 'Purpose of Study' for Music (2013) is actually quite promising and highlights the creative opportunities afforded by the subject. The introduction to this section of the National Curriculum states that music 'embodies one of the highest forms of creativity' (2013, p. 217) to increase self-confidence and a sense of achievement. On the surface this seems to allude to a curriculum area that provides the opportunity for an existential form of pedagogy as outlined above.

However further inspection highlights this new direction for music education as prioritising knowledge and skills whereas creative potentiality is afforded less significance. The document's rhetoric of history, evaluation and notation is accompanied by terms such as 'understand' and 'perform' (2013, p. 217). Teachers therefore, should teach children to read music, to perform as individuals and in groups, and to learn the characteristics of certain composers in different periods of musical history. Composing activities should reflect the theoretical input concerning composers, musical elements and music technology, and performing from notation is encouraged rather than freedom of expression. Although each element here provides a formal foundation for music appreciation, the spiritual aspects of connectedness, open-ended creativity and transcendence are noticeably absent. Rather than promoting a pedagogy of potentiality that pertains to learners in their Being and allows for the possibility of any outcome, this form of learning implies the prioritising of measurable attainment.[2]

This is a real cause for concern as it seems that the opportunity for spiritual development is blocked in this particular curriculum area. Without having a wider perspective on the spiritual and existential value of music education, there is a danger that opportunities for self-reflection in relation to identity and meaning become lost in the need to identify 'achievement' and the requirement that learners 'have the opportunity to progress to the next level of musical excellence' (2013, p. 218). As well, without opportunities for collaboration and open-ended creativity, the potential for the overcoming of separation as highlighted above is limited. As this discussion later illustrates, the action of creative collaboration *can* transcend religious, cultural and gender differences and contribute to a wider perspective on the part of individual learners; however, such opportunities in music classes in the England are limited.

It is argued here that policy makers, school leaders and teachers need to re-think how music education contributes to the spiritual life of a school and, in particular, learning that fosters belonging, identity and meaning-making. Transcending but not negating the externally set learning objectives, it is proposed that the element of 'standing out', which provides the opportunity for reflection and response can facilitate a personal impact on the creative learner when embedded into the lesson as a whole. This is education's transformative telos.

Illustrating an existential pedagogical process that has been used in schools, it is argued that the creative activity of collaborative musical composition *can* provide the inspiration for the spiritual development already outlined in this chapter. As well, a more existential understanding of both spirituality and creativity might allow for the music classroom to become a safe spiritual space. Using Heideggerian terms, it is possible to identify how a learner's essential state of Being is prior to and present throughout the process as well as how potentiality becomes manifest authentically through the progression of self through to response. This process is dynamic and continuous and is discussed below.

## A musical pedagogy of potentiality

### Being and presence

Creating space for the spiritual in school allows for learning to start with Being. Most importantly this occurs when teachers recognise themselves as spiritual Beings and intentionally prepare the ground to recognise the Being of the learner. Since the primary school classroom is the location for most of children's learning, space and time can be given to creating special areas or moments for the spiritual and to allow the children to 'be'. In the music classroom, learners enter the learning environment as potentiality-for-Being and although learning objectives are shared, the existential outcome of the session is undefined. The class is then given a stimulus: a piece of music plays as they sit in stillness and learners attend to who they are in their own Being.

### Awareness

Learners are given time to allow the stimulus to bring their own potentiality to awareness. Sitting in stillness and quiet, and allowing their imaginations to recall their own experiences, they are encouraged to highlight their emotions as they listen, think of words to describe how they feel and create a mental picture based on what they hear. Awareness of the way music can move or inspire is brought to consciousness and this forms the basis for creative engagement.

### Engagement

Next, the children are provided with tools for their creations. These might include formal musical instruments, classroom percussion instruments, computers, 'found sounds' from the classroom, or their own bodies. In small groups the children share their own ideas in order to create a musical composition that reflects their emotional responses to the stimulus. Learners engage with each other, express their own feelings and thoughts, listen to and respect each other, and bring their response to their previous or current experiences of the world to the activity. Together they discuss, plan, experiment with sounds, create and evaluate. What was within and ahead of the learning situation as potentiality is now expressed externally.

## Standing out

The children rehearse then share their music. A period of quiet follows each performance to allow both performers and listeners to reflect on the music. This quiet time allows learners' thoughts and feelings to integrate as they 'stand out' from what they have created. The opportunity to reflect on the activity enables children to make connections with the aspects of their lives that they have brought to the learning process and the thoughts they now have. When they recognise what 'stands out' (Heidegger, 1978, p. 230) for them, a response can be made. This often leads to existential questioning or even theological reflection.

## Care

Children are finally encouraged to articulate their responses privately or publicly. This continues the movement from being a part of who they are in their own potentiality to something made manifest in care (Heidegger, 1962, p. 236). Furthermore, it represents something that can make a difference. As the children are able to express the results of their learning they are encouraged to take these feelings, thoughts and ideas with them into their next learning situation and so the process is repeated.

## Examples from practice

The following examples from two different contexts of children's reflections in response to a music-making activity provide evidence of this process in practice. The responses highlighted here concern belonging, identity and meaning-making in order to inspire change.

## English context

The first example represents the responses of children aged 8 and 9 from a large UK primary school. This school is diverse in terms of ethnicity and over 25 languages are spoken by its 400 children. Most children use the term 'God', and this has a personal meaning for each individual. Spirituality is strongly evident and one of the school's aims is to teach children an awareness of their role in the wider world.

The music lesson described here formed part of a series of lessons undertaken with the same children on the theme of 'Water'. As the children entered the room, the piano piece 'Reflects dans l'eau' by Debussy was playing on a CD and a PowerPoint presentation with a range of water scenes unfolded on a screen. The children were invited to sit in stillness on the carpet, to listen and watch. Following this, a time of quiet encouraged them to become aware of their stillness and to bring to mind any images, feelings and thoughts inspired by the stimulus. The task was then outlined: to compose a piece of music called 'The power of water'. The children were divided into small groups and provided with a selection of instruments, white boards, time for planning and the opportunity to experiment with sounds. The children worked collaboratively to create unique pieces of music which were rehearsed and performed; however, it is important to note that during this activity, conversations turned to themes wider than the task, inspiring deep questioning about the world.

Following the creative session, the children were asked to individually reflect on the task they had undertaken. In the discussion, children indicated how they had enjoyed the session and found experimenting with sounds fun. A popular response was that it made them feel happy or proud. Other children highlighted the value of the collaborative aspect of the activity, indicating how each participant had a part to play: no one was left out and all ideas were heard. One child commented on how this activity helped him to understand how he could make friends with children from a different class, and one suggested that he was happy to make friends with children from a different religion. He explained that the activity had united them in a way that playing in the playground could not. The children also commented on how much they enjoyed the group activity, as much of their usual class time was spent in individual work.

Some children's reflections widened out to more existential thinking. Some indicated that the activity had extended their thinking about themselves and their place in the world. In the wider discussion some commented on the destructive power of water, mentioning the recent Tsunami that had been in the news. Some commented that it was unfair how people's lives had been lost and one questioned why God would allow this. Another explained how she was reminded that all humans are equal and two children indicated they would be committed to research ways to help others in the local Indian community and abroad.

It might be argued here that this collaborative activity inspired reflection on the themes of identity and belonging in terms of their cultural and religious affiliations in order to effect an understanding of how separation might be overcome and unity in diversity gained. The session, for some, reinforced the school aim of developing a sense of global responsibility and while existential questioning did not provide any answers to their questions about God, their minds were opened to critical evaluation regarding world events. Meaning-making for some inspired action and for almost all, the session had some form of personal significance.

## Croatian context

The second example represents the responses of young people aged 15 and 16 from a state-funded secondary school in Croatia. As most of the population of students and staff came from Catholic backgrounds, the term 'God' was understood in terms of the God of the Catholic faith which had personal meaning for some. Music education focused on the more cognitive aspects of the subject and in this classroom there was little evidence of corporeal or collaborative aspects of learning. Furthermore, the Balkan War of the 1990s, through which Croatia gained independence from other Yugoslav states, was a living memory for these young people. Their views on identity and belonging are, thus, shaped by these events more so than their religious identity and this contingent influence was evident in their responses.

The activity session had similarities to the session undertaken in Englan. As a stimulus, a song about the beauty of creation was played on a CD. The students were then allowed to experiment with the range of sound sources available before composing a teacher-led class composition called 'Creation'. Responses were then gained from the students.

A key theme in the responses was inclusion, with one student explaining how each member of the 'band' was important: 'even the player of the triangle is important'. Another student equated the collaborative aspect of the activity with unity, indicating how the music allowed the group to be 'as one'. It was also noted how the music inspired cross-cultural unity. Allusion was made towards the differences between members of Balkan states, and the students were given the opportunity to reflect on their identity and their views on difference in the light of their responses to the music, leading to the comment: 'it makes you think about the purpose of your life'.

Religious responses were also made and one student explained that the activity enabled him to think about the 'fruits of the spirit' from the book of Galatians in the Bible which outlines qualities such as patience, joy, kindness, goodness and self-control. The student explained that all these qualities were needed when working with others, and that 'God gives you the spiritual tools to be able to carry out the task'. Finally, the students were able to identify music as a universal language that transcends cultural and language barriers. Parallels to their own experiences of cultural barriers were drawn, and as they considered the way they felt about people from other Balkan countries, appropriate personal responses or prayers were offered in the quiet time that concluded the session.

Finally, it might be argued that this creative activity inspired authentic reflection on the themes of identity and belonging in the students' immediate cultural context. As well, it allowed for the evaluation of their opinions of others and of their roles as local and global citizens. Meaning-making on these themes was able to challenge some particular worldviews as well as promote understanding on how the spiritual dimension of life can afford unity and peace.

## Concluding comments

As outlined above, the existential spiritual dimension of Being exists ahead of the application of knowledge and inheritance of beliefs or values. Acknowledging the potentiality-for-Being of each learner is vital in providing educational experiences that go beyond knowledge and skills, and attend to their innate creativity and capacity to reflect. It is argued here that the spiritual notions of belonging, identity and meaning-making that are essential for children and young people's wellbeing and ethical lives might be inspired in the creative classroom. It is also proposed that school leaders and teachers need to think about how to educate not only from within but also 'beyond' the rather restrictive government policies that currently focus on cognitive learning and testing, thereby discouraging creativity and spiritual wellbeing.

As such, considering these limitations within current school-based teaching and Initial Teacher Training courses, continued research is required to highlight how such a perspective of education might be applied in such contexts. The aim of this research going forward is to consider how a creative pedagogy might allow for a more organic and open-ended dimension to learning yet within the remits of current expectations. As a result, if such education nurtures individual creativity and spirituality, it is proposed it will contribute to the wellbeing of students and lead to the development of empathetic yet critical global citizens.

## Notes

1   In this article it is gender separation that is highlighted; however as will be outlined later in this chapter, cultural and racial separations are also noted to have been effected through music-making.
2   For example, the document states that children should learn to read musical notations, develop an understanding of the history of music, and recall sounds with increasing aural memory (2013, p. 218).

## References

Begbie, J. (2008). *Resounding truth: Christian wisdom in the world of music.* London: SPCK.
Carlton, M. (1987). *Music in education.* London: The Woburn Press.
Coles, R. (1990). *The spiritual life of children.* London: Harper Collins.
Department for Education. (2013). *National Curriculum in England: music programmes of study.* https://www.gov.uk/government/publications/national-curriculum-in-england-music-programmes-of-study/national-curriculum-in-england-music-programmes-of-study accessed on 25/08/2016.
Hart, T. (2003). *The secret spiritual world of children.* Makawao, HI: Inner Ocean Publishing.
Hardy, A. (1979). *The spiritual nature of man.* Oxford: Clarendon Press.
Hay, D., & Nye, R. (2006). *The spirit of the child.* London: Jessica Kingsley Publishers.
Heidegger, M. (1962). *Being and time.* Oxford: Blackwell Publishers.
Heidegger, M. (1978). Letter on humanism. In M. Heidegger (ed.), *Basic writings* (pp. 213–256). London: Routledge.

Hyde, B. (2008). *Children and spirituality: Searching for meaning and connectedness.* London& Philadelphia: Jessica Kingsley Publishers.

James, W. (1982). *The varieties of religious experience.* London: Penguin Books.

Nortge, E., and L. Van der Merwe. (2016). Young children and spirituality: understanding children's connectedness in a group music class. *International Journal of Children's spirituality,* *31*(1): 3–18.

Office for Standards in Education (Ofsted). 2016. *School Inspection Handbook.* Manchester: Ofsted.

Otto, R. (1950). *The idea of the holy.* London: Oxford University Press.

Wills, R. (2011). The magic of music: A study into the promotion of children's well-being through singing. *International Journal of Children's Spirituality,* *16*(1), 37–46.

# 10

# SEEING WHAT IS TRUE AND HOLY IN OTHERS

*Rev. Associate Professor John Dupuche*

## Introduction

While religions can be studied from many points of view – historical, geographical, sociological and philosophical – my contention is that they are most intimately concerned with what is deemed to be 'true and holy' (Vatican Council II, 2016). They also presuppose forms of perception and faculties that differ from the five senses and the reasoning mind. Religions are lived realities that involve ordinary people as well as highly gifted 'saints'. This chapter seeks to explore how 'seeing what is true and holy in others' can be a framework for interreligious education. The first part explores the terms 'in others', 'seeing', 'true' and 'holy' and the second part presents a portrait of students receiving such an interreligious education. Finally, I discuss the possible benefits of such a program on students' wellbeing and for their broader societies.

## Part I

### a. 'In others'

Some scholars argue that human beings are inherently spiritual before receiving any instructions from a tradition or belief system. For example, Daniel Scott (2006, p. 1118) states that: 'Spirituality is as normative and natural as physicality or emotionality. Children are spiritual. Children are physical. Children are emotional'. Moreover, he notes that it is spiritual experiences that give rise to religious traditions, which are their expression in words, art and ritual.

Although Scott (2006, p. 1117) believes that religion and spiritual awareness are intimately connected, he holds that this awareness is not the exclusive property of 'religions' and can be present even in those who consider themselves to be irreligious. He therefore contends that it is important not to confuse 'God-talk' with spirituality.

Even though many scholars recognise that spirituality is highly significant in the rounded education of the young, they have not succeeded in defining it. This lack of success is also evident in confusion regarding what religious education is supposed to achieve (Erricker, 2006, p. 1308).

However, not all have accepted the view of an inherent spirituality. According to Dietrich Bonhoeffer (1906–1945), the Lutheran theologian, 'the idea of the innate religiousness of man [sic], the religious *a priori*, must be rejected' (Hamilton, 2016). Yet Bonhoeffer did not go so as far as Friedrich Nietzsche (1844–1900) who put into the mouth of Zarathustra the dramatic words: 'God is dead!' (Nietzsche, 1961, p. 41). The 'Death of God' movement flourished in the USA in the 1960s. Among its major proponents were Gabriel Vahanian, Paul van Buren, William Hamilton, John Robinson and Thomas Altizer.

By contrast, *Nostra Aetate*, (Latin for In our Time), the Declaration on the Relation of the [Catholic] Church with Non-Christian Religions of the Second Vatican Council released in 1965, presumes that the religious quest is universal and justified. It begins by listing some questions:

> [People] expect from the various religions answers to the unsolved riddles of the human condition, which today, even as in former times, deeply stir the [human heart]: What is the [human being]? What is the meaning, the aim of our life? What is moral good, what is sin? Whence suffering and what purpose does it serve? Which is the road to true happiness? . . . whence do we come, and where are we going?'
>
> (Vatican Council II, 2016)

It then succinctly describes Hinduism, Buddhism and Islam, without going into detail on how they might answer these questions, and then makes the momentous statement that 'the Church does not reject what is true and holy in these religions' (Vatican Council II, 2016). The emphasis here is laid on religion. However, religions are not just abstractions or organisations; they are lived realities. They consist of ordinary men and women. What have they experienced? What draws them to religion? What gives them a satisfaction that this world cannot give? What is the quality of their wisdom and humility, their joy and peacefulness, their mutuality and compassion? For what are they willing to surrender their lives? The traditions that have stood the test of time have something valuable to say to every time. What is it? I argue that attention in religions is ultimately focused on persons, on 'others'.

Emmanuel Levinas (1906–1995) has much to say in this regard, and makes use of an image of the 'face'. He states that the person facing me is the most fundamental experience I can undergo. That person is transcendent and yet present, with claims that demand a response. Levinas proposes that meaning is not derived from the self but is received from the other. He notes that the individual autonomous subject at the foundation of so much Western philosophy has marginalised the other. His is a teaching on the primacy of love that leads beyond a world fashioned by individualist concerns (Cassidy, 2006, pp. 877–879)

Martin Buber (1878–1965) speaks in similar terms that the 'instinct of communion' is 'in the gift of every child'. It is precisely this openness to others 'that defines the human being'. He warns of the mentality that reduces the other to an object or an idea (Cassidy, 2006, p. 880). Therefore, Buber's focus is on the other, not just on the tradition to which they belong as though their transcendent otherness were of no concern and that they must abandon their uniqueness in favour of a standardised outlook.

Buber notes that this awareness of the 'you', namely of the other human person, gives a fleeting glimpse of the eternal 'You', who is called 'God'. The human being reveals the Invisible. He adds that this 'You' has been named by many names, and that over time attention has moved from the 'You' to the names; that people began to reduce the 'You' to an 'It', namely an idea or construct. The names remain sacred nevertheless because they are not only used to speak about God but also to speak to God (Cassidy, 2006, p. 881).

Paolo Freire also notes that openness to the 'other' is universal, and attends to the most dissimilar: the humanist, the agnostic, the atheist, the animist, the syncretist and the polytheist (Byrne, 2011, p. 56). This attentiveness is an attitude of tolerance (Cullen, 2006, p. 993). It involves profound humility and the abandonment of any sense of superiority (Byrne, 2011, p. 57). Indeed the feeling of superiority precludes meeting and understanding. However, openness does not remove the right to disagree (Byrne, 2011, p. 56). Indeed, this critical faculty is necessary if there is to be any learning, a critical faculty that is directed to one's own tradition as well as to the other's tradition (Cullen, 2006, p. 993). Tolerance is not naivety.

These views have significant consequences. I assert that it is others, in all their uniqueness and transcendence that provide the suitable context for religious and spiritual education. The study of doctrines and traditions, of art and ritual, does not suffice. Nor is spirituality best found in retreat into privatised meditation (Cassidy, 2006, p. 882). It is the 'other' that above all can communicate a sense of the divine.

## b. 'Seeing'

There are countless aspects to the work of education, but one of the most fundamental is to awaken the students' faculties. Sport develops socialising skills as well as physical coordination. Mathematics develops the powers of abstraction and accurate observation. Poetry develops sensibility not only to words but also to the range of emotions and images. Following this argument, I propose that education in its fullest sense means enabling students to develop their capacity to see others in their fullness, not just their intelligence but also what is true and holy in them.

This approach immediately raises questions. What realities and dimensions do we allow for in education, in faith-based and secular settings? Do we, *a priori*, exclude certain forms of perception, deeming them to be useless and false, just make-believe and whim? Do we open the students' minds to many forms of realisation, allowing at least in theory the possibility of religious awareness?

The act of 'seeing' is complex. With whose eyes do the students see? With their parents' eyes? With the eyes of their peer group? Do they see only with the eyes of the media, the Internet, the TV, the darker prejudices of culture? Do they see through the coloured glasses of unresolved conflicts or weaknesses of character? Do they allow their deepest and true self to see?

## c. 'True'

Ignatius of Loyola (1491–1556), the founder of the Society of Jesus, which has developed a highly regarded worldwide network of Jesuit, Catholic schools, composed his *Spiritual Exercises* in 1522–1524. Towards the start of this influential work he stated that one must presume there is truth in what another person holds (Ignatius, 1952, p. 12). This attitude does not mean agreeing, but it does require attending to the other with more than mere civility. He elaborated that 'if he cannot save it, let him enquire how he understand it; if the other understand it wrongly, let him correct him with love' (Ignatius, 1952, p. 12).

This openness is particularly remarkable as it was propounded at the start of the heated controversies of the Protestant Reformation. It contrasts with the outlook of René Descartes (1596–1650), a student at the Jesuit College at La Flèche, who preferred doubt. Descartes wrote his *Discourse on Method* (1637) during the Thirty Years War. Confronted by the opposing religious forces and the many other currents of thought, theistic and atheistic of his day, he sought to find the truth, and in order to reach this objective he developed his 'methodic doubt', wishing to defeat scepticism by means of scepticism (Kemerling, 2011) and so demanding unassailable truth before granting his assent.

In Descartes' second Meditation, he states, 'Archimedes used to demand just one firm and immovable point in order to shift the entire earth; so I too can hope for great things if I manage to find just one thing, however slight, that is certain and unshakable' (Descartes, 1954, p. 67). He believed he had found this in the famous 'I think therefore I am'. In the third Meditation he set about to prove the existence and God, and then the existence of other realities (Descartes, 1954, p. 76ff.).

Immanuel Kant (1724–1804) held that the noumenon – the transcendent God – cannot be known. It is only the phenomenon that can be known with certainty. All this philosophising was dismissed by Auguste Comte (1798–1857) who rejected the mythical dreaming of religions, as well as the philosophies of the Enlightenment, and argued that science alone is the source of valid knowledge. Karl Popper (1902–1994), however, countered this confidence by saying that: '. . . anything like a conclusive proof to settle an empirical question does not exist'. (Popper, 1983, p. xxii) and 'All knowledge remains fallible, conjectural' (Popper, 1983, p. xxxv). This increasing uncertainty was compounded by Jacques Derrida's (1930–2004) philosophy of deconstruction in linguistics and Jean-François Lyotard's

(1924–1998) post-modernist rejection of grand metanarratives in favour of each individual's own 'small narratives' (*petits récits*).

The Cartesian dream has failed if it is taken to mean acquiring knowledge by some objective method that is independent of the knower (Mulherin, 2016, p. 9). Yet the alternative of subjectivism, Christopher Mulherin (2016, p. 35) proposes, is equally unfounded, and he provides a succinct definition of the extremes of objectivism and subjectivism respectively as 'a naive optimism, based on method and the disengaged human subject, or . . . a relativism that cannot make universal truth claims'.

Mulherin (2016, p. 9) takes a middle position, following on Martin Heidegger's phrase that 'interpretation is the basic form of all knowing', that the human is essentially an interpreting being. Mulherin also follows Karl Polanyi (1886–1964) and Hans–Georg Gadamer (1900–2002) who see objectivity and subjectivity not as competing but as complementary and mutually reinforcing (Mulherin, 2016, p. 31).

These thoughts have a curious connection with quantum mechanics. Albert Einstein (1879–1955) held to objective realism and rejected quantum mechanics stating that: 'I like to think the moon is there even if I am not looking at it'. Other significant figures in the development of quantum mechanics held that observation was an essential part of reality. For example, Martin Rees (b. 1942) made the astounding comment that: 'The universe could only come into existence if someone observed it . . . The universe exists because we are aware of it'. John Bell (1928–1990) even went so far as to say: 'Suppose that . . . we find an unmovable finger obstinately pointing outside the subject, to the mind of the observer, to the Hindu scriptures, to God, or even only Gravitation? Would that not be very, very interesting?' (Rosenblum and Kuttner, 2011).

Interpretation, it must be clearly said, is not mere fancy. It is not make-believe. It is truly seen, but from one perspective. It is the result of the complementarity of subject and object. Such interpretation, Polanyi and Gadamer held, is not just 'true for me' but is universally true (Mulherin, 2016, p. 31). It is a perception that one can offer to others for their consideration and from which they can learn. It is what Mulherin calls a 'robust' truth, namely a truth which is universal and true for all, irrespective of what any individual or group may think (Mulherin, 2016, p. 78).

Understanding involves a continual process of interpretation. Through the knowledge of another tradition, and of another person's understanding of their tradition, there is an enhanced understanding of one's own, a new interpretation (Meijer, 2016, p. 322). It is a continual learning, a constant correction and refinement. Re-interpretation involves historicity because it means tapping into the experience and understanding of many others that have gone before, a critical reflection in the light of many sources. It can lead to the realisation of one's own identity (Jackson, 2006, p. 297–298). It is a reshaping of outlook, and therefore of those choices and actions that flow from understanding. It is education in its finest sense.

Indeed, it is what is called comparative theology, which,

> . . . marks acts of faith seeking understanding which are rooted in a particular faith tradition but which, from that foundation, venture into learning from one or more other faith traditions.
>
> (Clooney, 2010, p. 10)

Raimundo Panikkar corroborates this approach. He coins the term 'intra-religious' dialogue where the worldview of the other is allowed to enter into one's being and by learning about the other one discovers one's own identity. It is a demanding process (Boys, 2010, p. 26), which can only occur in the context of trust and friendship. Cullen refers to what the literary critic Patricia Spacks calls 'gossip strategy' where the interlocutors 'swap stories' about their religious tradition and attitude in a manner that is not trivial but light-hearted (Cullen, 2006, p. 997).

This process of learning is not syncretistic, however, or a sort of 'mix and gather', a point made by HH the XIVth Dalai Lama. While acknowledging that Buddhists and Christian share many things in common, he warns against uncritical combination that he likens to putting a yak's head on a sheep's body (Lefebure, 2005, p. 87).

The Bible makes its own contribution to the question of what is true. The word 'true' or 'truth' does not refer so much to ideas as to relationships. The Hebrew word for 'truth', *amen*, derives from the Semitic root *a-m-n* meaning 'to be reliable', 'to be trustworthy', 'to confirm', 'support'. When used adverbially it indicates agreement (Online Etymology Dictionary, 2016a). When applied to God it usually signifies his faithfulness. To be true means to be in right relationship. Humans are called to faithfulness. They are true to each other if they are benevolent and just. The New Testament follows on the Old Testament. It reaches its climax in the teaching that Jesus is the truth but not in some Platonic or gnostic sense. The evangelist proclaims, '. . . we have seen his glory . . . full of grace and truth' (Jn 1:14). Christ himself states, 'I am the way, and the truth, and the life' (Jn 14:6). Jesus reveals God fully and perfectly and therefore those who enter into right relationship with Jesus enter into right relationship with God, with humans and all that is.

However, competing views of what is true have led to wars and divisions of every sort. The search for religious truth is beset by scandals of every sort that have discredited it completely in the eyes of many. Again, the plethora of opinions has so complicated things as to be self-defeating. What is true? Why do those who say they have found the truth, belittle those who have arrived at different conclusions? It is a sorry tale that cannot be concealed from the students.

To what extent should students be exposed to the acrimonious debates between Jews and Muslims, Catholics and Protestants, atheists and theists, between science and religion, and so on? Will education in religions become so thoroughly confusing as to be dismissed by students altogether?

## d. 'Holy'

*Nostra Aetate* was made possible by a change in Catholic theology on the relationship between nature and grace. Whereas these had once been opposed, now grace is seen to be omnipresent (Lane, 2006, p. 910). As Karl Rahner put it, the grace of God is 'given always and everywhere to all human beings' (Rahner, 1986, p. 75). The great Protestant theologian Paul Tillich likewise saw other religions as formed by the action of the Holy Spirit (Lane, 2006, p. 912).

The term 'holy' is explicitly religious. It comes from the Old English *halig* that derives its meaning from Hebrew, Greek and Latin. The Hebrew word *qadhosh* originally referred to the separation of ritual objects from mundane objects, with any confusion between them causing impurity. *Qadhosh* attaches primarily to YHVH – the Hebrew representation of God – who is beyond all limited things, and secondarily to the people and objects associated with him (International Standard Bible Encyclopaedia Online, 2016). It also has an important ethical dimension. The Chosen People are not to act like others who have no knowledge of YHVH, for they have been 'set apart' (Lev. 20:26).

The Greek term *hágios* essentially means 'different'. Thus a temple was *hágios* because it was 'different' from other buildings. It was 'other' because it was 'special' to the Deity. By extension it involved 'likeness of nature with the Deity' and 'difference from the world'. In the New Testament, *hágios* shifts from its cultic meaning; it acquires a stronger ethical sense and refers to those who, despite their weaknesses, are where the Holy Spirit has taken up his abode (International Standard Bible Encyclopaedia Online, 2016).

The equivalent term in the Vulgate is the Late Latin *sanctus*, 'consecrated', 'sacred', 'inviolable' (Online Etymology Dictionary, 2016c).

To render the term *sanctus* at the time of the Christianisation of the Germanic peoples, the Old English *halig* was used. It meant 'consecrated', 'sacred'; it derived from the Proto-Germanic *hailaga*. It is not possible to determine the primary (pre-Christian) meaning, but probably it referred to something 'that must be preserved whole or intact, that cannot be transgressed or violated' (Online Etymology Dictionary, 2016c).

The same idea is found in Arabic. In the teaching of Ibn 'Arabī, the term *walāya* can mean 'helping' and is an attribute of Allah who is the helper of mankind. It is also applied to the holy person (*awliyā'*) where it refers to his/her proximity to Allah, the transcendent (Chodkiewicz, 2015, p. 57). According to Michel Chodkiewicz (2015, p. 29), '[t]he essential feature of the *awliyā'* is the transparency which makes them the privileged vehicles of theophany'.

In short, the word 'holy' is widely and constantly connected with the sense of the transcendent. It refers to something beyond the ordinary and the usual, something fundamentally 'other'. The term 'holy' is not to be confused with 'virtuous'. In his *Nicomachean Ethics* Aristotle defines the nature of happiness and presents the various virtues, moral and intellectual, which lead to it (Aristotle, 1953, Books 1, 3, 4 and 6.) In Book IV, 426–435 of *The Republic* Plato examines the idea of the good and notes that 'it must have the four virtues (*aretai*) of wisdom, courage, temperance and justice' (White, 1979, p. 112) but these do not capture the meaning of 'holiness'.

Throughout his work, *The Idea of the Holy*, Rudolf Otto (1923) reflects on the holy as a *mysterium tremendum et fascinans*. It is *mysterium*, that is something beyond the capacity of the human mind fully to grasp. It is known but not comprehended. It is not a mystery, as in a crime novel, or a riddle or a puzzle or a problem. Rather, the *mysterium* goes beyond the limits of human cognisance, and pertains to the domain of the spirit. Though it is beyond understanding, it is communicated through rituals and art, saints and sacred texts and so. The 'holy' is experienced; all attempts to define it are inadequate, and all attempts to control it are vain, for it is not subject to human thought or will. The holy is *tremendum*; it is overwhelming because it is beyond human control. It is unsettling and introduces the altogether other. It is *fascinans* because it captivates and intrigues in ways that logic and reason do not.

Buber experienced something of this *mysterium* in his encounter with different religious systems, stating:

> I do not rest on the broad upland of a system that includes a series of sure statements about the absolutes, but on a narrow, rocky ridge between the gulfs where there is no sureness of expressible knowledge but [only] the certainty of meeting what remains undisclosed.
>
> (Buber, 1947, p. 184)

In Biblical terms, God manifests his holiness in his act of creation and in the liberation of his People from the all-powerful Pharaoh. His holiness is expressed above all in love and forgiveness, which surpasses all that humans can do. The People to whom he shows himself are thereby holy (Ex 19:6). In the Christian tradition, Jesus is the Holy One of God (Jn 6:69) for his holiness is identically that of God himself. Christians who are one with him by baptism receive the Holy Spirit and are classed as 'saints'. They may not be virtuous, but they are in communion with the Holy One.

Holiness is thus particularly linked to the transcendent, which is acknowledged even by some declared atheists. A. C. Grayling, for example, opposes religion but in keeping with his Stoic outlook does acknowledge a transcendent dimension of reality. After the frontispiece of his *The God Argument: The Case against Religion and for Humanism* he quotes Seneca's *De Constantia* XIX. 4 '*esse aliquid invictum*' ('there is something unconquered') (Grayling, 2013, p. v). In his *The Book of Atheist Spirituality* André Comte-Sponville (2009) speaks of his 'oceanic feeling', which he acknowledges is deeply spiritual, and which Romain Rolland (1866–1944) defines as '*the feeling of the "eternal"*' (italics in original) (Parsons, 1999, p. 36).

Something remarkable occurs where people from different holiness traditions meet. Mary Boys (2010, pp. 21–22) compares it with what is called 'thin' space in Celtic mythology, namely where the boundary between this world and the transcendent is almost 'translucent'. She goes on to say that this 'thin' place needs a 'thick' religiosity, where the interlocutor is firmly grounded in the texts and rituals, the history and culture of their tradition (Boys, 2010, p. 25).

And yet, there is scandal. The crimes of spiritual leaders are particularly heinous. They speak of holiness and seem to lead holy lives, but too often they are hypocrites, deceiving and manipulating their followers in order to satisfy their desires. These scandals are well known and cannot be ignored. Students must face them, and learn how to distinguish between the holiness of a tradition and the unholiness of some of its members.

How can we prepare students to face the horrors done in the name of religion? How can we tackle the scandals of corruption, greed and misconduct that can affect all human activities, religious and non-religious alike? On 8 November, 1793, during the French Revolution whose motto was 'Liberty, Equality, Fraternity', Madame Roland cried out as she faced the guillotine, 'O Liberty, O Liberty! What crimes are committed in thy name!' (Abbott, 1904, p. 300). Her cry could be adapted: 'O Christianity, O Islam, O Buddhism!'

## Part II: a portrait

We have examined aspects of the phrase 'seeing what is true and holy in others'. What might students be like who come to see others in this way? How would they see others? How would they see themselves? In what ways would their minds be freed and not just trained, in what ways enlightened and not just informed? How would they see the world? What contribution may they make to a world beset by conflict, often along religious lines? This second part attempts to sketch such a portrait.

It would be hoped that from the outset such students would presume that others speak the truth. They would reject the presumption of error that leads to a culture of doubt and contention. They would not be gullible, accepting everything that is asserted. Neither would they *a priori* exclude forms of perception other than their own. They would keep an open mind. The presumption of truth is not naivety, for it is not uncritical. They would presume the truth but also wish to see it for themselves.

Students would attach primacy not to the spoken but to the speaker. They would allow themselves to be intrigued by the other, challenged by new ways of thinking. They would not see the other as a mere object, someone to be marginalised in favour of one's own individualist concerns, but as a person to be respected with their own unique views and gifts. While preserving their strong self of self-worth, students would be humble before the other, who would gift them the most intense human experience and call them to respond in justice and truth. They would begin to see the depths that lie hidden in the other, and realise that they are windows onto something that far exceeds human limitations, however this is understood.

Many students may be strongly linked to a religious tradition or to a spirituality not linked to any tradition, or not identify as spiritual at all. They would learn about other religions but would not be pressured to abandon their own beliefs and worldviews. The students would remain rooted in their own faith or non-faith tradition, if they have one, and appreciate its richness and depth all the more.

The teacher would serve as a role model. Because the teacher would welcome the truth and holiness of others, students would all the more easily adopt the same attitude.

Students would consider those who, to a remarkable degree, have been engaged with the transcendent. For example, Sri Rāmana Mahārṣi (1879–1950) for Hinduism, Said Nursî (1877–1960) for Islam, Dom Thomas Merton ocso (1915–1968) for Christianity, Achaan Chah (1918–1992) for Buddhism, to name just four possibilities. Something happened in these great figures that profoundly moved them. What was it?

Students would also meet living practitioners of these religions, Rabbis, Imams, Priests, Pastors, Brahmins, Monks, Humanists and Secularists, including exemplary lay people whose very person manifests the truth of their traditions.

Some students may enter more deeply into this inquiry through the practice of meditation, where they come to stillness and attentiveness, and where they may discover deeper meanings and connections. This approach may not suit all students but could suit many.

Students would also visit temples, synagogues, mosques, *gurdwara*s and churches, viewing their layout, meeting religious and community leaders, and realising that religions are a lived reality. They would also view something of the ritual, calendar, architecture, art, calligraphy, sculpture, music, chants and pilgrimages that come from religious experience and can lead to it. Students can do so through real-life and online interactions.

The students may experience something of the delight, even the ecstasy that others throughout the ages have experienced in encountering such exquisitely beautiful and moving places and art work. Would their spirits soar also? Perhaps. At least the opportunity would be given to them and possibly prepare them for a later time when this might happen.

The students would consider the essential doctrines and teachings of diverse worldviews. These would necessarily be presented only in bare outline, but at least they would be presented clearly and accurately. In this way they would be disabused of the false views that are presented by unsympathetic opponents or religions and religious extremists. They would also be informed about the beliefs held by other members in their class and by people they will meet later in life.

Through all these encounters, the students would begin to discern their own selves more clearly. They may consider some of the following. What do you see? What touches you strongly? What does that reveal about your own being? What is your deepest and most authentic self? How are you challenged? How have you changed and grown by seeing what is true and holy in others? What answers have you found to the questions that, as stated in *Nostra Aetate*, have always been put to religions? What is your considered interpretation? What meaning has the other given to you? What can you now state with conviction? What can others see or hear that is trustworthy in you?

Students would face the scandals but not be blinded by them; they could still see what is valuable in the mess. So further questions may be put to them: How do you respond to the scandal of evil? What truth do you find within the horror?

As students would be encouraged to acquire an open and responsible mind, they would not let themselves be put into the Procrustean bed of fundamentalism that can be found in every sphere, religious and non-religious alike.

Through this whole process, students would be taken into four forms of transcendence: 'upwards to the One who surpasses all', 'outwards to the other', 'within to the unplumbed depths of one's own tradition', and 'onwards to a future which is beyond human imagining' (Faith and Order Commission, 2005, p. 14).

They would acquire a sense of awe and wonder at their own infinite worth. They would also acquire deeper qualities of soul, becoming sensitive and alert, tranquil and forgiving, but above all discovering the depths from which they themselves and this world have sprung.

This approach has consequences beyond the immediate ambit of the student. Such educating, in the words of Paulo Freire, the proponent of liberation theology, is not in order to 'replicate' society but to 'recreate' it. The educator is not imposing the dominant ideology, but awakening the student's mind to social, political, spiritual and religious dimensions (Byrne, 2011, p. 48).

John D'Arcy May sees,

> . . . the depths of the religious traditions the whole of humanity has inherited
> . . . as non-renewable *spiritual* resources which, far from being irrelevant to
> our problems or even the cause of them, offer an unparalleled possibility of
> filling the vacuum left by social dislocation and materialistic excess.
>
> (May, 2016, p. 177)

In short, by participating in such an educational approach, students would acquire an outlook that will be productive throughout life. They will be continually enriched in their own persons and they will help create a harmonious society that is no longer polarised into opposing camps or confused by the diversity of beliefs and worldviews.

## References

Abbott, J. (1904). *Madame Roland, makers of history*. New York: Harpers & Brothers.

Aristotle (1953). *The ethics of Aristotle: The Nicomachean ethics*, (Trans. J. A. K. Thomson). London: Penguin Books.

Boys, M. (2010). The promise and perils of inter-religious education. *Toronto Journal of Theology, 26*(1), 21–32.

Buber, M. (1947). *Between man and man*. (Trans. Ronald Gregor Smith). London: Kegan Paul.

Byrne, K. (2011). Freirean critical pedagogy's challenge to interfaith education: What is interfaith? What is education? *British Journal of Religious Education, 33*(1), 47–60.

Cassidy, E. (2006). Journeying towards the 'other': a challenge for religious, spiritual and moral education. In M. de Souza, G. Durka, K. Engebretson, R. Jackson & A. McGrady (eds), *International handbook of the religious, moral and spiritual dimensions in education* (pp. 869–884). Dordrecht The Netherlands: Springer.

Chodkiewicz, M. (2015). *Seal of the saints: Prophethood and sainthood in the doctrine of Ibn 'Arabī.* Srinagar (Kashmir, India): Gulshan Books.

Clooney, F. (2010). *Comparative theology: Deep learning across religious borders.* Chichester, UK: Wiley-Blackwell.

Comte-Sponville, A. (2009). *The book of atheist spirituality.* (Trans. Nancy Huston). London: Bantam Books.

Cullen, S. (2006). The role of the school in promoting inter-religious and inter-cultural dialogue. In M. de Souza, G. Durka, K. Engebretson, R. Jackson & A. McGrady (eds), *International handbook of the religious, moral and spiritual dimensions in education* (pp. 993–1000). Dordrecht, The Netherlands: Springer.

Descartes, R. (1954). *Descartes: Philosophical writings.* (Trans. Elizabeth Anscombe & Peter T. Geach). Sunbury-on-Thames, Middlesex: Thomas Nelson and Sons.

Erricker, J. (2006). Engaging children in spiritual discovery in a multi-faith approach. In M. de Souza, G. Durka, K. Engebretson, R. Jackson & A. McGrady (eds), *International handbook of the religious, moral and spiritual dimensions in education* (pp. 1307–1320). Dordrecht, The Netherlands: Springer.

Faith and Order Commission of the Victorian Council of Churches (2005). *One Faith – Multifaith: A theological basis for interfaith gatherings.* Melbourne: Victorian Council of Churches.

Grayling, A. (2013). *The God argument: The case against religion and for humanism.* London: Bloomsbury.

Hamilton, W. (2016). *Dietrich Bonhoeffer.* Retrieved 17 October, 2016, from www.religion-online.or/showchapter.asp?title=537&C=591.

Ignatius of Loyola (1952). *The text of the spiritual exercises.* (Trans. John Morris et al.) London: Burns & Oates.

International Standard Bible Encyclopaedia Online (2016). *Holiness.* Retrieved 18 January, 2016, from http://internationalstandardbible.com/H/holiness.html

Jackson, R. (2006). Introduction to section two: Religious education and debates about plurality and culture. In M. de Souza, G. Durka, K. Engebretson, R. Jackson & A. McGrady (eds), *International handbook of the religious, moral and spiritual dimensions in education* (pp. 295–306). Dordrecht, The Netherlands: Springer.

Kemerling, G. (2011). *Philosophy pages.* Retrieved 13 January, 2016, from Encyclopaedia Britannica website http://philosophypages.com/hy/4c.htm

Lane, D. (2006). Expanding the theological imagination in the service of inter faith dialogue: Impulses from Vatican II. In M. de Souza, G. Durka, K. Engebretson, R. Jackson & A. McGrady (eds), *International handbook of the religious, moral and spiritual dimensions in education* (pp. 905–916). Dordrecht, The Netherlands: Springer.

Lefebure, L. (2005). The contribution of H.H. the XIVth Dalai Lama to interfaith education. *Cross Currents,* 55(1), 83–89.

May, J. (2016). *Imagining the ecumenical journey.* Northcote, Vic: Morning Star Publishing.

Meijer, W. (2016). Plural selves and living traditions: A hermeneutical view on identity and diversity, tradition and historicity. In M. de Souza, G. Durka, K. Engebretson, R. Jackson & A. McGrady (eds), *International handbook of the religious, moral and spiritual dimensions in education* (pp. 321–332). Dordrecht (The Netherlands): Springer.

Mulherin, C. (2016). *Truth and knowing after method: A hermeneutic, universal, fiduciary, and provisional approach to truth.* Unpublished doctoral dissertation, University of Divinity, Melbourne, Australia.

Nietzsche, F. (1961). *Thus spoke Zarathustra*. (Trans. R. J. Hollingdale). Harmondsworth, Middlesex: Penguin Books Ltd.

Online Etymology Dictionary (2016a). *amen*. Retrieved 20 October, 2016, from http://etymonline.com/index.php?term=amen

Online Etymology Dictionary (2016b). *holy*. Retrieved 20 October, 2016, from http://etymonline.com/index.php?allowed_in_frame=0&search=holy

Online Etymology Dictionary (2016c). *sanctus*. Retrieved 20 October, 2016, from http://etymonline.com/index.php?allowed_in_frame=0&search=saint

Otto, R. (1923). *The idea of the holy*. (Trans. J. W. Harvey). Oxford: Oxford University Press.

Parsons, W. (1999) *The enigma of the oceanic feeling: Revisioning the psychoanalytic theory of mysticism*. Oxford: Oxford University Press.

Popper, K. (1983). *Realism and the aim of science*. London: Hutchinson.

Rahner, K. (1986). In P. Imhof & H. Biallowons (eds), *Karl Rahner in dialogue: Conversations and interviews 1965–1982*. New York: Crossroad.

Rosenblum, B., & Kuttner, F. (2011). *Quantum enigma: Physics encounters consciousness*. Oxford: Oxford University Press. Retrieved 22 October, 2016 from. http://quantumenigma.com/nutshell/notable-quotes-on-quantum-physics/

Scott, D. (2006). Spirituality and identity within/without religion. In M. de Souza, G. Durka, K. Engebretson, R. Jackson, & A. McGrady (eds), *International handbook of the religious, moral and spiritual dimensions in education* (pp. 1111–1125). Dordrecht, The Netherlands: Springer.

Vatican Council II (2016). *Declaration on the relation of the church with non-Christian religions (Nostra Aetate)*. Retrieved 20 October, 2016, from http://vatican.va/archive/hist_councils/ii_vatican_council/documents/vat-ii_decl_19651028_nostra-aetate_en.html

White, N. (1979). *A companion to Plato's Republic*. Oxford: Basil Blackwell.

# 11

# CHILDHOODS PAST AND PRESENT

## A reflexive approach to enhancing children's spiritual wellbeing

*Kate Adams*

## Introduction

When reading any education policy document which makes reference to children's spirituality, one can be forgiven for being uninspired. While some texts may well be more engaging than others, it can be difficult for the authors to capture the potential for the delicate, intangible, mysterious nature of spirituality, particularly when the audience may be seeking a pragmatic explanation of what it is and how they can apply it to the classroom. Educators' responses to the inclusion of spirituality in policy are inevitably divergent, ranging from whole-hearted embrace to ambivalence through to hostility, and those individual responses inevitably translate into practice in the classroom. In countries such as England and Wales, where spiritual development has had long-standing links with education for over 70 years, practice today still varies widely in schools – a result of complex socio-cultural factors which will be outlined in this chapter. In the UK, where the policy language is rooted in the history of the education system, it is perhaps easier for those who oppose it to ignore it rather than exert any energy into contesting it. In contrast, for countries such as Australia, where the inclusion of spirituality is relatively new outside of the faith schools sector, we see added layers of complexity related to igniting of debates as to why it is even necessary at all, and if so, why now: debates which are intensely passionate and heartfelt on both sides.

England's education system has become, like those in the USA and Australia, increasingly performativity-oriented (see Polesel et al., 2012). With heavy foci on test and exam results, which are publically available and have strong bearing on a school's reputation, there is anxiety that the whole child is being lost (Peterson et al., 2014). This is of considerable concern on two counts. First, reports indicate that the education system itself appears to be causing increasing levels of anxiety among children (NSPCC, 2015). This finding sits alongside other statistics which show rising rates of obesity among children (Bradshaw & Mayhew, 2005; Coster, 2007) and fears for children's safety which are leading to increased indoor activities (Coster, 2007) among other issues. Second, this has led to a strong, albeit contested, discourse about the so-called 'loss of childhood' (Kehily, 2009) which I have explored from children's perspectives elsewhere (Adams, 2013). These issues are far from being exclusive to England and Wales but are also reported in other economically advanced countries. Furthermore, the plight of war-torn countries and increasing poverty and economic decline in others serves to remind us of the myriad of problems facing children on a global level. Hence the nurturing of children's spiritual wellbeing is becoming increasingly important, set against a backdrop of a planet which appears increasingly complex and pressured in endless ways.

This chapter takes a reflexive theoretical approach to understanding researchers and teachers' varied views on the relationship between education and children's spiritual wellbeing. Roni Berger (2015) highlights how reflexivity has become an important vehicle for ensuring quality in qualitative research. Reflexivity relates to the researcher's social position (e.g. gender, age, race, immigration status, sexual orientation), personal experiences, and political and professional beliefs and how these impact on all aspects of their research. This is far from a straightforward process, as Berger (2015) illustrates with examples of how researchers may share the experience of the participants so that they may move from the position of an outsider to the position of an insider in the course of a study; or they may have no personal familiarity or experience with what is being studied. In many topics, but particularly those relating to the delicate topic of spirituality, this process can be imbued with sensitivities. Indeed, Melvin Pollner (1991) defined reflexivity as 'an unsettling', describing it as 'an insecurity regarding the basic assumptions, discourse and practices used in describing reality' (p. 370). The notion of an unsettling is pertinent to spirituality, as it is inherently personal and linked to meaning-making and sense of purpose – our own views of which are regularly challenged, adapted and reviewed in the course of life.

In this chapter I argue that the aligned concept of the reflexive practitioner (Atkinson, 2004), detailed below, is also essential if educators are to enhance children's spiritual wellbeing. But first, I begin by highlighting the influence of each individual's personal history on their research and practice with a brief sketch of my spiritual autobiography.

> I grew up in a suburb of a major city in England, into a family which was not particularly religious. My primary school had links with the local Anglican church where we went to celebrate Easter, Harvest Festival and Christmas. I remember sitting in this vast building, often cold, both physically and emotionally, being unable to engage with or understand the vicar's words. Like all children, I sought to find purpose and meaning in my life but for me, from an early age, it seemed unlikely that I would find it in formalised religion.

As I transitioned to secondary school, I was captivated by my Religious Education (RE) lessons. A young and enthusiastic newly qualified teacher, Mr Gent, offered an interactive, multi-faith syllabus. Our school and immediate local community was largely mono-cultural but Mr Gent took us into the city to *gurdwaras*, mosques, synagogues and a range of different churches where we were welcomed by all. It was in my RE lessons that my eyes were opened to a divergence of ways of making meaning. Simultaneously though, I was also interested in alternative ways of thinking about life, the universe and everything – anything which may help to find answers to the big questions in life.

A few years later I became a primary teacher with a specialism in RE. In turn this interest led me to undertake a small piece of research into children's spiritual dreams which subsequently led to becoming a full-time PhD student exploring the same theme. This set me on the track of becoming an academic. As Marian de Souza (n.d.) came to find, I was becoming one of the growing number of people who defined themselves as 'spiritual but not religious'. When I undertake research I remain conscious of my childhood influences and also of my openness to the myriad of ways in which children may experience, express or define spirituality, whether religious or not.

The main influences of our childhoods on our religious and/or spiritual beliefs are essential shapers of our adult lives, sometimes affirming or sometimes diverging from our upbringing. Reflection on these influences is important, but so too is the recognition of how the wider social infrastructure and policy have also impacted us, albeit subconsciously. These broader influences are vital to reflexive practitioner approaches (see Atkinson, 2004), as will become apparent later. First, then, I will visit the policy developments which affected my own education as a child and my adult roles as practitioner and researcher.

## Spiritual development and religious education in England and Wales

England and Wales have a very long history in relation to spirituality and education. The two concepts first appeared in legislation in the 1944 Education Act which obliged education authorities to contribute to the spiritual, moral, mental and physical development of the community. For countries which have no mention of spirituality in the curriculum, this may appear a curious situation and leads to the question, why has this been so strongly embedded in our system to the present day?

At the time, the Church of England had a clearly established and dominant position. Indeed, the origins of schools for the masses in England lay with the church (Marples, 2005). In the 1940s, Christianity still dominated and this was directly reflected in the school system where religion and spirituality were synonymous. Furthermore, Religious Instruction was taught in schools. As the name implies, it was based on confessional Christian teaching.

The current system, however, has different conceptualisations as a result of significant shifts in population composition. As the population became increasingly multicultural, particularly through immigration from the 1950s onwards and increasing secularism in latter years, these changes were reflected in the curriculum over time. For example, Religious Education became the successor of Religious Instruction whereby children were to be educated about the main world religions to gain understanding about them and learn from them. It was Religious Education which I, as a child, encountered in my schooling and then as a teacher, became a specialist in, personally holding an interest in the diversity of world religions offered on our syllabi.

Although the nature of Religious Education changed, the term 'spiritual development' has remained constant through successive Education Acts. Currently, the wording in policy in England is 'spiritual, moral, social and cultural development', known as SMSC. A key change came in 1992 when a new schools' inspection body came into being, known as Ofsted, which was required to inspect a range of elements across schools, including children's spiritual, moral, social and cultural development. Of course, knowing that they would be inspected (and with inspections being such a high-stakes affair), many teachers' minds became focused on SMSC, but confusion about it was rife and educators sought clarity.

In the eyes of current policy, spirituality and religion are not synonymous. This fundamental philosophy has important implications for spirituality's relationship with RE. While there is no doubt that RE has a special relationship with spiritual development, policy makers are clear that spiritual development should be cross-curricular. Indeed, Ofsted (2010) reported the strengths and weaknesses of RE in primary and secondary schools based on visits to 94 primary and 89 secondary schools in England. A key finding was that RE made little contribution to students' spiritual development – a finding that applied to 6 out of 10 secondary schools. A second, related, key principle is that spiritual development applies to all children – of all faiths and none.

Ultimately, the most enduring challenge for policy makers lies in attempts to convey what spiritual development is. Successive governments have provided teachers with guidance on its meaning (e.g. NCC, 1993; Ofsted, 2004, 2011) which has changed over time (see Adams, 2014). The most recent Ofsted (2015) description states that students' spiritual development is demonstrated by their: 'ability to be reflective about their own beliefs' be they religious or not, which 'inform their perspective on life'; their 'interest in and respect for different people's faiths, feelings and values'; their 'sense of enjoyment and fascination in learning about themselves, others and the world around them'; and their 'use of imagination and creativity in their learning willingness to reflect on their experiences'. However every definition or description will inevitably prompt contestation and to try to create a definition which applies to children of all faiths and none, as policy makers have attempted, has been a significant challenge which has led to accusations of policy offering vague definitions which actually say little. Indeed, the debate about the meaning of spirituality, as to whether or not it can be defined, and if so whether or not a universally agreed definition can be attained continues.

The key issue on current thinking for this chapter, while recognising that any country's policy definition will inevitably impact on the researchers and practitioners working within it, is to also highlight the reflexivity required by those individuals in illuminating their own understandings of the meaning of spirituality. Personal conceptions may or may not concur with those embedded in legislation and the former may well drive practitioners' actions in the classroom. As a school pupil myself, while multi-faith RE was a self-evident part of what I studied, I was not aware that spiritual development was also a component. This might of course have been a reflection that spiritual development is not intended to be a separate, taught component of the curriculum and hence its existence may have been imperceptible to me as a pupil. Alternatively it may be that my own school, like many others, did not have any understanding of it, or chose to ignore it, particularly as those were the days before it was inspected in schools like mine that had no faith affiliation.

While I worked for 10 years as a primary teacher and RE Co-ordinator, in retrospect I realise that my understanding of spirituality at that time was not as well formed as I thought it was. It was only through subsequent years as an academic, conducting in-depth research for my doctorate and beyond, that I have come to more fully understand my own positionality and the personal history that has shaped it.

## Changing demographics

As noted above, the changing demographics have been reflected in new approaches to RE and spiritual development over preceding decades. Returning to the present day, the most recent Census of England and Wales, conducted in 2011, revealed a population of 56,075,912. The census contained a question asking 'What is your religion?' Essentially this asked about religious affiliation, referring to how people connect or identify with a religion, irrespective of their actual practice or belief. The Census Office recognises that religion is a multifaceted concept and there are other aspects of religion such as religious belief, religious practice or belonging which were not covered in their analysis. Importantly this question was the only voluntary question on the 2011 Census and 7 per cent of respondents chose not to answer it.

Of those who answered, 59 per cent reported themselves as Christian. The next largest religious group was Islam, with 5 per cent reporting themselves as Muslim. These were followed, in size order, by Hindus, Sikhs, Jews, 'other religions' and Buddhists. However, a quarter stated that they did not have a religion. This latter number had increased across all age groups since the previous Census in 2001, particularly in the age groups of 20–24 and 40–44. This increase occurred alongside a decline in the number of Christians, which appeared primarily in people under the age of 60 (Office for National Statistics, 2013).

In terms of the curriculum, the six main world religions represented in the population are also reflected in the content of most RE syllabi. In addition, the fact that one quarter of the population do not align themselves with any religion is also of crucial importance for spiritual development's relevance to children of all faiths and none.

## Understanding childhoods past and present

Just as our own personal understandings of the term spirituality are shaped by our experiences, beliefs and environment, so too are our understandings of childhood. Within the field of spirituality research, very little attention is paid to notions of childhood. Yet study of it is essential because we cannot understand 'children's spirituality' without carefully considering both elements in the phrase.

At first glance the notion of childhood appears more straightforward to unpack. After all, it is very obvious that children are different from adults in many ways. However since the early 1990s, authors writing under the banner of the 'new sociology of childhood' have problematised the concept (see James & Prout, 1997; James & James, 2004; James et al., 2006). They have exemplified how complex the notion of childhood(s) is/are. Their main theoretical underpinnings lie with social constructionism which holds that childhood is co-created within societies and can change over time even within the same culture. For example in England in the 1900s, children were seen as empty vessels which needed to be filled and were largely to be seen but not heard. In comparison, children today are seen as active agents who have negotiating powers over the meaning of their lives. They also have other identities such as consumers, and have met with various media labels such as deviants.

Our own notions of childhood are directly linked to our ideas about children's spiritual wellbeing, since for many of us, the former embody our personal and collective views of what a good childhood should consist of. An example relates to how many people in economically advanced countries perceive childhood to be a time to play and attend school which will prepare them to become adults who will enter paid employment and become responsible citizens. Any model of childhood which is considerably different inevitably causes strong reactions, as well as demonstrating the range of social constructions globally. Kate Cregan and Denise Cuthbert (2014) demonstrate these in their case studies of diverse childhoods which include foci on child soldiers and child labour. The latter theme is an important one for showing how adverse reactions in the economically developed world may contrast with those in the less economically developed world where child labour may be a routine part of daily life, and often one that is essential to staying alive. While moral responses lead the way, alongside campaigns to end child labour globally, there are other elements to consider. Some research in these communities has illuminated quite different understandings, including from the children themselves. For example Rosemary D. F. Bromley and Peter K. Mackie (2009) interviewed 100 children who worked as street traders in Peru. While the children (age 6–16) recognised the inherent dangers in their job, they also highlighted the positive elements such as employment, economic empowerment, agency and self-esteem. Marit Ursin (2011) explored the narratives of 'home' of young people living on the streets of Brazil and discovered why some had deliberate~~~, ~~sen the street as a place to call home. Spirituality and spiritual wellbeing for children in these communities will be quite different to those living in other contexts.

These examples are not intended to condone childhoods which are characterised by work or poverty, but are instead used to illustrate how vastly differing concepts and realities exist around the world and that our own concepts are, in the first instance, shaped by what we ourselves have experienced. This experience will be primarily of our own lived childhood, no matter where in the world that was situated, but also through other experiences such as travel, charity work, the virtual world or perhaps vicariously through friends' lives. Yet, no matter how our views of childhood were formed, the key issue for researchers and practitioners is to be able to identify and articulate their personal views, together with the reasons for them. Without doing so, notions of children's wellbeing – what constitutes a 'good childhood' – cannot be fully grounded.

Of course, illuminating one's own position can be painful because many childhoods, past and present, have been blighted with darkness, some with serious trauma, no matter where in the world they took place. Re-visiting such experiences brings its own difficulties and needs to be managed with care and sensitivity if being facilitated in a college, university, school or other professional development setting. Not, of course, that any such conversation is intended to act as therapy. Rather, it should be designed to encourage illumination of thoughts, ideas and the challenging of assumptions which may have hitherto gone unchallenged.

## The reflective and reflexive practitioner

How then does a reflexive approach to enhancing children's spiritual wellbeing apply to practitioners? Just as the notion of reflexivity in research has become increasingly recognised and valued, the notion of the 'reflexive practitioner' has also gained some momentum in professional settings, but first let's consider the more familiar notion of the reflective educator.

In education, the concept of the reflective practitioner, drawn initially from John Dewey (1933) and Donald Schön (1983), has been long established in teacher training. From the outset, student teachers are encouraged to reflect on their own practice in various ways with the aim of facilitating greater insights and improved future practice as a result. Reflective practice has been theorised in numerous ways. For example, Dewey (1933) made a distinction between routine action which is guided by tradition, routine habit and institutional expectations that remain relatively static, and reflective action – a willingness to engage in constant self-appraisal and development. The latter requires social awareness, flexibility and rigorous analysis. Schön (1983) explored notions of reflecting-in-action and reflecting-on-action in the classroom. More recently, Tony Ghaye (2011) highlights that reflective practice enables practitioners to understand the links between what they do and how they might improve that effectiveness, embodying a focus on taking action in order to become more effective. In education circles, therefore, reflective practice is focused on practical issues which enable teachers to improve what they do, supported and directed by self-awareness, as well as being shaped through dialogue with mentors and peers.

Reflective thinking is essential. However, I argue that particularly in matters of spiritual wellbeing, reflexive thinking and action are also crucial. Dennis Atkinson (2004) develops the notion of the 'reflexive practitioner' in the context of developing teacher identity, arguing that while it involves rational reflection upon classroom practice and one's own beliefs, attitudes, assumptions, prejudices and suppositions that inform teaching, it also requires attention to the effect of institutional structures on teaching. If we apply this idea to children's spiritual wellbeing, we need therefore to also consider respective policy structures which shape the spiritual or religious dimensions of curricula, as well as how and why those policies came into being, as outlined above for England and Wales. Further-more, we need to also evaluate our own responses to those policies and explore the reasons for them: reasons which will inevitably differ in either subtle or sig-nificant ways from those offered by colleagues. On a personal level, I concur with England and Wales' policy of religion and spirituality not being synonymous as it fits into my own identity as spiritual but not religious, yet fascinated by many belief systems. Nevertheless, I respect the views of others who would disagree with this stance.

However, reflexivity involves more than consideration of the relevant policy structure. Ann Cunliffe (2004) applies the concept of the reflexive practitioner to management education. She views reflexivity in practitioner settings as relating to 'the subjective understandings of reality as a basis for thinking more critically about the impact of our assumptions, values, and actions on others' (p. 407). She contends that reflexive practice can support people in becoming critical thinkers and moral practitioners. Again, if this notion is applied to educators engaged in nurturing children's spiritual wellbeing, there is a case to be made that through undertaking this approach, greater insights into our own dispositions and associated actions (both conscious and unconscious) can be gained.

Let's explore this idea through three examples of educators' narratives, beginning with a boy's spiritual experience which affected his spiritual wellbeing for many years into adulthood and shaped his philosophy of education. The narrative belongs to Matt, an American teacher working in the UK who recounted a childhood experience at the age of nine, which was to impact on him into adulthood. He recalled:

'It was late spring and there were beautiful cloud formations. The sun was low and the clouds looked red. I was gazing and I saw a whole city in the clouds. It looked like Jerusalem – there were houses in the hillside. . .'

Matt explained that this was not a simple case of seeing pictures in the clouds. Instead, this was an incredibly intricate image which looked like a drawing rather than a photograph. It was a 'profound' moment. He eagerly ran indoors to tell his parents who said 'that's nice, what did it look like?'

Matt ran back outside to see if he could still see it, which he could. But his parents remained in the house 'and didn't come out to validate it'. The next morning at school, during a show and tell session, he eagerly explained his experience to the whole class. 'And that was the most stupid thing I ever did,' he said. 'I told other people'. The teacher, a nun, was very patronising and said 'Oh I am sure you didn't see that' at which point all of his classmates 'roared with laughter'. Matt said that that moment in school was 'the moment of socialisation' for him and he no longer told people of personal experiences such as this for fear of a similar response. In fact, I was the first person with whom he shared this encounter in 35 years.

(Adams, 2010, pp. 56 and 130)

Matt was an inherently reflective and reflexive practitioner-researcher and these elements of his personality, combined with this defining moment in his childhood came to shape his approach to working with children in the classroom. While Matt went on to teach in Catholic schools, he was also open to, and welcoming of, different faiths and alternative understandings of spirituality. He had remained highly sensitive to listening to the varied experiences of the children in his care. Remembering how his own teacher had dismissed his experience out of hand made him determined not to do that to his pupils. Furthermore, he consciously created an ethos in his classrooms in which children were facilitated to listen and respect the religious and spiritual views and experiences of their classmates.

A second example comes from Safa, a teacher in an inner-city secondary school in England who grew up in the Sikh community. Central to her childhood, and faith, were gatherings in the *langar* (kitchen) in her local *gurdwara*. She recalled her regular childhood visits to the *langar* where people from all backgrounds were offered a free meal, and ate together. She explained,

At the time, as a young girl, I remember this overwhelming feeling of being part of something that was much bigger than my family and my neighbours who were mostly Sikh. Because the *gurdwara* welcomed people from all walks of life, where everyone was equal, I met with them often in the *langar*, there was a sense that I was part of something much bigger, that I was somehow connected to a bigger world.

Safa's overriding memories of connection to others and the world directly influenced her philosophy of education when she became a teacher. She works in a school which draws on a diverse population comprising several different ethnicities, faiths and secular populations. Tensions between some ethnic groups are apparent both among the children in school and also adults in the local community so in the classroom she emphasises their place in the wider world, as part of a global community.

In a chapter on reflexivity it would be appropriate to also include my own experience of how self-awareness influenced my practice as a primary teacher.

As noted above, I worked in a state-funded school in England which had no religious affiliation. Like Safa, I was uneasy about conflicts between different faiths and I sought to emphasise the similarities in teachings across different religions while also recognising and respecting the distinctive nature of them.

With regards to spirituality, my personal history of being open to many ways of viewing the world and meaning and purpose in life was also explicit in the classroom. I was in accordance with the country's non-confessional policy on RE but, perhaps more importantly, my own childhood meant that I was attuned to children's openness to a wide variety of spiritual worldviews, many of which did not align to conventional religious teachings. Hence I, like Matt, created spaces within the classroom for their ideas to be expressed and explored in an environment where they would feel safe to contemplate and, if they wished, share their thoughts without fear of the ridicule which had done so much damage to Matt and many other children around the world.

A reflexive approach such as this, as exemplified by Matt, Safa and myself, moves beyond a teacher reflecting on a lesson in which a child may have shared a meaningful encounter and they, the teacher, may have inadvertently or overtly dismissed it, resulting in laughter from peers. In such a case, a teacher may have reflected-in-action or on–action (Schön, 1983), and realised that they had handled the situation poorly and vowed to act differently next time. This would have been a useful outcome. However, by adopting a reflexive approach to practice, a teacher would have potentially gained a much stronger insight into their actions and those around them, all of which have been shaped to some extent by their own personal histories and societal influences including policy.

Our own past experiences of childhood and our current constructions of contemporary childhood(s) can be difficult to reconcile. A key difficulty is in being able to accurately recall our past and as we grow older we inevitably come to see the world through adult lenses (Adams, 2010). Doing so can take us too far away from contemporary children's views; views which may be unexpected and not necessarily sit comfortably with adult taken-for-granted assumptions. Yet the very act of self and peer challenge can aid the processes of reflection and reflexivity and in the process aid personal growth.

## Moving forwards

Any policy requirement around spirituality does not inevitably mean that it is implemented well, nor in some institutions, implemented at all. Furthermore, the additional complexities inherent in spirituality, such as lack of agreement over its definition make the area far from straightforward. Yet in the discourse about children's spirituality, concepts of childhood are also essential for, without articulating what we mean by both terms, we are neglecting an important part of the topic. Work by the new sociologists of childhood has demonstrated, through a highly critical approach, how complex the terms 'childhood' – and also 'child' and 'children' – are. Similarly, meanings of the term 'wellbeing' are also open to debate. Theoretical considerations of all these issues are vital in order to add depth of understanding, and to inform practice with the ultimate aim of supporting and nurturing children through education.

The term 'spirituality' ignites a range of emotions in people from complete acceptance, curiosity through to antagonism and outright rejection. Whichever view people take, it is inevitably going to lead to contestation and fuelled debate, especially when it first emerges in an education system. Unlike the idea of teaching language or maths, which stimulates debate over teaching methods but not over their very existence, the inclusion of children's spirituality in a curriculum will remain controversial for many. It is partly for this reason that all stakeholders, irrespective of their views, need to explore reflexive approaches in order to more fully understand and articulate their own positions. In so doing they may choose not to apply a spiritual approach to their role, but will nonetheless be better placed to know how best to support children as they navigate their way through an ever increasingly complex and confusing world. Children need to know who they are; to have a strong sense of connectedness and meaning and purpose. They need to be creative, to wonder at the mysteries of life . . . to be 'whole' people. Educators are one key to helping children on their journey, and getting to know themselves better will ultimately help them know children better too.

# References

Adams, K. (2010). *Unseen worlds: Looking through the lens of childhood.* London: Jessica Kingsley.

Adams, K. (2013). Childhood in crisis? Perceptions of 7–11 year olds and the implications for education's well-being agenda. *Education 3–13: International Journal of Primary, Elementary and Early Years Education,* 41(5), 527–537. doi:10.1080/03004279.2011.613849

Adams, K. (2014). Spiritual development in schools with no faith affiliation: The cultural ambivalence towards children's spirituality in England. In M. de Souza, A. Trousdale & J. Watson (eds), *Global perspectives on spiritual education* (pp. 21–32). Abingdon: Routledge.

Atkinson, D. (2004). Theorizing how student teachers form their identities in initial teacher education. *British Educational Research Journal,* 30(3), 379–394.

Berger, R. (2015). Now I see it, now I don't: Researcher's position and reflexivity in qualitative research. *Qualitative Research,* 15(2), 219–234.

Bradshaw, J., & Mayhew, E. (eds). (2005). *The well-being of children in the UK.* London: Save the Children.

Bromley, R. D. F., & Mackie, P. K. (2009). Child experiences as street traders in Peru: Contributing to a reappraisal for working children. *Children's Geographies,* 7(2), 141–158.

Coster, W. (2007). Childhood in Crisis? In P. Zwozdiak-Myers (ed.), *Childhood and youth studies,* p.26. Exeter: Learning Matters.

Cregan, K., & Cuthbert, D. (2014). *Global childhoods: Issues and debates.* London: Sage Publications.

Cunliffe, A. (2004). On becoming a critically reflexive practitioner. *Journal of Management Education,* 28(4), 407–426.

de Souza, M. (n.d.). A concept of human spirituality. *International Association for Children's Spirituality.* Retrieved 3 July, 2016, from: http://childrenspirituality.org/documents/concept-of-spirituality.pdf

Dewey, J. (1933). *How we think: A restatement of the relation of reflective thinking to the educative process*. Chicago, IL: Henry Regnery.

Ghaye, T. (2011). *Teaching and learning through reflective practice: A practical guide for positive action*. Abingdon: Routledge.

James, A., & James, A. L. (2004). *Constructing childhood: Theory, policy and social practice*. London: Palgrave Macmillan.

James, A., & Prout, A. (eds). (1997). *Constructing and reconstructing childhood: Contemporary issues in the sociological study of childhood*. Abingdon: RoutledgeFalmer.

James, A., Jenks, C., & Prout, A. (2006). *Theorizing childhood*. Cambridge: Polity Press.

Kehily, M. J. (ed.). (2009). *An introduction to childhood studies*. Maidenhead, UK: Open University Press.

Marples, R. (2005). Against faith schools: A philosophical argument for children's rights. *International Journal of Children's Spirituality, 10*(2), 133–147.

National Society for the Prevention of Cruelty to Children (NSPCC), (2012). NSPCC factsheet: an introduction to child protection legislation in the UK. Retrieved June 11, 2012, from www.nspcc.org.uk/Inform/research/questions/child_protection_legislation_in_the_uk_pdf_wdf48953.pdf

NCC (1993). *Spiritual and moral development: A discussion paper*. York: National Curriculum Council.

Office for National Statistics (2013). Full story: What does the Census tell us about religion in 2011? Retrieved 15 August, 2016, from: https://ons.gov.uk/peoplepopulationandcommunity/culturalidentity/religion/articles/fullstorywhatdoesthecensustellusaboutreligionin2011/2013-05-16

Ofsted (2004). *Promoting and evaluating pupils' spiritual, moral, social and cultural development*. London: Ofsted.

Ofsted (2010). *Transforming religious education: Religious education in schools 2006–09*. London: Ofsted.

Ofsted (2011). *The framework for school inspection from January 2012*. London: Ofsted.

Ofsted (2015). *School inspection handbook*. London: Ofsted.

Peterson, A., Lexmond, J., Hallgarten, J., & Kerr, D. (2014). *Schools with soul: A new approach to spiritual, moral, social and cultural education. Report*. London: RSA.

Polesel, J., Dulfer, N., & Turnball, M. (2012). *The experience of education: The impacts of high stakes testing on school students and their families*. Sydney: The Whitlam Institute.

Pollner, M. (1991). Left of ethnomethodology: The rise and decline of radical reflexivity. *American Sociological Review, 56*, 370–380.

Schön, D. (1983). *Educating the reflective practitioner*. San Francisco: Jossey-Bass.

Ursin, M. (2011). 'Wherever I lay my head is home': Young people's experience of home in the Brazilian street environment. *Children's Geographies, 9*(2), 221–234.

# 12

# EDUCATIONAL REFORMS IN JAPAN

## Are they contributing to a sense of wellbeing and happiness among young people?

*Dorothea Filus*

## Introduction

Japanese education has been praised for producing excellent academic outcomes in the areas of mathematics, science and reading, as is evident in comparative international achievement tests. However, critics of Japanese education have argued that its major focus on preparing students for university entrance exams has resulted in an emphasis on rote learning and memorisation, rather than contributing to developing students' analytical, critical and independent thinking, or their creativity and ability to express themselves. Some commentators claim that the high academic performance of Japanese students should be attributed to private cram schools (*juku*); this is often referred to as 'shadow education'. The critics further argue that in the era of globalisation, such obsolete pedagogy is inefficient in preparing students to compete in the global economy, and ineffective in meeting the needs of a global and multicultural society (Park, 2013, pp. 1–6, 75–77).

Furthermore, rigid Japanese education, which places great pressures on students and demands high levels of conformity, has been blamed for the growing alienation of students and alarming social problems, such as high rates of bullying, violence, suicide and chronic truancy which often results in social withdrawal and self-seclusion (*hikikomori*). *Hikikomori* is a phenomenon peculiar to Japan, where young people retreat into their bedrooms and may stay there for years (Gifford et al., 2014, pp. 86–87; Cabinet Office, 2013, p. 21).

As a result, in the late twentieth century it became clear that Japanese education was in urgent need of reform. A series of changes have since been introduced, promoting a more diversified, flexible and individualised education known as 'relaxed education' (*yutori kyoiku*). These new reforms also targeted students' psychological and spiritual wellbeing, with calls for the introduction of religious education in schools, and improvement in moral guidance. Yet, as the Japanese Constitution forbids the teaching of religion in public schools (Filus, 2006, pp. 1039–1043; Filus, 2010a, pp. 779–781), instead, various moral education programs were introduced, such as 'heart education' (*kokoro no kyoiku*) and 'life and death education' (*inochi no kyoiku*) to combat juvenile problems (Saito, 2015; MEXT, 2009, p. 4). However, it is questionable whether the new reforms and programs have produced any positive changes in students' wellbeing, as will be discussed below.

This chapter will first examine the recent changes to the Japanese education system. This will be followed by a review of a recent comparative survey on the attitudes of young Japanese people, in order to evaluate whether Japanese education contributes to the psychological wellbeing of Japanese youth, and in particular their sense of identity, belonging and happiness. The chapter will also examine how the Japanese education system prepares students for the challenges of globalisation and living in a multicultural society.

## Recent changes to the Japanese education system

The postwar Japanese education system was established in 1947 with the enactment of the Fundamental Law of Education adopted under American supervision. This Law was thoroughly revised in 2006. Chiho Mori and Ian Davies (2015, p. 171) argue that:

> One of the aims of the revision of the Fundamental Law of Education in 2006 was to remove some of the alleged excessive individualism imposed by the US occupation and to supplant "respect for the individual" emphasising "love for one's homeland" instead.

The new Fundamental Law of Education opened the door to teaching traditional values and nationalism in schools. Educational reforms, conducted approximately every 10 years, have resulted in new Courses of Study (teaching guidelines) being prescribed by the Ministry of Education, Culture, Sports, Science and Technology (MEXT). The most recent Courses of Study were prescribed in 2008–2009 (MEXT, 2011, 2016a).

Traditionally, the goal of education in Japan has been defined as a three-fold development of personality, namely, intellect, morality and physical strength. This is in accord with the three pillars of education as delineated by Herbert Spencer's 1860 *Education: Intellectual, Moral, and Physical* (Spencer, 1860). Spencer's ideas became influential in Japan at the end of the nineteenth century and have been the basis of teaching guidelines ever since (Nagai, 1954). In the twenty-first century, MEXT once again used Spencer's ideas to formulate educational policies, but enriched Spencer's ideas with the principle known as 'zest for life' (*ikiru chikara*) as a core objective of education (MEXT, 2008, 2011; Cabinet Office, 2013, pp. 60–61; Maruyama, 2013, pp. 2–3). The idea of 'zest for life' was first coined in 1996 by the Central Council for Education (*Chuo Kyoiku Shingikai*), advisory

committee of the then Ministry of Education, as the main goal for Japanese education in the twenty-first century, so that young Japanese can learn and think
independently in order to solve problems they encounter living in a rapidly
changing society (Chuo Kyoiku Shingikai, 1996). Thus the latest Japanese model
of education still uses Spencer's old ideas, and also the slogan 'zest for life'.

In accord with Spencer's views that the cultivation of morality is as important
as the cultivation of the intellect, moral education, known as *Shushin*, was
introduced into Japanese schools in 1873, and eventually became the core subject
in the Japanese curriculum until 1945. However, in 1945, *Shushin*, which was used
as a vehicle for ultranationalist and militaristic propaganda during the war, was
banned from schools by the American Occupation authorities (Maruyama, 2013,
pp. 1–2). After the Occupation ended in 1952, moral education under the name
of *Dotoku* was reinstated in schools in 1958, when conservative politicians were
bemoaning a decline in morals among young Japanese, which was allegedly
responsible for juvenile problems (Duke, 1967, pp. 35–37). When high suicide
rates, violence and truancy continued in the 1960s and 1970s, and education became
synonymous with rote learning, thereby suppressing students' independent critical
thinking and the development of their individuality, calls for a less stressful
education began. Originally the aim was to reduce school to 5 days per week and
to decrease the curriculum content. Those goals were finally realised in 2002, when
the 5-day-school-week was fully implemented and the curriculum content was
reduced by 30 per cent. The new changes also involved the redefinition of the
role of teacher in the classroom in order to promote 'active learning', a shift from
teacher-led instruction to children learning autonomously. This new type of
education became known as 'relaxed education' (Ikeno, 2011; Park, 2013).

However, soon after relaxed education was introduced, the academic ability of
Japanese students deteriorated, as was evident most conspicuously in the 2003 and
2006 Programme for International Student Assessment (PISA) tests results. The
PISA tests have been conducted every 3 years from 2000 to 2015 (OECD, 2013b).
Relaxed education was blamed for the decline of academic achievements and critics
argued that relaxed education was failing students as it was creating a gap in scholastic
ability between affluent and poor students. As students were not learning sufficiently
at school, they had to rely on privately owned and expensive *juku*, cram schools,
to supplement their learning. Apparently only high performing students from
socioeconomically advantaged families have benefited from relaxed education,
while socioeconomically disadvantaged students, who could not afford *juku*, have
become victims of growing inequality (Miki, 2014; Park, 2013, pp. 23–24,
113–130). However, proponents of relaxed education, argued that it was not the
new curriculum *per se*, but the way it was taught that caused problems. They claimed
that, in particular, the changed role of the teacher in active learning, from providing
knowledge to merely supervising students' own study, had been misinterpreted by
teachers (Park, 2013; Ikeno, 2011; Mori & Davies, 2015, pp. 153–154).

In reaction to the negative effects of relaxed education, in 2008 MEXT
developed the Basic Plan for the Promotion of Education and revised the Course

of Study. The new legislation also aimed at alleviating persistent juvenile social problems, such as bullying, violence, suicide, truancy and hikikomori. The Course of Study re-evaluated the role of the teacher in the classroom and placed the teacher at the centre of learning as a knowledge provider. The subsequent improvement in students' academic ability was striking, as evident in the 2009 and 2012 PISA results. Among 35 OECD countries, in 2012 Japan ranked first in both reading and science, and second in mathematics performance (OECD, 2013a, 2013b; Cabinet Office, 2013, p. 11). In just released 2015 PISA results (6 December, 2016), Japan ranks first in mathematics and science, and sixth in reading (National Institute for Educational Policy Research of Japan [NIER], 2016).

However, the alleviation of juvenile problems was not that easily achieved. In spite of new moral education programs, such as 'heart education' and 'life and death education', statistics indicate that neither bullying nor juvenile suicides have declined (Cabinet Office, 2013, pp. 2, 13, 21; Cabinet Office, 2016, pp. 5, 17). The recently released Report on Juvenile Problematic Behaviour (MEXT, 2016c, p. 1) shows alarming statistics, namely in 2015 bullying at school increased by 19.4 per cent when compared to 2014, and school violence increased by five per cent. A slightly older UNICEF research report states that: 'More than a quarter of children aged 13 to 15 in Japan report being bullied' (UNICEF, 2013, p. 28), while another UNICEF report states that the number of 15-year-old Japanese students who felt 'awkward and out of place' at school (18 per cent), and those who felt lonely (30 per cent) was the largest by far among the developed countries (UNICEF, 2007, p. 38). Shinichi Ishikawa, Satoko Sasagawa, Junwen Chen and Cecilia Essau (2016, p. 158) claim that 22.8 per cent of adolescents in junior high schools and 11.6 per cent of elementary school children aged 10–12 years suffer from clinical depression, and that the depressed children have a much higher propensity to attempt suicide, as high as 31.3 per cent. In spite of the fact that adult suicide rates have been decreasing in Japan, children's suicide rates remain unchanged at a rate of 2.5 per 100,000 people (Cabinet Office, 2016, p. 17). Moreover, a report of the Commission on Measuring Wellbeing (2011, p. 2) states that 'suicide is the most common cause of death among males in their 20s to early 40s, and among females in their late teens to early 30s', and that 'one in three people in their 20s and 30s have reported that they have seriously considered committing suicide in their past' (also Cabinet Office 2013, pp. 4, 6, 14).

Therefore, once the academic abilities of Japanese students had improved, MEXT shifted its attention to solving juvenile problems. In 2013 MEXT developed the Second Basic Plan for the Promotion of Education, with its main objective that of improving the morals of the young people, apparently as a remedy to juvenile issues. In order to do so, MEXT has begun to promote moral and citizenship education to a degree not seen since the end of World War II. Officially, the goal has been to increase students' normative consciousness, social competence, sociability, consideration for others, self-esteem, self-discipline, respect for life, self-motivation, and interest in social participation and volunteer activities (MEXT,

2013; Cabinet Office, 2013, pp. 56–57). In fact many proposed solutions are simply a return to traditional conservative values.

The Second Plan also expressed the need to enhance students' 'experiential activities', e.g., providing opportunities for students to experience nature (MEXT, 2013, Section 2–5; Cabinet Office, 2013, pp. 57–59). This may seem unrelated to moral education, but in fact it is in accord with the Japanese sense of spirituality and religiosity aiming at developing morality through aesthetic experiences. This is known as *joso kyoiku*, education in Japanese religious sentiments and ideals, and is the source of continuing debate as to whether or not its teaching should be permitted in public schools. If religious sentiments and ideals are inseparable from religious convictions, as some scholars argue, then under the current Constitution, they are forbidden to be taught in public schools. However, in MEXT's Second Plan, they are camouflaged as simply experiencing nature, while in fact they are linked to the essence of Shinto (see Iwata's chapter in this volume).

An analysis of the content of the moral education teaching materials, *Kokoro no Noto* (literally, 'Notebook for the Heart') (MEXT, 2002), demonstrates that the Japanese educational method of teaching morality is through evoking emotions, and not through rationalising what is wrong or right (Otsu, 2010, pp. 54–55). This is closely related to the Japanese concept of god and religion, and is very different from the Western Judeo-Christian tradition. In Shinto there is no guiding set of commandments or code of ethics for followers. *Kami* (gods) are neither perfect, nor omnipotent, nor absolute. They can be both benevolent and malevolent, and are not required to act morally. The Japanese sense of morality reflects this and there is no clear distinction between good and evil. Morality is relative and context-based. What guides individuals in their moral choices is their 'pure heart' and sincerity (*magokoro*), which can be attained through experiencing the beauty of nature, or purification (Filus, 2006, pp. 1043–1045; Filus, 2010b, pp. 143–153).

It is noteworthy that morals in Japan refer primarily to public morals and civic virtues (*kotoku*). Thus, what is meant by moral education in Japan might be defined in Western countries as an amalgamation of moral education and citizenship education. The 2008 Courses of Study and the 'Notebook for the Heart' delineate the content of moral education in terms of the relationships that individuals have with other people, with nature and 'sublime things', and with society in their public duties as citizens (MEXT, 2002, 2016a). In the face of mounting globalisation, citizenship education is gaining increased prominence. In Japan citizenship education is taught alongside moral education throughout the curriculum, in subjects such as Moral Education, Social Studies, Period for Integrated Studies and Special Activities in elementary and junior high schools, and in senior high schools in a Civics Course (consisting of Ethics, Contemporary Society, Politics and Economy), and also in History, Geography, Period for Integrated Studies and Special Activities (Kimura, 2011; Kobara, 2011; Mori & Davies, 2015; Davies et al., 2010; Otsu, 2010; Fujiwara, 2011).

While citizenship education is ideally concerned with preparing students to live in a global multicultural society, in Japan it emphasises nationalism and national unity as expressed in the slogan 'one nation, one language, one ethnicity' used frequently by Japanese politicians (Fujiwara, 2011, p. 111). Lynne Parmenter (2006, p. 147) argues that:

> Worthy of note is the fact that global citizenship, or citizenship as a 'member of international society', are [sic] not the aims [sic] . . . The clearly defined, explicit aim of citizenship education within the social studies curriculum is to develop Japanese citizens with a sense of patriotism who are willing to interact cordially with people of other cultures, not to develop intercultural citizens.

In fact, whenever MEXT mentions globalisation, love for the country, its culture and tradition are emphasised (MEXT, 2006). Thus the goal of citizenship education is to strengthen nationalism, which comes before any goal of global citizenship or multiculturalism. Even more confusingly, multicultural education is understood in Japan as involving studying about Japanese regional cultures. The goal is to assimilate those various cultures into one national Japanese culture (cf. Fujiwara, 2011, pp. 111–114; Saito, 2015). Such an assimilation policy can hardly be called multiculturalism as it is understood in other contexts.

MEXT's unprecedented preoccupation with moral and citizenship education is further evident in the most recent plan to upgrade Moral Education to an official school subject for credit at elementary schools from 2018 and junior high schools from 2019. Currently, Moral Education is an informal subject; teachers do not grade students and there are no official textbooks. Making it a subject for credit will entail written evaluations entered in students' records, used when applying for high schools, universities or employment. As textbooks must be approved by MEXT, the current Conservative government may use this opportunity to further inculcate children with a sense of nationalism and uniform moral codes reminiscent of those of the pre-1945 period (Ito, 2015; 'Moral education's slippery slope', 2014; Kumashiro, 2016). Masahiko Takanaka (2014), Chairman of the Tokyo Bar Association, opposes making Moral Education an official subject on the grounds that it may violate freedom of speech, thought and religion. However, some scholars advising the Central Council of Education, most notably Shigeki Kaizuka (2012), argue that making Moral Education a proper subject will contribute to the development of the discipline of moral studies, and will allow academic research into its theories, which will result in developing more adequate curriculum and teachers' training.

It is noteworthy that pre-war moral education, *Shushin*, which once had the lowest position among teaching subjects, from 1890 onwards was gradually moved to the highest position to promote the Confucian code of ethics, imperialism, ultranationalist propaganda and militaristic expansions of Japan (Maruyama, 2013, p. 2). Thus, the proposed elevation of the status of Moral Education to an official subject understandably causes anxiety among critics and parents. Ever since Moral Education was reinstated in 1958, the government attempted to imbue it with nationalistic instruction. In 1966 the Ministry of Education implemented a document known as 'The Image of an Ideal Japanese' (*Kitaisareru Ningenzo*), which indoctrinated young people to believe that love for the country and for the Emperor are synonymous and inseparable, and that '[i]t is through the state that we find the way to enjoy our happiness' (Chuo Kyoiku Shingikai, 1966, Section 4, translated by Duke, 1967, p. 34). Many Japanese people fear that the imposition of uniform principles extolling nationalism and conservative Confucian virtues may thus interfere with the principles of democracy.

MEXT's preoccupation with moral and citizenship education does not stop with reforms in elementary and junior high schools. MEXT is also proposing to change the Senior High School Civics Course by replacing the current subject Contemporary Society with a new compulsory subject *Kokyo*, literally 'Public', as of 2020. The new subject aims to develop students' political literacy, as the voting age in Japan changed in 2016 from 20 years to 18. However, some critics doubt whether *Kokyo* will increase young people's political participation, while others express confusion as to why this new subject is needed, given Contemporary Society is already taught (Jinnai, 2015; Takahama, 2016). Within the reformed Civics Course, students will be able to choose Ethics or Politics/Economy. Ethics will include instruction on what is good/appropriate, on issues of justice, the duty of citizens, happiness and some aspects of religious ideas and beliefs, details of which are still under discussion (MEXT, 2016b, document 27; S. Senoue, personal communication, 30 September, 2016).

If the proposed changes to moral education are implemented, it will take a few years before their influence on the wellbeing of young Japanese can be evaluated. However, as the proposed changes are reactionary in nature, put forward by conservative politicians with limited creativity and little vision for the future of global society and the role of the Japanese people in it, it may be predicted that clinging to the past will not bring any improvements in young people's psycho-logical wellbeing. According to traditional Japanese values, the cohesion of the group has always been emphasised at the expense of individual needs. Individualism is still strongly abhorred in Japan. Moreover, the social pressure to sacrifice one's ego for the benefit of the group is often the reason behind suicide, and is an obstacle to finding solutions to bullying (Filus, 2010b, pp. 141, 154–156). Ishikawa et al. (2016, pp. 159–161) argue similarly, when they blame the 'valuing of conformity' and the 'dominance of collective values' for difficulty in preventing and treating depression in Japanese children. Consequently, applying traditional values and solutions may exacerbate, and not solve the problems.

This was confirmed by the recent 2013 report on the International Survey of Youth Attitudes, which demonstrates that education fails the young Japanese, by hardly contributing to their sense of wellbeing, belonging, identity and happiness. It also doesn't adequately prepare them for the challenges of globalisation and living in a multicultural society.

## The 2013 international survey of youth attitudes

The International Survey of Youth Attitudes (Cabinet Office, 2013) is an excellent source of information on how young people in seven advanced countries see the reality of the world they live in. It is a comparative study involving the youth of Japan, Korea, the United States, the United Kingdom, Germany, France and Sweden. The survey was conducted in November–December 2013. A sample of each country consisted of 1,000 people, aged 13–29. The young people were asked about their views on life, school, family, community, nation, society, politics and volunteering. While differences in attitudes between the European/American young people and the East Asian young people may have been expected, it was surprising that the disparity between Korean and Japanese young people was so striking. Except for their concerns/worries and some attitudes towards family, in which the Japanese and Korean youth showed similarities, in all other respects the Korean young people were much closer to their European counterparts, while the Japanese youth demonstrated a very disheartened and pessimistic outlook. Furthermore, young Japanese people presented themselves as very insecure and uncertain as to how to conduct their lives in a globalised world.

The first part of the survey was concerned with young people's self-esteem and self-confidence, with Japanese youth being the least satisfied with themselves (45.8 per cent), which was in stark contrast to the youth of all the other countries participating. Interestingly, Japanese junior high school students showed a much higher level of satisfaction with themselves (64.3 per cent) which decreased with age.[1] Thus for senior high school students, the level of self-satisfaction dropped to 48.1 per cent, and for tertiary students to 39.5 per cent. These findings suggest that education may have a negative influence on Japanese students' self-satisfaction. In addition, a breakdown by degree of satisfaction with school life showed that those satisfied with school life also indicated a higher sense of satisfaction with self. Only 46 per cent of the Japanese young people thought they were intelligent. Many of them admitted that they were unable to make decisions (56.7 per cent), or express themselves and communicate with others (52 per cent), and many were unsure how to differentiate between right and wrong (42.5 per cent) (Cabinet Office, 2013, pp. 10–18, 31–36, 42, 115).

When asked about their state of mind during the previous week, Japanese youth revealed that they were the most depressed (77.9 per cent), unmotivated (76.9 per cent), saddest (72.8 per cent) and loneliest (54.9 per cent) by far, among the seven surveyed countries. The Japanese young people showed a very high degree of worries, had little hope, and pictured the bleakest vision of their future. A breakdown by educational background showed again that the junior high school students had the most optimistic image of the future, and that this decreased as they grew older (Cabinet Office, 2013, pp. 23–33, 43–48). The young Japanese also demonstrated that they lacked personal freedom and felt constrained by their families and society (Cabinet Office, 2013, pp. 54, 69, 73).

Only 31.5 per cent of the Japanese youth said that they were satisfied/somewhat satisfied with their society, and only 28.8 per cent (the lowest by far) thought that their country's future is bright. The young Japanese showed the lowest interest in political participation and a lack of confidence in their ability to change society, when compared with the youth of other countries. Also they indicated the lowest interest in volunteer activities (35.1 per cent) (Cabinet Office, 2013, pp. 74–86, 101). Few young Japanese thought that their countrymen were prepared to be members of the global community (24.3 per cent, the lowest percentage among the seven countries), and very few (14.5 per cent) thought that the public policy needed to equip citizens with a global perspective was adequately provided (again the lowest percentage by far) (Cabinet Office, 2013, pp. 91–94). This shows that the young Japanese are aware that citizenship education to prepare them to live in a global society is ineffective.

In summary, the Japanese young people are by far the most frustrated and depressed among the seven countries surveyed. They are also the least decisive, as they had the highest percentage for 'don't know' answers (61.3 per cent) among the seven nations. It is noteworthy that the aims of the Japanese Courses of Study as revised in 1988, 1998 and 2008 specifically targeted students' ability to express themselves, think for themselves, and develop self-confidence. Clearly these goals are far from being realised.

The answers of these young Japanese thus reveal a rather gloomy picture. Japanese youth seem apathetic, pessimistic, lack enthusiasm and the 'zest for life', emphasised in the revised education laws and Courses of Study. The Japanese young people are dissatisfied with themselves, with their education system and school life, with their country's politics and future outlook. They are the saddest, most depressed, unmotivated and insecure of the young people surveyed. The happiest young people in Japan, who are also those with the most optimistic dreams, are junior high school students. It may be argued that further education may have a negative influence on the happiness of Japanese students. This is contrary to popular belief that education enhances happiness (Chen, 2012).

Analysis of the survey's questions reveals that the Japanese Government, who commissioned the survey, is not particularly interested in children's wellbeing *per se*, but rather is searching for solutions that would assist in healing Japanese social malaises, such as a rapidly aging society, low child birth rates, economic stagnation and rising unemployment. Thus, it may be argued that the most recent changes in the curriculum, while conducted under the pretext of improving the morals of young people, in fact, have purely economic and political objectives, i.e. to make the young people subservient to traditional norms in order for them to serve the economic and political goals of the government and broader society.

## Conclusion

The Japanese education system is experiencing major changes. As globalisation, multiculturalism and the digital revolution advance, the need for educational reforms is inevitable. However, in Japan these developments appear regressive, particularly in the area of moral and citizenship education. Regarding the proposed educational goals and the solutions to juvenile problems, it is evident that MEXT is recycling old ideas, slogans and traditional conservative values, and putting a new spin on them. MEXT's vision of educational policies offers no new solutions or incentives, and if the politicians and educators, the products of Japanese education, lack creativity in proposing new ideas, this may actually be the best proof that there is a problem with the Japanese education system.

Ayako Tanimura (2004) argues that all educational reforms since the end of the American Occupation in 1952 were an attempt to reverse the American-style democratisation imposed upon Japan during the Occupation. American-style democracy, she argues, is blamed for Japan's loss of identity and cultural heritage, which are seen as being responsible for the lack of morals among Japanese young people. The 1966 'Image of an Ideal Japanese' and other educational reforms that followed aimed at reviving patriotism, national pride and traditional values. Tanimura's argument was confirmed in 2006 when The Fundamental Law of Education was revised and phrases in relation to patriotism were added, which then allowed for the introduction of a new Course of Study in the spirit of promoting nationalism. Thus MEXT, under the pretext of the lack of moral principles among the young people, makes every effort to reinforce nationalism and traditional moral codes, while paying lip service to democratic values.

Education in Japan, as in many other societies, is a constant battlefield between conservative and progressive political forces. Children become victims of such endless political polemics and dilemmas. Christopher Gifford, Andrew Mycock and Junichi Murakami (2014, p. 91), discussing the structural changes in contemporary Japanese society, the prolonged economic stagnation and the disintegration of the traditional employment system, all of which affect young people, argue that:

> [T]he structural dislocation and disadvantage experienced by Japanese young people is redefined as a problem of individual character and cultural instruction, i.e. of not being Japanese . . . Education has therefore been utilised to reassert notions of duty and obligation among young people as a solution to social problems.

Whether in the 1960s or in the 2010s, Japanese politicians are using the same recipe for social malaises: they revert to nationalism, to a conservative Confucian ethic, and feudal values, in contrast to the reality of an increasingly global and diverse world united by digital technology. It is the lack of vision, fear of novelty or any significant changes, and traditional xenophobia that halts progress in Japan. There are empty words promoting independent thinking while abhorring individualism. There have been no visible changes in young people's sense of psychological wellbeing and happiness, therefore, in the last 50 years. Their pessimistic outlooks and negative attitudes, as demonstrated in the International Survey of Youth Attitudes (2013), are not surprising. Japanese youth seem disenchanted with their society, country and education system. They are apathetic and disengaged from their community and state politics, and unwilling to participate in democracy or voluntary activities. They see their own future and the future of Japan as bleak. Analysis of the questions asked in the International Survey of Youth Attitudes (2013) reveals that the government isn't prioritising solving young people's problems but rather, it is more concerned with using their young people to assist with solving the problems of an aging society and economic stagnation.

The opening statement of MEXT's educational policy says: 'Education is an endeavour that aims to fully develop the personality of each and every child, and is essential for children to lead happy lives in the future'. (MEXT, n.d.). However, education in Japan fails to produce happy youth. As 98.3 per cent of children go on to high school (Cabinet Office, 2013, p. 9), basically every Japanese young person becomes a victim of the education system.

## Note

1   Tomohiko Asano (2016, p. 14), in his recent study argues that the sense of happiness of the junior high schoolers has been improving (also Cabinet Office, 2013, p. 34). This may be the case, but in comparison with other countries, the level of happiness of Japanese youth is still very low.

## References

Asano, T. (2016). Seishonen kenkyukai no chosa to wakamono ron no konnichi no kadai (Research and theories on young people today). In M. Fujimura, T. Asano & I. Habuchi (eds), *Gendai wakamono no kofuku: Fuankan shakai o ikiru* (Happiness of Japanese youth today: Living in an uncertain society) (pp. 1–23). Tokyo: Koseisha.

Cabinet Office Japan (2013). *International survey of youth attitudes.* Tokyo: Author. Retrieved 12 April, 2016, from http://cao.go.jp/youth/english/survey/2013/pdf/contents.pdf; http://cao.go.jp/youth/english/survey/2013/pdf/part1.pdf; http://cao.go.jp/youth/english/survey/2013/pdf/part2-1.pdf; http://cao.go.jp/youth/english/survey/2013/pdf/part2-2.pdf

Cabinet Office Japan (2016). *Sanko zuhyo* (Suicide statistics). Tokyo: Author. Retrieved 11 April, 2016, from http://mhlw.go.jp/file/06-Seisakujouhou-12200000-Shakaiengokyoku shougaihokenfukushibu/h27kakutei-sankou.pdf

Chen, W. (2012). How education enhances happiness: Comparison of mediating factors in four East Asian countries. *Social Indicators Research, 106*(1), 117–131. doi:10.1007/s11205-011-9798-5

Chuo Kyoiku Shingikai (1966). *Kitaisareru ningenzo* (The image of an ideal Japanese). Tokyo: MEXT. Retrieved 2 May, 2016, from http://mext.go.jp/b_menu/shingi/chuuou/toushin/661001.htm#51

Chuo Kyoiku Shingikai (1996). *21 seiki o tenboshita waga kuni no kyoiku no arikata ni tsuite* (Japanese education in the 21st century). Tokyo: MEXT. Retrieved 11 April, 2016, from http://mext.go.jp/b_menu/shingi/chuuou/toushin/960701.htm

Commission on Measuring Wellbeing Japan (2011). *Measuring national wellbeing: Proposed wellbeing indicators.* Tokyo: Cabinet Office. Retrieved 11 April, 2016, from http://cao.go.jp/keizai2/koufukudo/pdf/koufukudosian_english.pdf

Davis, I., Mizuyama, M., & Thompson, G. H. (2010). *Citizenship education in Japan. Citizenship, Social and Economics Education, 9* (3), 170–178. doi.org/10.2304/csee.2010.9.3.170.

Duke, B. (1967). The image of an ideal Japanese. *The Educational Forum, 32*(1), 31–37. doi.org/10.1080/00131726709340336

Filus. D. (2006). Religious education in contemporary Japan. In M. de Souza, K. Engebretson, G. Durka, R. Jackson & A. McGrady (eds), *International handbook of the religious, moral and spiritual dimensions of education* (pp. 1039–1053). Dordrecht: Springer.

Filus, D. (2010a). Interreligious education and dialogue in Japan. In K. Engebretson, M. de Souza, G. Durka & L. Gearon (eds), *International handbook of interreligious education* (pp. 779–804). Dordrecht: Springer.

Filus, D. (2010b). Dotoku kyoiku to "shukyo o kangaeru kyoiku" wa donna kankei ka (Moral education and "education that respects religion"). In N. Suzuki (ed.), *Shukyo o kangaeru kyoiku* (Education that respects religion) (pp. 138–163). Tokyo: Kyobunkan.

Fujiwara, T. (2011). International, global and multicultural education as an issue in citizenship education. In N. Ikeno (ed.), *Citizenship education in Japan* (pp. 107–115). London: Continuum.

Gifford, C., Mycock, A. & Murakami, J. (2014). Becoming citizens in late modernity: A global-national comparison of young people in Japan and the UK. *Citizenship Studies, 18*(1), 81–98. doi:10.1080/13621025.2013.820393

Ikeno, N. (2011). Postwar citizenship education policy and its development. In N. Ikeno (ed.), *Citizenship education in Japan* (pp. 15–27). London: Continuum.

Ishikawa, S., Sasagawa, S., Chen, J. & Essau, C. (2016). Prevention programs for depression among children and adolescents in Japan. In R. H. Shute & P. T. Slee (eds), *Mental health and wellbeing through schools: The way forward* (pp. 157–170). Abingdon, Oxon: Routledge.

Ito, F. (2015, June 26). Tokubetsu no kyoka ni kaku age dotoku (Moral Education as an official subject). *Yomiuri Online*. Retrieved 1 September, 2016, from http://yomiuri.co.jp/kyoiku/special/CO015552/20150619-OYT8T50027.htm

Jinnai, A. (2015, 1 November). Atarashii kokosei no seiji kamoku "kokyo" wa honto ni hitsuyo ka (Is the new senior high school subject "kokyo" really necessary?). *Bengoshi.com News*. Retrieved 1 September, 2016, from https://bengo4.com/other/n_3880/

Kaizuka, S. (2012). *Dotoku kyoiku no toriatsukai setsumeisho: Kyokaka no hitsuyosei o kangaeru* (Moral Education: Arguments for making it an official subject). Tokyo: Gakujutsu Shuppankai.

Kimura, H. (2011). The history of citizenship education in the postwar course of study: Moral education and other topics. In N. Ikeno (ed.), *Citizenship education in Japan* (pp. 55–71). London: Continuum.

Kobara, T. (2011). The evolution of postwar guidelines for teaching social studies and citizenship education in Japan. In N. Ikeno (ed.), *Citizenship education in Japan* (pp. 73–83). London: Continuum.

Kumashiro, T. (2016). Yori mashina aku toshite no dotoku no hyoka (Problems with grades for moral education). *Kyoiku, 849*, 65–72.

Maruyama, H. (2013). *Moral education in Japan*. Tokyo: National Institute for Educational Policy Research of Japan (NIER). Retrieved 10 April, 2016, from https:/nier.go.jp/English/educationjapan/pdf/201303MED.pdf.

MEXT (2002). *Kokoro no noto: Chugakko* (Notebook for the heart: Junior high school). Tokyo: Author. Retrieved 12 April, 2016, from http://mext.go.jp/a_menu/shotou/doutoku/detail/1302318.htm

MEXT (2006). *Basic Act on Education*. Tokyo: Author. Retrieved 10 April, 2016, from http://mext.go.jp/english/lawandplan/1303462.htm

MEXT (2008). *Basic plan for the promotion of education*. Tokyo: Author. Retrieved 10 April, 2016, from http://mext.go.jp/en/policy/education/lawandplan/title01/detail01/1373797.htm

MEXT (2009). *Kodomo no jisatsu no jittai* (Juvenile suicide). Tokyo: Author. Retrieved 12 April, 2016, from http://mext.go.jp/component/b_menu/shingi/toushin/__icsFiles/afieldfile/2009/04/13/1259190_4.pdf

MEXT (2011). *The revisions of the courses of study for elementary and secondary schools.* Tokyo: Author. Retrieved 11 April, 2016, from http://mext.go.jp/en/policy/education/elsec/title02/detail02/__icsFiles/afieldfile/2011/03/28/1303755_001.pdf

MEXT (2013). *Second basic plan for the promotion of education.* Tokyo: Author. Retrieved 12 April, 2016, from http://mext.go.jp/en/policy/education/lawandplan/title01/detail01/sdetail01/1373805.htm

MEXT (2016a). *Genko gakushu shido yoryo: Ikiru chikara* (Current course of study: Zest for life). Tokyo: Author. Retrieved 17 April, 2016, from http://mext.go.jp/a_menu/shotou/new-cs/youryou/1304417.htm; http://mext.go.jp/a_menu/shotou/new-cs/youryou/1304424.htm; http://mext.go.jp/a_menu/shotou/new-cs/youryou/1304427.htm

MEXT (2016b). *Shakai, Chiri/Rekishi, Komin wakingu gurupu ni okeru shingi-no torimatome* (Summary of discussions of the working group on Social Studies, Geography/History and Civics). Tokyo: Author. Retrieved 14 September, 2016, from http://mext.go.jp/component/b_menu/shingi/toushin/__icsFiles/afieldfile/2016/09/12/1377052_02_2.pdf

MEXT (2016c). *Heisei 27 nendo "Jidou seito no mondai kodo to seito shido jo no sho mondai ni kansuru chosa" soku ho chi* (Report on juvenile problematic behaviour). Tokyo: Author. Retrieved 28 October, 2016, from http://mext.go.jp/b_menu/houdou/28/10/__icsFiles/afieldfile/2016/10/27/1378692_001.pdf

MEXT (n.d.). *Education: Overview.* Tokyo: Author. Retrieved 9 April, 2016, from http://mext.go.jp/en/policy/education/elsec/title01/detail01/1373834.htm

Miki, T. (2014). Japan finds inspiration in its PISA results. OECD Education Today Blog. Retrieved 11 April, 2016, from http://oecdeducationtoday.blogspot.com.au/2014/01/japan-finds-inspiration-in-its-pisa.html

Moral education's slippery slope (2014, 26 October). *Japan Times.* Retrieved 10 July, 2016, from http://japantimes.co.jp/opinion/2014/10/26/editorials/moral-educations-slippery-slope/#.V-VvO_B97IU

Mori, C., & Davies, I. (2015). Citizenship education in civics textbooks in the Japanese junior high school curriculum. *Asia Pacific Journal of Education, 35*(2), 153–175. doi:10.1080/02188791.2014.959468

Nagai, M. (1954). Herbert Spencer in Early Meiji Japan. *The Far Eastern Quarterly, 14*(1), 55–64. doi:10.2307/2942228

National Institute for Educational Policy Research of Japan (NIER) (2016). *OECD seito no gakushu totatsu do chosa PISA 2015 no pointo* (OECD PISA 2015 results). Tokyo: NIER. Retrieved 7 December, 2016, from http://nier.go.jp/kokusai/pisa/pdf/2015/01_point.pdf

OECD (2013a). Japan: Results from PISA 2012. OECD. Retrieved 11 April, 2016, from http://oecd.org/pisa/keyfindings/PISA-2012-results-japan.pdf

OECD (2013b). *PISA: Key findings.* OECD. Retrieved 11 April, 2016, from http://oecd.org/pisa/keyfindings/

Otsu, T. (2010). Moral and global citizenship education in Japan, England, and France. *Research Bulletin of Education, 5,* 53–60. Retrieved 12 April, 2016, from http://mukogawa-u.ac.jp/~edugrad/506otsu.pdf

Park, H. (2013). *Re-evaluating education in Japan and Korea: De-mystifying stereotypes.* Florence: Taylor and Francis.

Parmenter, L. (2006). Beyond the nation? Potential for intercultural citizenship education in Japan. In G. Alred, M. Byram & M. Fleming (eds), *Education for intercultural citizenship: Concepts and comparisons* (pp. 144–163). Clevedon: Multilingual Matters.

Saito, T. (2015). "Inochi no kyoiku" wa sho chugakko de dono yoni jissen sareteiru ka (How has "life and death education" been taught at elementary and junior high-schools?). *Taisho Daigaku Shukyogaku Nenpo, 30*, 25–51.

Spencer, H. (1860). *Education: Intellectual, moral and physical.* New York: D. Appleton. Retrieved 20 June, 2016, from https://ia800503.us.archive.org/3/items/spencereducation00spen/spencereducation00spen.pdf

Takahama, K. (2016, February 16). 'Gendai shakai' haishi o kento, hisshu kamoku 'kokyo' shinsetsu de Monkasho (MEXT considers abolishing 'contemporary society' and introducing 'kokyo' as a compulsory subject). *Asahi Shimbun.* Retrieved 10 July, 2016, form http://asahi.com/articles/ASJ2J65X6J2JUTIL05P.html

Takanaka, M. (2014). *Dotoku no kyokaka ni tsuite no iken* (An opinion on making moral education an official subject). Tokyo Bengoshi kai (Tokyo Bar Association). Retrieved 10 July, 2016, form http://toben.or.jp/message/ikensyo/post-368.html

Tanimura, A. (2004). Chuo Kyoiku Shigikai toshin o chushin ni mita sengo Nihon kyoiku kaikaku no kadai (The problem of educational reforms in Japan after World War II: Reports of the Central Council for Education in Japan). *Kyoto Daigaku Daigakuin Kyoikugaku Kenkyuka Kiyo, 50*, 317–330. Retrieved 17 April, 2016, from http://repository.kulib.kyoto-u.ac.jp/dspace/bitstream/2433/57515/1/eda050_317.pdf

UNICEF Innocenti Research Centre (2007). *Child poverty in perspective: An overview of child well-being in rich countries.* Florence: UNICEF Innocenti Research Centre. Retrieved 11 April, 2016, fromm https://unicef-irc.org/publications/pdf/rc7_eng.pdf

UNICEF Office of Research (2013). *Child well-being in rich countries: Comparing Japan.* Florence: UNICEF Office of Research. Retrieved 11 April, 2016, from https://unicef-irc.org/publications/pdf/rc11_comparing%20japan_fnl.pdf

# 13

# REFLECTIONS ON GENDER DISCRIMINATION IN THE SPIRITUAL LIFE OF A MUSLIM COMMUNITY

## Gender in elementary and middle school religion textbooks in Turkey

*Mualla Yildiz*

## Introduction

An individual's spiritual world begins to take shape at a very early age (Selcuk, 2000, p. 347). In a child's early years, his or her spiritual views are most often shaped by the information that the child's parents, older relatives, or other close adults communicate to the child about God (Yildiz, 2012). A number of studies have investigated the image children hold of God. Of these, Yavuz (1987) and Abanoz (2008), who studied the development of children's beliefs, found that a child's gender played no important role in his or her perceptions of God. Other studies, however, have found evidence of gender playing an important part in spiritual perceptions, but these have been based either on adolescents solely or on mixed groups of adolescents and pre-adolescents (Kusat, 2006). They indicate that a child's gender becomes an important factor, both in terms of one's image of God and one's psychological health, with the onset of puberty (Ozturk, 1981).

Moreover, the discriminatory postures and policies regarding race, religion, language, or gender in any given society tend to be reproduced and legitimised in and by the educational institutions of that society (Guvenç Çetinkol, 2008). In Turkey, the gender-discriminatory aspects of the educational tradition have led to a pronounced distinction between the way men and women relate to religion as well as the support and coping devices they derive from it. This has distinct implications on the emotional and spiritual wellbeing of female students. In order to better understand the impact of education in this regard, this chapter will first present the findings from a number of studies pertaining to gender, youth and religion in Turkey. It will then discuss the role of textbooks in communicating ideas about social roles and finally, it will examine evidence of gender discrimination in pictures included in religious education textbooks used in state schools.

## Gender, youth and religion in Turkey

In terms of an adolescent's spiritual life, females are more likely to hold an image of a protective God, while males are more likely to hold an image of a punishing God. The difference between the image of God held by male and female adolescents seems to reach its peak at 16 years. This is the age where males score lowest and females score highest in terms of their image of a protective God, and this is also the age where females begin to perceive themselves as less religious (Kusat, 2006). In a study investigating the role of gender differences in connection to self-respect and religious coping mechanisms in adolescence, it was found that females have higher levels of religiosity and lower levels of self-respect than males. In terms of coping mechanisms, male students scored higher on focusing on a problem, and refusing to seek help. Female students scored higher on seeking support from their peers, focusing on their feelings, and needing acceptance. Finally, male students were found to have higher levels of positive religious coping (to believe God will help them when they in trouble) while female students were found to have higher levels of negative religious coping (to believe God punished them because of sin when they in a trouble) (Çevik Demir, 2013).

These gender-based differences become more pronounced as children grow older. Nalbant (2010) for instance, found a positive correlation between religiosity and personal perceptions of success in university students, with male students more likely than female students to view themselves as successful. In a recent study that examined the relationship between religiosity and psychological resilience, Erdogan (2015) compared groups of students in various years of their studies at education and theology faculties respectively. In this study, male students had a greater overall level of psychological resilience than female students. Of the male students, those in theology were found to have the highest level of psychological resilience. Female students in theology, however, had the lowest levels of psychological resilience. In a similar vein, a study carried out on students at the Selcuk University Faculty of Theology found that female students experienced higher levels of fear of God than their male peers (Sahin, 2006).

A number of other studies have pointed to similar gender-based disparities between adults. Cirhinlioglu and Ok (2011) found that women experience a greater degree of worry and ambiguity in relation to religion than men. Kurnaz (2015) indicated that adult females are both more religious and unhappy than males. Kavas (2013) also discovered that women turn to religion in troubled times at a higher rate than men. Similarly, Gok's (1995) study showed that women suffering from depression tend to use religious coping strategies, and Kavas (2013) concluded that Gok's findings could be attributed to women's feelings of weakness and power-lessness.

In a meta-analysis of 78 different field studies carried out in Turkey on differences related to gender and religiosity, Yapici (2005) found that males ranked higher in the dimension of 'information', while females ranked higher in the dimensions of 'belief', 'worship', 'emotion' and 'affect', thus, indicating that they were more religious than men overall. In terms of the respective religiosity of each group, males tended towards a more 'internally motivated' and 'dogmatic' religiosity, while females tended towards a more 'externally motivated' and 'popular' religiosity. The study also found that females' spiritual worlds were generally shaped by mythical, magical and mystic knowledge and a sense of sinfulness. Ultimately, Yapici argues that the way young girls are educated and raised is an important factor in their tendency to be more religious as adults. It is also Yapici's contention that this trend is fostered by society for the purposes of ensuring the continuity of the institution of the family since women who are poorly educated tend to be more religious than men, while women who are better educated tend to be less religious.

## Gender in textbooks

Beginning in childhood, gender roles are one of the most important things that people learn in their social lives. The family plays an important role in communicating these roles, as do television-viewing habits, one's education, and a variety of other factors (Miller, 2008, pp. 270–271; Misra, 2013; Stericker & Lawrence, 1982). As a result of these social factors, individuals are directed towards adopting certain life goals, social roles and gender-based behaviour patterns (Oskamp et al., 1996). Recently, an increasing number of studies have been devoted to analysing how 'gender', a term used to convey the cultural and societal differences between males and females (Giddens, 2008, p. 505), is reflected and reproduced in school textbooks. Since gender is something that children learn and a category which they employ before they reach the stage of adolescence, the question of how the textbooks used in elementary schools portray gender is one that deserves closer study (Çubukçu & Sivaslıgil, 2007; Helvacıoğlu, 1994; Asan, 2006) since they are likely to have some impact on the wellbeing of the students.

Analysing textbooks written from 1928 to 1994 in terms of their portrayal of gender, one sees that an early emphasis on women as free individuals gave way by mid-century to steadily less progressive depictions of women's roles. For example, in the textbooks prepared during the early years of the Republic of Turkey, prior to 1945, there was a strong emphasis on the role played by women in the establishment of Turkey as an independent country. From 1945 to 1950, in contrast, women were no longer depicted on the front lines, but rather in the kitchen, wearing aprons, with their young daughters at their side helping them. From 1950 onward, visual materials in textbooks almost invariably portrayed women inside the home (Helvacıoğlu, 1994). Such restrictive depictions can only impede the wellbeing of female students since they suggest that women have limited opportunities for their careers. In turn, and given these are religious education textbooks, such thinking does little to promote the spiritual lives of these students.

An examination of the visual materials contained in the textbooks used between 2005 and 2007 reveals that the books use traditional gender roles to convey different messages. For instance, there is a predominant focus on male children who are portrayed more often and more frequently alone and outside the home. Fathers are shown as the head of the household while mothers are pictured with babies on their laps. The father motif is used to convey messages stressing the importance of economic independence. The mother motif, in contrast, is used to emphasise the importance of having children, caring for them, and performing household chores. Women are portrayed as housewives, teachers, nurses and in other capacities in line with their domestic roles. In turn, men are portrayed as, for example, administrators or repairmen, in line with the strength and authority of the roles attributed to them (Yorganci, 2008).

The textbooks used from the first to the fifth grade in primary schools in 2005–2006, both in terms of their visual and written components, indicate that while they contain less overtly sexist content than books used in earlier years, they are still far from free of such content (Asan, 2006). Professionals in fields requiring a certain amount of training or specialisation, for example in technical fields or in the government, are portrayed as men, while teachers and health workers are portrayed as women (Aykac, 2012). While the texts of these books do not explicitly praise men or elevate them above women, they contain text that express these messages indirectly and they contain visual materials that make the same statement (Guvenc Cetinkol, 2008). Once again, such portrayals of women suggest to girls that their lives are restricted and they are not free to pursue their own special interests and yearnings. Restrictions such as these do not offer much positive nurturing of the emotional aspirations and wellbeing of female students.

One study on gender in Religious Culture and Moral Knowledge textbooks compared them with the textbooks used in Traffic Safety, Social Studies and Turkish Language in the fourth and fifth grades in elementary schools. The study found that their written content was internally consistent and contained less gender bias than the textbooks used in other classes, but also found that these virtues did not extend to the main lessons the books were trying to convey or to the visual materials they included (Bulut, 2008).

Following the above discussion, this chapter complements these research studies since it reports on the findings from a study that focused on gender. It discusses and analyses the periodisation and gendered content of the visual material contained in 15 different Religious Culture and Moral Knowledge textbooks used between 1982 and 2012 (see Yavuz & Gunay, 1982; Şener & Karmış, 1982; Bilgin, 1982; Fığlalı, 1982; Komisyon, 2003; Akgul, 2012).

## Research process

The study discussed here has employed a quantitative approach based on content analysis in the collection of its data, its analysis of that data, and its evaluation of visual material. Content analysis, while generally used for messages expressed in written form is, in principle, open to all messages, including those conveyed by visuals (Bilgin, 2006). In this study, then, content analysis was utilised in an effort to identify the implicit and explicit messages concerning gender conveyed by the visual materials in textbooks. In order to achieve an effective process in the analysis and to clarify the findings, these visuals were categorised according to their historical period.

The study was designed on the basis of a descriptive survey of the relevant textbooks. On the basis of this original survey, the textbooks that were in widest circulation and which were found to be most representative of their periods were selected for inclusion. In order to ensure the integrity of the survey and selection process and to secure the most useful data, both steps were carried out in close coordination with experts in the field of religious education.

In determining the coding to be used in this study, previous studies relating to textbooks were consulted. Under the selective code 'visuals with messages about gender roles', several axial codes were identified: 'people at prayer', 'professionals', 'important historical figures', 'people outside the home', 'people at home', and 'people in need'.

The coding process was carried out four times, and a consistency percentage was derived from the correspondence between each coding attempt. The result of this was a score of 0.80, which indicated that the identified categories were consistent.

More specifically, the study was based on the visual material contained in textbooks used in Religious Culture and Moral Knowledge classes at the elementary and middle-school level. The MAXQDA 11.0 packet program utilised in content analysis was first employed to identify open codes, then to identify axial codes, and finally to identify the selective code (see Punch, 2011). The codes were then analysed and presented in cross-table form. In the end, there were 261 visuals analysed in this study.

## Findings

### Distribution of visuals of people at prayer by gender

Of the 55 visuals depicting people at prayer, 45 were of males and 10 were of females. Of these ten, half depicted those (5) engaging in votive prayer (*dua*), and the other half depicted them (5) performing the ritual prostrations while at prayer (*namaz*). The ones of men were more varied, depicting them worshipping as part of a larger mosque congregation (14), engaging in votive prayer (13), performing ritual prostrations (9), reading the Qur'an (5) and performing their ablutions (3).

### Distribution of visuals of professionals by gender

The 15 textbooks examined in this study contain a total of 88 visuals depicting professional men and women. Of these, 12 were of female professionals. The images of women showed two as farmers, one was a scientist, four were teachers and five were health workers. Out of all the professionals depicted in these pictures, every health worker (a total of five), most of the teachers (four) and half of the farmers (out of a total of four) were women.

## Distribution of visuals of important historical figures by gender

There were a total of 25 images of important historical figures. Of these, three were women. There was one picture of a young woman carrying an artillery shell and one picture of a woman carrying ammunition in an ox cart and one picture of women looking after wounded soldiers during the Turkish War of Independence. There were no pictures of female religious or spiritual leaders who influenced the moral values of society or of prominent female figures from the War of Independence.

## Distribution of visuals of people outside the home by gender

There were a total of 136 images of people outside the home. Of these, 27 were of women and 109 were of men. Of the pictures depicting people engaged in intellectual exchange, four were of men and two were of women. Of the pictures of people looking at and contemplating nature, 10 were of men and one was of a woman. Of the pictures of people at work, 76 were of men and 12 were of women. Of the pictures depicting people alone outside the home, 12 were of men and five were of women. Of the pictures of people spending time with children in parks or other places, seven were of men and three were of women. Of the pictures of people shopping for groceries at markets, bakeries, or elsewhere, all four were of women.

## Distribution of visuals of people at home by gender

A total of 72 images depicted people inside the home. All of those pictured cooking (a total of two) were women. Of those pictured caring for or looking after others, one was a man and six were women. Of those pictured attending to their personal hygiene, three were women and three were men. Of those pictured cleaning the home, two were men and six were women. Of those pictured at home alone with a child, five were men and nine were women. Of those serving food or tea, three were men and five were women. Of those pictured helping someone else study, one was a man and four were women. Of those pictured studying, 15 were male and seven were female. Of the females pictured studying or reading, virtually all were young students, the sole exception being one picture which showed an adult woman reading a book in the library.

## Distribution of visuals of people in need by gender

Of the 29 images of people caring for others in need, 18 were of men and 12 were of women. All of the people pictured with physical disabilities (a total of three) were men. Of those pictured with illnesses, four were men and three were women. Of those pictured in poverty, six were men and three were women. Of the pictures of elderly people, five were men and five were women.

## Discussion

According to the stages of psycho social development in Erickson's theory of development, children between the ages of 7 and 12 are in a stage where they begin to attend school and work to earn acceptance through academic success by, for example, learning to read and write and solving mathematical problems (Bee & Boyd, 2009, p. 523). This period is also one where children have the potential to develop a negative self-image, a confused gender identity, and problems that may lead to fears of socialising (Corey & Corey, 2006, p. 46). The mental schemas that children develop during this period will affect their later psychological health and spiritual wellbeing which will impact on their future decisions (Crabb & Marciano, 2011), and for this reason the choice of images to be included in textbooks that many children will be exposed to is an important one.

Many contemporary social problems like radicalisation, racism and violence are affecting the lives of children and young people. Therefore, we need to explore an understanding of spirituality and its role in promoting wellbeing (de Souza et al., 2016, p. 3) more than before. 'To better serve the needs of young people, the field of adolescent spirituality and education needs to embrace and carefully explore the benefits and challenges of its interdisciplinary nature work at integrating research data and disciplinary frameworks in more coherent ways' (Yust, 2016, p. 81).

In terms of elementary and middle-school level Religious Culture and Moral Knowledge textbooks, a need has already been identified to improve the correspondence between the visual images they contain and their textual content (Bulut, 2008). The results of the present study reveal that men and women are not given equal space in the images these texts contain of the performance of religious activities. In terms of the images they contain of people at prayer, only those dealing with votive prayers and the performance of ritual prostrations include women. This may be interpreted as a result of the tendency of other religious activities, such as attending Friday prayers or funerals, to be male-dominated affairs, at least in Turkey. While certain religious activities—such as the *tarawih* prayer performed during the month of Ramadan—are generally attended by a high number of women and children, nevertheless, they are not included in the visual material for these textbooks.

Further, the Religious Culture and Moral Knowledge textbooks picture women in only a very limited number of professions: as teachers, farmers, health workers. Other studies, too, have shown that in Turkish school textbooks, men tend to be portrayed in fields requiring a certain level of specialisation, while women tend to be portrayed as teachers and health workers (Aykac, 2012). Such unbalanced representation has important consequences in terms of shaping social expectations about gender roles which may have implications for spiritual nurturing. Individuals' perceptions of their own capabilities and self-sufficiency in different areas are significantly influenced by such expectations, and they can have important consequences for people's professional lives and psychological health (Miller, 2008, pp. 270–271). In what can be interpreted as a consequence of these sorts of expectations, one study has shown that young children in Turkey, when asked to draw a picture of a scientist, are much more likely to draw a man than a woman (Buldu, 2006). Such responses may also reflect the child's awareness that gender inequalities exist where boys are perceived as being superior to girls. Such understandings may have a negative impact on female students' identity and sense of belonging within their communities, thereby affecting their future relationships and their spiritual identity and wellbeing.

Another problem is the fact that these textbooks also fail to offer girls pictures of a female figure of historical importance with whom they can identify, aside from a few nameless women carrying munitions for men or tending to their wounds after they have been hurt (Oguzkan, 1997, p. 325). Instead, young female readers are offered images of women leaving the home only to do the grocery shopping, and of women at home contenting themselves with preparing meals, cleaning, or looking after children. Pictures of women reading or studying are few and far between. One of the few areas where equal visual space is given to men and women is in images portraying people in need. All of this results in a lopsided and negative representation of women and their social status. Such images, and the encouragement and models they embody, not only affect children's behaviour, but also serve to shape their expectations and intellectual horizons (Bee & Boyd, 2009, p. 511).

In addition, studies have shown that children model the gender roles they are shown in the visuals contained in books (Crabb & Marciano, 2011), and that personal identification with such images is one of the most important factors in the establishment of children's gender identities (Yorukoglu, 2008, p. 238; Oguzkan, 1997, p. 325). Yet, given the limited visuals of women in the textbooks under investigation in this study, it is only possible for a young female reader to identify with or model caring or home roles. Thus, the books' visuals convey distinct implicit messages which reflect particular thinking and attitudes where female roles are restricted (Johnson, 2016, p. 109). When liberty is curtailed, the spirituality of a person may become affected in terms of withdrawal and disconnectedness and with constant restrictions on their own hopes for the future, their emotional and mental wellbeing may well be affected.

Negative characterisations of the members of certain groups in particular fields can lead to unhealthy stereotypes and serve to stigmatise and alienate members of that group, both of which can have a negative impact on the way they perform in certain conditions (Bee & Boyd, 2009, p. 407; Steele & Aronson, 1995). Such negative characterisations and stereotypes can be and are passed along to young students through their textbooks so that their spiritual nurturing is impeded.

In a similar fashion, the portrayal of the place of women in social life offered by seventh-grade Social Studies textbooks is also far from an accurate representation of women's actual place in social life. An image they offer of a madrassa in Edirne, for example, contains only men. In an entire section dealing specifically with women, there is not a single picture of a woman. In another section, a picture depicting a publicly held guild ceremony for the promotion of a journeyman to the status of master does not contain a single obviously female spectator; there are certainly none among the people in the front rows, which are reserved for particularly important spectators. In the section detailing the foundation of the Republic of Turkey, no women are depicted in the picture of the first major congress during the War of Independence. This is despite the fact that women were indeed present there, and that Turkey was among the first countries in the world to give women the right to vote and be elected. Although Turkey has many female judges and prosecutors, in a picture of a courtroom the only female present is the court stenographer, with the judge and attorneys all portrayed as males. In a picture of a young female student trying to choose her profession, her parents and other older relatives are shown present at her side and attempting to make the decision for her; a young male student in the same situation is pictured alone in front of several large machines (Guvenc Cetinkol, 2008). All of this goes to show that in Turkey, the position of women in social life, at least as it is depicted in the country's textbooks, is one of backwardness and obscurity which has serious consequences for their sense of identity and belonging. This, in turn affects their spiritual wellbeing.

In this context, it is worth noting just how true the observation is that: 'Most children's books are written by adults, and children's literature serves as a form of education and socialisation that conveys society's deepest hopes, fears, expectations, and demands' (Boutte et al., 2008, p. 943). Given the influences of these biased images and role models offered to female students, it is not surprising that, in Turkey, females experience an increasing rate of psychological problems from adolescence onwards (Taskin & Cetin, 2006) which affects their spiritual wellbeing. Accordingly, female students in high school and university are much less successful in coping than male students at the same levels (Bugay & Erdur-Baker, 2011). These facts alone are sufficient to show that sexism in some form or another is operative in the sphere of education and that it impacts on the emotional and spiritual health of female students. Religious education is but a small part of a much larger educational system, and it would perhaps be naive to expect it to be more progressive than the broader system of which it is part. But the problem is not simply that the field of religious education mirrors this broader system. While the system might set troubling standards, the real issue is that religious education actually goes beyond other curriculum areas in encouraging gender stereotypes which lower the status of women. The prevalence of such sexist attitudes and gender stereotypes throughout their schooling, ultimately, have a negative impact on the self-image and identity of female students, thereby affecting their spiritual wellbeing.

Self-reflection permits human beings to examine their thoughts, feelings and motives, and to develop their strengths, weaknesses and capability, as well as to explore their life targets and improve a sense of individual identity and integrity (Johnson, 2016, p. 109). Under these circumstances, it is unlikely that these textbooks will have a beneficial effect on the spiritual wellbeing of young women in terms of nurturing in them a positive sense of identity which may be linked to having equality in gender roles in society. In conclusion, then, the findings of this study point to the fact that these textbooks support traditional prejudices about gender identity in Turkish society which, ultimately, have implications for the psychological and spiritual health of female students.

## Acknowledgement

This chapter draws on an earlier article: Yildiz, M. (2013). Analysis visual components of elementary and middle school religious culture and moral knowledge textbooks in terms of gender. *Religious Studies*, *16*(42), 143–165.

## References

Abanoz, S. (2008). 6–12 Yas arasi çocuklarin dini ve ahlaki gelisimlerinde anne ve babalarin rolü (İzmir ve Sakarya örnegi). *MA Thesis. Department of Philosophy and Religious Sciences Institute of Social Sciences of Sakarya University*, Sakarya.

Akgul, M. (2012). *Ilkogretim din kulturu ve ahlak bilgisi ders kitabi 4–8.sinif.* Ankara: Basak Matbaacilik.

Asan, H. T. (2006). Gender differences in textbooks and teachers' gender perceptions. *Fe Journal: Feminist Critique*, *2*(2), 65–74.

Aykaç, N. (2012). Evaluation of life sciences and social sciences course books in term of social sexuality. *Hacettepe University Journal of Education*, (43), 50–61.

Bee, H., & Boyd, D. (2009). *Cocuk gelisim psikolojisi*, Istanbul: Kaknus Yayinlari.

Bilgin, B. (1982). *Ilkokullar icin din kulturu ve ahlak bilgisi 5. sinif.* Istanbul: TIFDRUK Matbaacilik.

Bilgin, N. (2006). *Sosyal bilimlerde içerik analizi*, Ankara: Siyasal Kitabevi.

Boutte, G. S., Hopkins, R., & Waklatsi, T. (2008). Perspectives, voices and worldviews in frequently read children's books. *Early Education and Development*, *19*(6), 941–962.

Bugay A, Erdur-Baker, O. (2011). Age and gender differences in rumination, *Türk Psikolojik Danışma ve Rehberlik Dergisi*, *4*(36), 191–201.

Buldu, M. (2006). Young children's perceptions of scientists: A preliminary study. *Educational Research*, *48*(1), 121–132.

Bulut, S. (2008). İlköğretim ders kitaplarinin görsel boyut ve içerik tutarliligi açisindan incelenmesi. *Ma Thesis Department Education Institute of Social Sciences of Nigde University*, Nigde.

Çevik Demir, S. (2013). Self-esteem and religious coping in adolescences, *PhD Thesis Department of Philosophy and Religious Sciences Institute of Social Sciences of Uludag University*, Bursa.

Cirhinlioglu, F., & Ok, U. (2011). Kadinlar mi yoksa erkekler mi daha dindar? *ZFWT: Zeitschrift für die Welt der Türken*, 3, 121–141.

Corey, G., & Corey, M. S. (2006). *Choice.* Belmont: Thomson Brook Corporation.

Crabb, P. B., & Marciano, D. L. (2011). Representations of material culture and gender in award-winning children's books: A 20-year follow-up. *Journal of Research in Childhood Education, 25*(4), 390–398.

Çubukçu, H., & Sivasligil, P. (2007). Sexism in English textbooks. *Cukurova University Faculty of Education Journal, 34*(3), 25–33.

de Souza, M., Bone, J., & Watson, J. (eds). (2016). Contemporary spirituality: An introduction to understanding in research and practice. In M. de Souza, J. Bone, & J. Watson (eds), *Spirituality across disciplines: Research and practice*. Switzerland: Springer International Publishing.

Erdogan, E. (2015). The relationship of resilience with god perception forms, religion orientation and subjective religiousness: A sample of university students. *Mustafa Kemal University Journal of Social Sciences Institute, 12*(29), 223–246.

Fığlalı, E. R. (1982). *Ortaokullar için din kültürü ve ahlak bilgisi 3. sınıf*, Ankara: Türk Tarih Kurumu Basımevi.

Giddens, A. (2008). *Sosyoloji*, İstanbul: Kirmizi Yayinlari.

Gök, Ş. (1995). Anksiyete ve Depresyonda Stresle Başa Çıkma. *Doctoral Thesis Department of Psychiatry of Istanbul University*, İstanbul.

Guvenc Cetinkol, S. (2008). Türkiye'de egitime farkli bir bakis açisi: feminist pedagoji, *MA Thesis Department of Woman's Study Institute of Social Sciences of Istanbul University*, İstanbul.

Helvacioglu (Gümüsoglu), Firdevs (1994). Sexism in lesson book from 1928 to 1994. *MA Thesis Department of Politics Institute of Social Sciences of Istanbul University*, İstanbul.

Johnson, A. (2016). Spirituality and contemplative education. *Spirituality across Disciplines: Research and Practices*. Switzerland: Springer International Publishing.

Kavas, E. (2013). The relationship between religious attitude and coping with stress. PhD Thesis, *Department of Philosophy and Religious Sciences Institute of Social Sciences of Suleyman Demirel University*. Isparta.

Komisyon (2003). *Ilkogretim din kulturu ve ahlak bilgisi ders kitabi 4–8.sinif*, Ankara: MEB.

Kuşat, A. (2006). *Ergenlerde Allah tasavvuru, dindarlığın sosyo-psikolojisi*, Adana: Karahan Kitabevi yay.

Kurnaz, M. (2015). The relationship between religious tendency and happiness in early childhood. *MA Thesis Department of Philosophy and Religious Sciences Institute of Social Sciences of Süleyman Demirel University*, Isparta.

Miller, P. H. (2008). *Gelisim psikolojisi kuramlari*. In Bekir Onur (ed.), İstanbul: Imge Yayinlari.

Misra, N. (2013). Impact of gender and education on gender role identity, gender role perception and psychological mindedness of college students. *TIJ's Research Journal of Social Science and Management, 2*(12), 91–99.

Nalbant, H. (2010). A study on the relationship between religiosity and academic achievement at university students (MAKÜ example). *MA Thesis Department of Philosophy and Religious Sciences Institute of Social Sciences of Süleyman Demirel University*, Isparta.

Oguzkan, F. (1997). *Yerli ve yabanci yazarlardan örneklerle çocuk edebiyati*. Ankara: Emel Matbaacilik Sanayi.

Oskamp, S., Kaufman, K., Atchison, W., & Atchison, L. (1996). Gender role portrayals in preschool picture books. *Journal of Social Behavior and Personality, 11*(5), 27–39.

Ozturk, M. (1981). *Din egitimi ve çocuk ruh sagligi*. Paper presented at the Türkiye 1. Din Egitimi Semineri, Ankara.

Punch, K. F. (2011). *Sosyal arastirmalara giris nicel ve nitel yaklasimlar*. Ankara: Siyasal Kitabevi.

Sahin, A (2006). A study on the religion caused stress, *Selcuk Universitesi Ilahiyat Fakultesi Dergisi*, (21), 147–180.

Selçuk, M. (2000). Gençlik çağı ve inanç olgusu (inanç ve davranış bütünlüğü açısından bir deneme). Gençlik Dönemi ve Din Eğitimi, Istanbul: İSAV, 333–358.

Şener, A., & Karmış, O. (1982). *Ortaokullar için din kültürü ve ahlak bilgisi 1.sınıf.* İstanbul: Ogul Matbaacılık Sanayi.

Steele, C. M., & Aronson, J. (1995). Stereotype threat and the intellectual test performance of African Americans. *Journal of Personality and Social Psychology, 69,* 797–811.

Stericker, A. B., & Lawrence, A. K. (1982). Dimensions and correlates of third through eighth graders' sex-role self-concepts. *Sex Roles, 8,* 915–929.

Taşgın Esra, Çetin Füsun (2006). Major depression in adolescents: risk factors, protective factors and resiliency: A review. *Çocuk ve Gençlik Ruh Saglığı Dergisi,* 13 (2), 43–61.

Yapıcı, A. (2005). The children prayers and problems that are reflected to prayers from the point of motive and contents. *Cukurova University Journal of Faculty of Divinity, 5*(2), 57–93.

Yavuz, K. (1987). Çocukta dini duygu ve düşüncenin gelişmesi (7–12 yaş), Ankara: Ayyıldız matbaası.

Yavuz, K., & Günay, Ü. (1982). *İlkokullar için din kültürü ve ahlak bilgisi 4. Sinif.* İstanbul: Murat Matbaacilik.

Yildiz, M. (2012). Determination of primary school students' god image and studying it's according to some factors. *PhD Thesis. Department of Philosophy and Religious Sciences Institute of Social Sciences of Ankara University,* Ankara

Yorganci, F. (2008). The construction of the social sex roles in the primary-education textbooks. *MA Thesis. Department Sociology Institute of Social Sciences Kocatepe University,* Afyon.

Yorukoglu, A. (2008). *Çocuk ruh sagligi.* İstanbul: Özgür Yayinlari.

Yust, K. M. (2016). Adolescent spirituality and education. In *Spirituality across disciplines: Research and practice.* Switzerland: Springer International Publishing.

# 14

# YINGADI ABORIGINAL IMMERSION – A PROGRAM TO NURTURE SPIRITUALITY[1]

*Olga Buttigieg*

## Spirituality and childhood

Spirituality has been referred to as an 'is-ness for life' (Sinetar, 2000, p. 17). The child is animated with a sense of 'aliveness' or a heightened awareness reflected in inspired thought (Sinetar, 2000, p. 13). Marsha Sinetar (2000) asserts that heightened consciousness is related to a perception of unity which relates to the way we see ourselves and others. Rebecca Nye (2009) argues that spirituality is the natural capacity for awareness of the sacred quality of life's experiences and being in relation to something beyond the self. This awareness can be conscious or unconscious and can affect actions, feelings and thoughts. In childhood it is 'especially about being attracted towards "being in relation"' (Nye, 2009, p. 6). Nye conceptualises this as relational consciousness which is understood in terms of experiencing connectedness to others, Creation and the inner self.

Spirituality, then, is the connectedness that a child feels to himself/herself, to others, and to the world and beyond. It emphasises the potential of right relationships to be life-giving and transforming. Spirituality is concerned with the fundamental quality of what it means to be human (O'Murchu, 1997; Zohar & Marshall, 2000) which includes the search for unity or oneness with everything other than self (Adams et al., 2008).

Underlying this research is that all people are spiritual regardless of whether or not they belong to a particular religious tradition (O'Murchu, 1997). Recent research indicates that children are particularly spiritual (Hart, 2003; Hay & Nye, 2006; Hyde, 2008) and it is this inherent quality that can be nurtured if particular characteristics of children's spirituality are identified. Children have a more holistic way of seeing things. They are active, open and curious, and have a natural capacity to wonder and their emotional life works in conjunction with their intellectual life. They do not hide their feelings and are comfortable with the noetic, a feeling of being granted a new understanding. Contemporary literature emphasises that children are active participants and co-constructors of meaning (for instance, see Adams et al., 2008) which heightens the importance of nurturing spirituality in childhood to allow children's imaginations to question, explore and create a personal worldview (Hay & Nye, 2006). Further, Nye (2009) observes that children are hungry for a language to address their complex experiences and sense of being.

Another relevant concept is Marian de Souza's (2016) relational continuum which reflects human spirituality. On one side of the continuum there is a sense of being alone/separate, where the individual Self is separated from everything that is Other. Thus, as children grow in experience they may be led towards deeper connectedness which moves them further along the continuum and, ultimately, towards experiences of unity. It is de Souza's contention that spirituality is implicit in the relational dimension of Being:

> Spirituality is understood as a raised awareness/consciousness that individuals may have of themselves as relational beings; that is an awareness that the Self is Whole, which also comprises the Other and, for some, includes the Transcendent Other.
>
> (p. 36)

Given this understanding, it is important that learning opportunities are provided where young people are enabled to become more deeply connected to themselves, their communities and the wider world so that they feel a sense of belonging (Palmer, 1999). This is not something that is 'brought into' or 'added onto' the curriculum but should be at the heart of every subject that is taught.

## Spirituality in Australian education

In recent years, there has been an indication that spirituality is receiving some attention in Australian education. For instance, the Melbourne Declaration in 2008 recognised the importance of nurturing the spiritual as one of the school's legacies to young people.

> Schools play a vital role in promoting the intellectual, physical, social, emotional, moral, spiritual and aesthetic development and wellbeing of young Australians, and in ensuing the nation's ongoing economic prosperity and social cohesion . . . as well as knowledge and skills a school's legacy to young people should include national values of democracy, equity and justice, an personal values and attributes such as honesty, resilience and respect.
>
> (Ministerial Council on Education, Employment, Training and Youth Affairs [MCEETYA], 2008, pp. 8–9)

Spirituality is further acknowledged in the Declaration through its identification of successful learners: 'Successful learners . . . are able to think deeply . . . are creative, innovative and resourceful . . . are able to make sense of their world' (MCEETYA, 2008, pp. 4–5). These traits are usually perceived to be spiritual characteristics (Hyde, 2008; Nye, 2009; Sinetar, 2000) since they reflect a way of relating to the world through a spiritual lens in terms of relatedness or connectedness. Creative individuals display connectedness through their personal identity, revealed through their sense of self-worth and self-awareness which enables them to manage their emotional, mental, spiritual and physical wellbeing. As well, these traits makes us distinctively human. There is a focus on connectedness and interconnectedness in the Australian Curriculum where the interplay between cognition, affective and spiritual knowing is recognised in three dimensions:

- The discipline-based learning areas or traditional subjects.
- General capabilities, skills or attributes that are seen to be relevant to young people, which includes intercultural understanding, ethical understanding, critical and creative thinking, personal and social capability.
- Cross-curriculum priorities, which includes Aboriginal and Torres Strait Islander histories and cultures (Australian Curriculum, Assessment and Reporting Authority [ACARA], 2016).

Intercultural understanding is further explained so that it

> encourages students to make connections between their own worlds and the worlds of others, to build on shared interests and commonalities, and to negotiate or mediate difference . . . It offers opportunities for them to consider their own beliefs and attitudes in a new light, and so gain insight into themselves and others.
>
> (ACARA, 2016)

Hence, it is within the framework of the last two dimensions that there is potential to nurture young people's spirituality by encouraging spiritual qualities such as empathy, open-mindedness, inclusivity, relating well to others, self-worth, self-awareness, respect, personal identity, optimism, creativity, as well as managing emotional, mental, physical wellbeing.

Further implications of connectedness in the document are the prescription that education must respond and connect to what is happening in our world and the rapid nature of change. Therefore, there is a need to take just and sustainable action to address the effects of globalisation, climate change and technology are additional aspects. These are all areas where children's spirituality may be given movement for growth.

## Forging connectedness to the Other who is different

de Souza (2011) emphasises that in our contemporary world, too many religions emphasise the rules and regulations to the detriment of the spiritual dimension of their tradition. This has led to many people searching along spiritual pathways which are not aligned with mainstream religion. This can lead to disconnection which impacts on a young person's wellbeing. Children are searching for a language to address their complex experiences (Nye, 2009). The expressions of spirituality include emotions both positive, such as, reverence, joy and gratitude, as well as negative, such as sadness, disappointment and loneliness. To do justice to the spiritual emotional experiences of young people, 'their spirituality needs more than a language of love' (Nye, 2009, p. 81).

Spirituality is closely related to the psychosocial health of a person (Ellison, 1983). Spirituality may keep the mind-spirit-body connection in balance, especially during stressful times, by facilitating more adaptive coping styles and positive emotions (Koenig & Cohen, 2002). Mueller and colleagues (2001) found that most studies showed an association between spirituality and better health outcomes, including greater coping skills and less depression. Further statistics show that one in four young Australians aged 16 to 24 lives with a mental illness and one in three experiences moderate to high levels of psychological distress (Mission Australia, 2015, p. 5). Another site, Youth Beyond Blue, provides information and resources for young people dealing with mental health issues including depression, anxiety, bullying, self-harm, discrimination, alcohol and drug and suicide prevention.

> One in 16 young Australians is currently experiencing depression . . . One in six young Australians is currently experiencing an anxiety condition . . . One in four young Australians currently has a mental health condition . . . Suicide is the biggest killer of young Australians.
>
> (Youthbeyondblue, 2016)

These experiences relate to the shadow side of spirituality (de Souza, 2012) when disconnectedness may occur or relationships do not enable human flourishing. It is important to deal with the issues relating to disconnectedness that may further result in experiences of fragmentation, discontent, prejudice, racism, anxiety, fear, guilt, boredom and apathy (de Souza, 2016) and education is one platform where these elements can be addressed.

Another aspect that needs to be identified is the religious and cultural diversity that has become evident in Australian society. Living with difference, young people need to be skilled in interfaith and intercultural dialogue.

Interfaith dialogue involves humility and openness to the spiritual depths of other faiths. It takes place in confidence, without fear or arrogance, without dominating or glossing over differences, never excluding or patronising, neither assimilating nor ignoring (Ecumenical & Interfaith Commission [EIC], Catholic Archdiocese of Melbourne, 2009, para 12).

Interfaith dialogue is a spirituality of communion and a practical concern for every human being. It is not a means of assimilation but involves an openness to dialogue in order to learn, grow and change. During authentic interfaith dialogue we are able to let go of assumptions, judgements, habits, expectations and become more mindful of each other and the natural world. The ability to listen deeply to each other is displayed through body language, eye contact, feelings, emotions and the deepening of connectedness to each other and the ability to enter the second stage of dialogue. The opportunity for interfaith dialogue develops friendships, based on mutual trust. There is a 'spirituality of communion' when each individual is able to see the positive in the Other and to welcome it and not to be fearful of difference. Fear of difference leads to a devaluing and disempowering of Others by devaluing their identity. It destroys communal cohesion, creates fragmentation and is deeply rooted in the power inequalities in society that have become ingrained in the social fabric of individual's lives.

Ken Robinson (2009) highlights three principles that are crucial for human minds to flourish and maintains that they are contradicted by the current culture of education. He first emphasises the importance of diversity because human beings are naturally different and diverse and that real education, therefore, needs to be broad and diverse. Children prosper when there is a broad curriculum but the current culture of education is about conformity to a narrow curriculum. Second, children are natural learners and education needs to excite the imagination rather than its current emphasis on compliance and standardised testing. As Robinson asserts, education that awakens the powers of a child's creativity should not be about a culture of standardisation. Instead, education needs to nurture curiosity. It should be seen in terms of an organic human system which promotes conditions under which humans thrive, not a mechanical system which focuses on what is quantifiable. Ultimately, Robinson is seeking an education which enables the human person to flourish so that it offers diversity, curiosity and creativity in order to engage children and inspire in them a love of learning.

## The Yingadi program

It is my belief that the Yingadi program provides much of what Robinson has argued for. The word Yingadi is a Mutthi Mutthi word that means 'to come'. It is an invitation to come and connect to country, to share stories and to connect to culture. It challenges all who come to be fully present, to listen to the sacred stories of the land and to each other.

> Sacred psychology calls for the recovering and deepening of our own personal story. The deeper story sustains and shapes our emotional attitudes, provides us with life's purposes, and energises our everyday acts. It offers us both meaning and momentum. Everything comes together when the deeper story is present. Consciously or unconsciously, stories give us connectedness with one another. Relationships can be deeply nurtured in the shared story.
>
> (Pike, 2011, p. 17)

In particular, Yingadi recognises wholeness, connectedness, right relationships, belonging and different ways of knowing about the world which are aspects of spirituality as identified earlier. This is holistic learning where effective learning is a continuous stream between the cognitive, affective and spiritual dimensions of education, all three of which complement each another (de Souza, 2009).

Yingadi is a unique experience of aboriginal reconciliation. There are many opportunities to meet and learn from Aboriginal elders and embrace Otherness. It is a different way of learning about the Other and confronts the learner with their own prejudices, assumptions and ignorance.

The next section presents a detailed description of the program as well as the responses of a group of sixteen students from a Catholic secondary school in Victoria, from Years 9, 10 and 11, who travelled to Lake Mungo as part of their religious education program, to immerse themselves in the Yingadi program.

## Elements of the program

### The head

Ultimately, Yingadi is an immersion program that acknowledges the importance of embracing all sacred stories, including the dark side of spirituality. Reconciliation is about nurturing sacred stories that bring healing and hope. New relationships are fostered between Aboriginal and other Australians based on an interfaith pilgrimage to share each other's story and to be enriched and enlarged by each other. It draws on the interconnectedness of creation, the connection to land, stars, fire and water of the Mutthi Mutthi people where their way of life and identity is uniquely expressed through ways of being, knowing, thinking and doing. Yingadi invites young people to become advocates for the Earth and to develop a deeper understanding of the transformative power of the natural world. It aims to reconnect, restore and re-enchant the sense of belonging.

### The heart

One of the sacred sites visited is called the Dippo Tree in Balranald on the way to Lake Mungo. The smoking ceremony takes place here, where people are invited to cleanse themselves with the smoke. This ceremony is about preparation for the journey ahead. When we encounter the land as sacred, it 'bursts' and 'demands' to be recognised (Tacey, 1995). The following response was from one of the teachers who accompanied the students:

> Encountering the Dippo Tree was like connecting with the Sacred Feminine. A place full of mystery that speaks to your intuition, emotions, feelings but at the same time cannot be captured by words – it needs to be experienced. This sacred women's site was hidden, deep, along the banks of the Murrumbidgee River. The Dippo Tree, also referred to as the Birthing Tree, a place where sacred stories of ordeal, pain, darkness were transformed into stories of new life. The babies born under this Tree were taken to the River where their hands and feet were then 'dipped'. This ritual speaks of a forgotten wisdom – that the Earth is a living being to which we belong. . . The Earth

teaches us a spirituality that nurtures silence, stillness, patience, generosity, creativity and compassion. It calls us to live mindfully in the present moment and to be alive to the interconnectedness and sacredness of creation.

(Adult A, personal communication, 2014)

During the immersion experience there are opportunities for interfaith dialogue where students learn about the sacred stories from within the Mungo landscape. The heart of the interfaith dialogue during the Yingadi immersion is to experience deep, inner listening. Deep, inner listening is a spiritual experience. It invites you to be fully present. When we are fully present our attention is focused and our whole being begins to slow down. The ability to connect is nurtured through cultivating the spiritual characteristic of presence. A person can only be present to someone else to the extent that they are present to themselves. The wide, open, salt bush landscape invites people to slow down, be still and silent.

'To be genuinely spiritual is to have great respect for the possibilities and presence of silence' (O'Donohue, 1998, p. 99). Thus, the students begin Yingadi by slowing down. They are aware that they enter Lake Mungo as a guest. It is Vicki Clark's[2] country and the students are invited into her sacred space. The spiritual quality of slowing down and letting go creates a space for inner stillness and silence. The smoking ceremony emphasises these spiritual qualities as the participants let go of attitudes, feelings and thoughts that prevent them from fully engaging. This ritual liberates the 'bad spirits' and invites the participants to begin the journey with an open mind and heart.

Vicki Clark sees aboriginal reconciliation and interfaith dialogue as critical in the education of young people.

The challenge that confronted me was to change people's negative attitudes to positive relationships, built on understanding of my Ancestors, Elders, leaders and our young generation's stories . . . I've worked side by side with teachers as they explore their own racism. I've helped them deal with their anger towards systems that have let Aboriginal people down over 200 years and the statements I often hear 'nobody told us so, we were not taught about any of this' and 'I don't feel comfortable teaching Aboriginal culture' and I would always answer 'You should have asked the question . . . as an educator it is your responsibility'.

(Walker, 2009, para. 2 & 5)

The way of knowing offered through the Yingadi program requires a con-templative approach, which takes students beyond rational thought and connects them to eternal truths and mystery. The spirit is enticed and nurtured by beauty and this is one of the most fundamental and innermost spiritual aspects of one's being.

Students were able to engage with Vicki Clark's story through watching a film *Knowing Home* (Albert Productions, 2003). This provided an opportunity to explore concepts such as spirituality, aboriginality and issues such as cultural difference, assimilation, sacredness and environmental protections.

Stories allow us to see something familiar through new eyes. We become in that moment a guest in someone else's life, and together with them sit at the feet of their teacher. The meaning we may draw from someone's story may be different from the meaning they themselves have drawn. No matter. Facts bring us knowledge, but stories lead to wisdom.

(Remen, 2002, p. xxviii)

Engaging with the land was an important element of the program. 'The Australian landscape is our greatest asset . . . we need to become less human and more like nature: in that way we may become more fully human, and experience anew the sacred' (Tacey, 1995, p. 7). It is in those moments of stillness that the imagination is stirred to give birth to new ideas and creative solutions. Creativity is a pathway to the sacred, it puts us on a path of self-discovery that takes us deep within ourselves. This leads us into the next stage of interfaith dialogue – the dialogue of hands.

## The hands

The dialogue of the hands occurred when students joined together to create a more just world. They joined hands with the Other to heal the world. This joining or connecting was tangible in moments of experiencing beauty such as the sunrise and sunset on the same day, but also in times of quiet and stillness. Students appeared to perceive the gentle touch of the Spirit of Mungo, sometimes with a butterfly or a bird as it sang its presence. A symbol of resilience was provided by the wild grey-green saltbushes growing in profusion, thereby enabling students to see the landscape with new eyes and becoming aware of a tangible energy that was both wild and gentle.

## The holy

On arriving at Mungo, the sacred camp fire was lit. Significantly, it called and gathered people into a sacred space to be still and silent, to be present in the now. The message stick was covered with sacred symbols of animals, insects, waterholes, birds, stars, cross, all visual reminders of the sacredness of creation. The students were led to rediscover the ancient wisdom that nature can be an excellent spiritual teacher.

To reconnect is to re-discover beauty, mystery, wonder and awe and its capacity to surprise, engage, liberate and transform us. The Yingadi experience included watching the night sky and hearing the aboriginal star stories. We live in right relationship with the world when we show that we love the world. This intimate relationship with the land was captured by the words of Joan Robinson, Vicki Clark's mother on the DVD *Knowing Home* (Albert Productions, 2003):

The land is my mother, like a human mother the land is protection, enjoyment and provides for our needs. When the land is taken from us or destroyed, we feel hurt because we belong to the land and we are part of it.

Joan Robinson speaks about the land in terms of being deeply connected and sensitive to the natural world. The students' connection with these sacred spaces helped to move them forward towards some new growth in Becoming. This is the place where the invisible and visible within the human person connects. Smith (2006), an educator on ecology, writes that sacred spaces are about rediscovering our ecological self. When we relate directly with the natural world, the ego can be transcended and the self arrives at a position of being deeply connected and sensitive to the natural world.

> We cannot discover ourselves without first discovering the universe, the Earth, and the imperatives of our own being. Each of these has a creative power and vision far beyond any rational thought or cultural creation of which we are capable. Nor should we think of these as isolated from our own individual being or from humanity. We have no existence except with the Earth and within the universe.
>
> (Berry, 1988, p. 195)

The new cosmology claims that creation itself is the primary revelation. 'God's life and love become visible and tangible first and foremost in the unfolding of universal life' (O'Murchu, 1997, p. 96). Yingadi awakens this sense of being alive. It provides a new way of relating with the Spirit that enlivens the universe. The new cosmology thrives on relatedness and interdependence. It evokes deep sentiments of creativity, respect, care and love (p. 100). It invites us to outgrow the dualistic oppositions of the sacred and the secular.

The Aboriginal people are aware of the interconnectedness of all life and the sacred nature of the land. During Yingadi young people connected at a deep level. In the final ritual they were invited back on the dunes to take their shoes off, sit in the circle and reflect on their experiences at Mungo. They were also invited to reflect on their own relationships including people who have died. Each person, including Vicki Clark, wrote the name of a loved person, a past ancestor, as a way of acknowledging the sacredness of their life. They wrote the name of a loved one in the sand and this name then became part of the Mungo landscape. Thereby, two different sacred stories were connected to become one.

On the return journey there is a sacred smoking healing ceremony with Marilyne Nicholls at Wood Wood and the return of the Message Stick to Vicki Clark. Vicki Clark gifted each person with a message stone that she created at the end of the Yingadi immersion. The following poem is included with the message stone as a reminder of the sacredness of land and every person's responsibility to look after the Earth.

As you walk in the footsteps of
My ancestors
May each step you take be as gentle as

the sacred land that's under your feet
May the Spirits of our old people
watch over you and keep you safe.

## Discussion

The immersion program took place from 2–6 May 2016. Before travelling to Lake Mungo to visit the sacred sites and experience various rituals, the participants were invited to respond to two questions:

1 Why did you choose to participate in Yingadi?
2 What are your expectations of the program?

### *Before the program*

A range of responses before the immersion centred on gaining knowledge and experience about Aboriginal culture as well as a focus on a deeper understanding of own self. The excerpts below indicate the expectations before the immersion:

'. . . it would be a different learning experience and it's a different way of learning'.

(Student A, personal communication)

'I also wanted to have the opportunity to reflect on myself and how I can become a better person to myself and other people'.

(Student B, personal communication)

'. . . hear stories from Aboriginal elders (true source)'.

(Student C, personal communication)

'. . . to open my mind, heart and soul. . .'.

(Student D, personal communication)

'I need to remember how to live without technology. To live with people, to live with the land, to live with beauty and love, and Yingadi called me'.

(Student E, personal communication)

'I expect or wish to have discovered . . . an inner trust a peace with the land and become more of a calm person who will hold the spiritual stories . . .'.

(Student F, personal communication)

'In my life, I have not previously had any opportunity to learn about the true history of Australia, and the wonderful connection the Indigenous have with the land'.

(Student G, personal communication)

As well, there were some responses that included spiritual values such as love and respect:

'I hope I form a deeper knowledge and love/respect for the indigenous community and land we all live off'.

(Student H, personal communication)

To sum up, the expectations of the Yingadi program were seen by many as an opportunity to connect and experience the land as sacred and which would enable them to become part of a bigger sacred story.

### After the program

After the immersion program students responded to two further questions that aimed to determine if the following two outcomes of the program were achieved.

- Nurturing aboriginal reconciliation – through interconnectedness: sacred stories, sacred rituals, bush walks, dune walks, interfaith dialogue, slowing down, stillness, silence, creativity, inner deep listening of the landscape.
- Nurturing own spirituality – reflective journalling, quiet time, as well as various experiences as outlined above.

The questions were:

1 What did you experience/learn during Yingadi?
2 What will you do with this knowledge personally, in your community, globally?

Many of the students wrote about deep connections, experiences of beauty, stillness and spiritual values such as patience. They expressed their experiences creatively through spiritual activities such as Mandala paintings, reflective journalling, poetry, song and music. Many of them commented on how the experiences had touched them deeply. They used words like 'feelings and emotions were aroused' and 'being transformed'. It was an inner dialogue that entered their heart and they connected to the wisdom and beauty of the landscape. The following excerpts from some students capture these sentiments:

'It is very difficult for me to write down or even tell what I experienced because it's not the same thing as being in Lake Mungo . . . I learnt many things like star stories, fire, dadirri, your inner self and many more wonderful things'.

(Student I, personal communication)

'I'm not sure how to put it into words but I'll try. I feel so much passion, emotion and inside me . . . I also learnt how to better understand my feelings, emotions and my inner listening'.

(Student J, personal communication)

'I learnt more about the values of patience, respect for those wiser than me and value of family and friends. I have learnt much more than the expectation I ever thought of'.

(Student K, personal communication)

'Sit back and appreciate the beauty and stillness in the world'.

(Student A, personal communication)

'I learnt that the simple things in life such as, the land, the stars, the rivers and lakes, the sun, the moon and flora and fauna. All have a history and sacredness that people too often take for granted'.

(Student L, personal communication)

'We lost track of time on this journey. At times we travelled back 40,000 years, while at the other times we were present in the moment, truly present!'.

(Student L, personal communication)

'It was very touching and an amazing experience to be part of these important rituals'.

(Student M, communication)

'It was absolutely incredible. I gained a lot of 'academic knowledge' about Aboriginal country, culture, history, and traditions, but this was not the highlight nor the major benefit of the immersion. The experience really rocked my sense of identity and connection to the Australian land'.

(Student N, personal communication)

'My feet are lighter. I have bush eyes. I have a warm heart. My feet and hands have touched ancient lands. My nostrils filled with smoke and the early morning air. I have breathed deeply. My soul is lighter and it is singing'.

(Student O, personal communication)

## Final thoughts

To conclude, the experiences and responses of the young people suggested that the Yingadi program is a useful and inspiring resource which can be used to meet the requirements of the Australian Curriculum that children's spirituality should be addressed. Students were able to articulate what has touched them and how they had responded to the Other with wonder, empathy and compassion. Their awareness of and connection to the land had been nourished and ultimately, they revealed their spiritual wellbeing in their discernment, gratitude, appreciation and their capacity to notice and attend to the sacred.

## Notes

1   Many Aboriginal and Torres Strait Islander people prefer to be called Aboriginal Australians rather than Indigenous Australians. In acknowledgement of this, I have used 'Aboriginal Australians' in this chapter except where Indigenous has been used in a direct quote.
2   Vicki Clark is a Mutthi Mutthi/Wemba Wemba woman who was instrumental in establishing and coordinating Catholic Ministry in Victoria, Australia for 25 years. She is currently working in partnership with Amberley, Edmund Rice Spirituality Centre in Lower Plenty, Melbourne, in the Yingadi immersion program.

## References

Adams, K., Hyde, B., & Woolley, R. (2008). *The spiritual dimension of childhood*. London: Jessica Kingsley Publishers.

Albert Street Productions (Producer) (2003). *Knowing home: A reflection of a personal spirituality by a woman from the river country. [videorecording]*. Melbourne, Australia: Albert Street Productions.

Australian Curriculum, Assessment and Reporting Authority [ACARA] (2016). Intercultural-Understanding. Retrieved from http://australiancurriculum.edu.au/generalcapabilities/intercultural-understanding/introduction/introduction

Berry, T. (1988). *The dream of the earth*. San Francisco: Sierra Club Books.

de Souza, M. (2009). Promoting wholeness and wellbeing in education: Exploring aspects of the spiritual dimension. In M. de Souza, J. O'Higgins Norman & D. Scott (eds), *International handbook of education for spirituality, care and wellbeing* (pp. 677–692). Dordrecht, Netherlands: Springer Academic Publishers.

de Souza, M. (2011). Promoting inter-spiritual education in the classroom: Exploring the perennial philosophy as a useful strategy to encourage freedom of religious practice and belief. *Journal of Religious Education, 59*(1), 27–37.

de Souza, M. (2012). Connectedness and *Connectedness*. The dark side of spirituality: Implications for education. *International Journal of Children's Spirituality, 17*(3), 291–304.

de Souza, M. (2016). *Spirituality in education in a global, pluralised world*. New York, NY: Routledge.

Ecumenical & Interfaith Commission [EIC]. (2009, October). *Promoting Interfaith Relations.* [Brochure]. East Melbourne, Victoria: EIC

Ellison, C. W. (1983). Spiritual well-being: Conceptualization and measurement. *Journal of Psychology and Theology, 11*(4), 330–340.

Hart, T. (2003). *The secret spiritual lives of children*. Makawao, HI: Inner Ocean.

Hay, D., & Nye, R. (2006). *The spirit of the child*. London: Jessica Kingsley Publishers.

Hyde, B. (2008). *Children and spirituality: Searching for meaning and connectedness*. London: Jessica Kingsley Publishers.

Koenig, H. G., & Cohen, H. J. (2002). *The link between religion and health: Psychoneuroimmunology and the faith factor*. New York: Oxford University Press.

Ministerial Council on Education Employment Training and Youth Affairs (MCEETYA). (2008). *Melbourne declaration on educational goals for young Australians.* Retrieved 10th April, 2017 from www.mceetya.edu.au/verve/-resources/National_Declaration_on_the_Educational_Goals_for_Young_Australians.pdf

Mission Australia (2015). *Youth Survey Mental Health.* Retrieved from: https://mission australia.com.au/what-we-do/research-evaluation/youth-survey

Mueller, P. S., Plevak, D. J., & Rummans, T. A. (2001). Religious involvement, spirituality, and medicine: Implications for clinical practice. *Mayo Clinic Proceedings, 76*(12), 1225–1235.

Nye, R. (2009). *Children's spirituality: What it is and why it matters.* London: Church House Publishing.

O'Donohue, J. (1998). *Anam Cara: A book of celtic wisdom.* London: Bantam Books.

O'Murchu, D. (1997). *Reclaiming spirituality.* Dublin: Gill & Macmillan.

Palmer, P. (1999). The grace of great things: Reclaiming the sacred in knowing, teaching and learning. In S. Glazer (ed.), *The heart of learning: Spirituality in education* (pp. 13–32). New York: Tarcher/Putnam.

Pike, E. (2011). *The power of story.* Victoria, Australia: John Garratt Publishing.

Remen, R. N. (2002). *Kitchen table wisdom: Stories that heal.* Sydney: Pan Macmillan Australia Pty Ltd.

Robinson, K., with Arnica, L. (2009). *The element: How finding your passion changes everything.* Melbourne: Penguin Books.

Sinetar, M. (2000). *Spiritual intelligence: What we can learn from the early awakening child.* New York: Orbis Books.

Smith. C. (2006). Ecoliteracy: The most important literacy of all. In *EarthSong Journal,* Autumn, 2006, Melbourne, Australia.

Tacey, D. (1995). *Edge of the sacred: Transformation in Australia.* Victoria, Australia: Harper Collins Publisher.

Walker, V. (2009). *Yarra Healing: Towards reconciliation with Indigenous Australians. Stories and Voices, para 2 and 5* Retrieved from http://yarrahealing.catholic.edu.au/stories-voices/index.cfm?loadref=43

Youthbeyondblue (2016). *Stats and facts.* Retrieved from https://youthbeyondblue.com/footer/stats-and-facts

Zohar, M., & Marshall, I. (2000). *Spiritual intelligence: The ultimate intelligence SQ.* London: Bloomsbury Publishing.

# 15

# SPIRITUAL WELLBEING AND THE NATIONAL SCHOOLS CHAPLAINCY PROGRAM IN AUSTRALIA

*Avril Howard*

## A brief history of religion, education and the NSCP in Australia

Debates regarding whether religion and/or spirituality has a place in a 'free, compulsory and secular' education system have been ongoing in Australia since the introduction of state education in the late nineteenth century.[1] During the first part of the nineteenth century religious institutions provided education in Australia but during the latter half of the century there was a 'call for universal, free – that is state supported – and secular education' (Bouma, 2006, p. 181). Marion Maddox (2014) argues that secular state education was introduced to create a more inclusive educational environment, where students would not feel discriminated against on the basis of their religious affiliation. As the meaning of the term 'secular' was not originally clarified, Gary D. Bouma (2006) states that it left it wide open to interpretation. Indeed, a hard secular position excluded teaching about religion in Australian schools, or at least minimised content in this field until recently. Australian scholars, Humanists, rationalists and faith-leaders have recently advocated for Australian schools' curricula to promote an appreciation for religious and non-religious diversity through the introduction of educational programs about diverse religions and non-religious worldviews to foster social inclusion, drawing on international research and best practices in this field (Byrne, 2014; Halafoff, 2015). While limited progress has been made at the national level, the state of Victoria is currently leading the way by introducing a compulsory focus on Learning about World Views and Religions in its History and Ethical Understanding curricula (VCAA, 2015). This chapter proposes that the NSCP may offer a complementary avenue to foster social cohesion in a multifaith society and develop student's spiritual wellbeing, given that there is currently little attention placed on how to address the latter in Australia's national curriculum (Halafoff, 2015; Donnely & Wiltshire, 2014).

Chaplaincy was first introduced in government schools by the Council for Christian Education in 1955. This program, which had humble beginnings expanded to 555 school chaplains nationally by 2004. Schools so valued the support that chaplains were providing in the areas of spiritual and emotional well-being that funding for chaplains came from communities, local churches and the schools themselves (Hughes & Sims, 2009).

In 2007 the National School Chaplaincy Program (NSCP) was introduced by the Australian government to support the positive contribution chaplains were making to state schools. Both Maddox (2014) and Halafoff (2015) have, however, argued that the NSCP was established as part of the then Prime Minister John Howard's Liberal Government's conservative political agenda to return to traditional Christian values instead of advancing intercultural and interreligious understanding, although acknowledging that the program was voluntary and there was no stipulation on the religious affiliation of the chaplain (Maddox, 2014). The NSCP enabled 2712 schools (government, Catholic and independent) in the two rounds of funding in 2007 to access $20,000 per annum, the 'due date for funding being July 2008' (Hughes & Sims, 2009, p. 8). The need for greater attention to the spiritual wellbeing of students was also articulated in 2008 in the Melbourne Declaration on Educational Goals for Young Australians, which recognised that: 'Schools play a vital role in promoting the intellectual, physical, social, emotional, moral, spiritual and aesthetic development and wellbeing of young Australians . . .' (MCEETYA, 2008, p. 4). This reflected international trends, particularly emerging from the UK and EU, and discussed in Adams' chapter in this volume.

The NSCP was introduced, at least in part, to support schools in meeting the *Melbourne Declaration's* goal of nurturing spiritual wellbeing and also to provide pastoral care support services for students. However this federally and state government-funded program has generated much public debate and media coverage due to the perception of it undermining the secular traditions of public education. Since then additional mechanisms of accountability have been implemented to ensure that the program upholds the principles of secular education in Australian, notably for chaplains to sign a code of conduct that they will not proselytise their religious beliefs in schools (Victorian State Government, Education and Training, 2016a).

Maddox (2014) contends that the NSCP was fraught with controversy and complaints ranging from concerns of the Australian Psychological Society (APS) about chaplains' suitability and qualifications to assist with mental health issues, to worries about resources, which the Australian Education Union (AEU) argued could be better spent on providing qualified counsellors to schools. Maddox concludes: 'Let us reclaim the secular' (p. 203) in state education. Yet, by stating this she is adopting a very narrow and *exclusive* understanding of the secular, which is at odds with how it is understood in democracies where, according to Charles Taylor (2007), diverse religions can still be present and *included* in public spaces.

Moreover, an investigation conducted by the Commonwealth Ombudsman's office in 2010, on the administration of the NPCS program, noted a major criticism of it being that 'chaplains religious affiliations . . . [have] been a source of concern for some parents in public schools who believe there is no place for religion in a secular educational environment' (Asher, 2011, p. 5). Once again this criticism highlights a very narrow view of secular societies and education and limited understanding around more contemporary arguments regarding the place of religion and spirituality in education in Australia (de Souza, 2009). The Ombudsman's office made eight recommendations including: setting minimum qualifications for chaplains; a code of conduct for chaplains; and a formal system for management of complaints regarding chaplaincy. Overall both the Ombudsman's office and the then national Department of Education Employment and Workplace Relations agreed that the consultation process during the investigation had shown that the NSCP supported the spiritual development of all students as set out in the Melbourne Declaration (Asher, 2011, p. 23), thus strengthening the case for the continuation of the NSCP.

In August 2010, the then Labour, and traditionally more progressive, Australian Government announced that a further $222 million would be provided so that existing schools funded under the NSCP could have their funding extended to the end of 2014 (Asher, 2011, p. 7). In 2011/2012 due to community concerns over the religious nature of the existing program the Labour government amended the NSCP to make provision for both chaplains and secular workers to be employed under a new scheme called the National School Chaplaincy and Student Welfare Programme (NSCWP) (Australian Teacher Magazine, 2014, p. 20). The NSCWP was, however, a short-lived program as in 2014 the newly elected Liberal Party agreed to support the original program put in place in 2007 and legislated that the NSCP would replace the NSCSWP (p. 20). The debate surrounding the question as to whether a counsellor is qualified to meet the spiritual needs of students arose at this time, hence the question of the distinctive and complementary roles of chaplains and welfare workers is explored in more detail later in this chapter. In 2015 the Australian Government further extended the NSCP funds to be available until the end of 2018 (Australian Government, Department of Education and Training, 2016).

From the outset of the NSCP it was made clear in the guidelines that the program was distinctive, having the spiritual wellbeing of the students as its focus, and was to complement existing wellbeing services of counselling for students (DEST, 2007). Clearer guidelines were also provided about the role of chaplains in 2015, stating that NSCP chaplains may be of any faith and be recognised through formal ordination, endorsed by an accepted religious institution (DEST, 2007). These guidelines also emphasise that chaplains are not to 'take advantage of their privileged position to proselytise, evangelise or advocate for a particular religious view or belief' (Victorian State Government, Education and Training, 2016a). An additional measure of accountability to the current Department of Education has also been introduced whereby independent schools are now to provide a progress report on the NSCP to the Department at the end of each semester instead of an annual report. This includes attesting that all requirements have been fulfilled and reporting any issues or complaints that may arise in the school year in regards to chaplaincy (Victorian State Government, Education and Training, 2016b), thus ensuring that any breaches in the implementation of the program that do not uphold Australian democratic and secular principles can be quickly addressed.

The NSCP provides one avenue of support for school communities to respond to the national goals of the Melbourne Declaration (2008) to provide for the spiritual, social and emotional wellbeing of students. By continuing to fund the NSCP the current Coalition government believes it is creating opportunity for schools to nurture spiritual wellbeing in students. Its implementation, however, has been chequered by much political and public debate due to the program being perceived as undermining the secular traditions of public education in Australia (Maddox, 2014). To terminate the program, however, poses the risk of schools being forced to potentially neglect the spiritual wellbeing of students, as schools simply do not have the additional financial or human resources to respond to this need. Moreover, and as the Review of the Australian Curriculum (Donnely & Wiltshire, 2014) and Halafoff (2015) have noted, it remains unclear how precisely schools can nurture spiritual wellbeing within the new National Curriculum. The flow on effect is that without the NSCP the gap between the goals of the Melbourne Declaration (2008) for spiritual wellbeing in students will widen and Australia will fall further behind in offering a world-class education, compared to, for example, the English, Irish and Welsh systems which have incorporated spiritual wellbeing in school programs. For instance, James O'Higgins Norman (2014a) explains that: 'School Chaplains in Ireland have . . . been to the fore in engaging with the emerging interfaith context. . . . Many school chaplains have adapted their practice to cater for those of "other faiths" and "no faiths" and they make a significant contribution to the school as a welcoming place of people of every faith and culture . . .' (O'Higgins Norman, 2014b, pp. 280–281).

The next section of the paper concentrates on developing a greater understanding of nurturing spiritual wellbeing in secular, multifaith, and democratic educational settings drawing on the philosophical work of Kierkegaard (1813–1855), and contemporary educational scholars and researchers.

## Existential spirituality and the NSCP

Defining religion and spirituality has been a subject of great interest for scholars for centuries and there now exists an abundance of explanations regarding these two phenomena and the interconnections between them. While some frameworks posit people to be spiritual but not religious, others note that the boundaries between the two are porous and that many religious people also identify with spirituality (Singleton, 2014; Ammerman, 2013).

Søren Kierkegaard (1813–1855), for example, although he was Christian, posited that spirituality is a process of discovering individual purpose and meaning to life – of 'becoming' (Carlisle, 2005, p. 113). It is this description of spirituality and process of 'becoming an authentic self', which this chapter focuses on, as it can pertain to both the religious and the non-religious (Webster, 2004). Anders Holm (2013) explains how Kierkegaard argued that the process of 'becoming' may be experienced outside of the religious dogma offered by the institutional structure of the church as one develops an 'authentic self' and comes into direct relationship with God and others. Holm (2013) notes that Kierkegaard emphasised that the subjective existing individual self (inwardness) is more important than any 'objective' truths of doctrine and understood the self to be an activity, process and way-of-being rather than an object of study (pp. 6–10). Frederick Sotang (1979), Clare Carlisle (2005) and Scott Webster (2004, 2009) discuss Kierkegaard's concepts of 'freedom', 'personal choice' and 'spiritual relation' in developing a notion of selfhood as part of spiritual formation. They recognise that Kierkegaard argued for the importance of the task of becoming a self, which leads to a meaningful and purposeful existence. John Davenport (2013) in analysing Kierkegaard's ideas about 'selfhood and spirit' (p. 1) says that Kierkegaard posited that it is through coming to authentic selfhood or becoming a 'self' that individual purpose and meaning to life becomes clearer. The process of becoming a 'self' or developing a unified identity is reflected in one who recognises the finite (temporal and necessity) and the infinite (eternal and freedom) dimensions to life and is able to dwell in a relation with the two. Clare Carlisle (2005) sheds light on Kierkegaard's idea of 'movement' or 'becoming' through her discussion on his three spheres of existence: the aesthetic (knowledge and reflection), ethical (freedom and action) and religious whereby the religious was entered into via a 'leap of faith' that the individual progresses through (p. 113), yet as Webster (2009) points out, can move between all the time evaluating and exercising 'freedom of choice'. Exercising personal freedom and choice enables the individual to actively choose to be free from a 'mass herd' (religious system) mentality to become an individual 'self'. Kierkegaard observed that this takes courage because it requires the individual to exercise critical judgement and responsibility which are considered here to be the hallmarks of an educated person, and in particular a spiritually educated person (Webster, 2009).

Notably Kierkegaard's concept of 'subjective truth' did not mean that he claimed that all institutionalised religions were to be avoided but rather that it is our 'relation' to such institutions which is the important thing as he posited that knowing is relating to the existing of the knower. Thus through the process of 'becoming' we can by 'personal choice' decide to enter a relationship with the Transcendent or God, as the priority is on 'how' we relate to God and find meaningfulness in our lives (see Webster's chapter in this volume).

Scott Webster (2009), in interpreting Kierkegaard's philosophy, adopts the position that spirituality is best understood existentially and by using the term, 'existential spirituality', Webster argues that it is this ontological approach which is useful for understanding how existential questions can be responded to in a secular, multifaith and democratic education system such as Australia. Webster (2009, p. 65) suggests that existential spirituality can offer an inquiry based approach to learning which can be applied when engaging with existential questions, such as what is the meaning of life and what is the meaning of my life? (see Webster's chapter in this volume). O'Higgins Norman (2014b) also recognises that the types of issues that chaplains deal with do in fact relate to the deeper existential questions of life such as meaning and purpose. Existential spirituality can therefore potentially provide a useful framework for chaplains when supporting students through their search for making meaning of life.

Philip Hughes' (2009, p. 919) research findings in Australian secondary schools led him to conclude that

> spirituality education should assist young people in working through the big questions of life and the nature of the world in which they live. It should assist them in working on the basic existential questions of life and death, of reality and unreality and of good and evil.
>
> (Hughes, 2009, p. 920)

Hughes further notes that many Australian children come to school 'without a clear background in any religious or spiritual tradition. Therefore, education cannot begin with an assumed religious background but rather ought to begin with the more basic questions of human existence' (p. 920), a factor which school chaplains ought to take into account as they work with young people on spiritual health and wellbeing.

Moreover, and as discussed above, Kierkegaard contends that one becomes more authentic through relating with others and God (Transcendent Being). Marian de Souza (2010) similarly stresses the importance of such connectedness for young people in exploring spiritual dimensions saying that '. . . this connectedness helps them [the person] to make meaning of their lived experiences and provides them with a sense of purpose' (p. 3).

de Souza, Francis et al.'s (2009, p, 2) research reveals that 'many young people appear to experience disillusionment and a sense of hopelessness and disconnection and that they often contribute to the rising statistics of mental health problems in many Western countries'. They contend that spirituality as an 'integral component of human experience' is essential to educational programs which address topics of 'personal and community identity . . . and promote meaning and connectedness' (p. 3). The inclusion of such elements into educational programs, they argue, 'should make possible the care and wellbeing of all students' (p. 3).

Within this context, de Souza (2009, p. 677) acknowledges that wellbeing and education in Australia has also become a topical issue due to the increase of teenage disengagement and even suicide rates, and that schools are being highly recommended to run programs to build young people's resilience. de Souza also factors in 'the distancing of many young people from traditional institutions such as religious traditions which provided some meaning and purpose to the lives of past generations'. Young people seeking fulfilment in 'spaces without boundaries' has led de Souza to give consideration to spirituality in human life 'to argue for an education that nurtures and gives expression to the inner and outer lives of students so that there is a greater chance of promoting balance and wellbeing for students to live and function effectively within their communities' (p. 677).

However, programs focused on building resilience in secular school settings may not always draw upon spiritual resources. Indeed, there have been a number of significant recent studies undertaken in and beyond Australia on the effectiveness of chaplaincy and also of the differences and similarities between chaplains and counsellors in school settings, to assist with student's spiritual wellbeing.

## Chaplains, counsellors and the effectiveness of the NSCP

The discussion below explores the distinctive and complementary role of chaplains and school counsellors and examines the effectiveness of chaplains in the provision of spiritual wellbeing in schools. It also demonstrates that chaplains have an 'extra tool' (Life Matters, 2014) to counsellors in regards to nurturing spiritual wellbeing in students.

The goals and objectives of the NSCP point out the complementary role of chaplains and counsellors, as chaplains are described as working 'closely with wellbeing and allied health staff in schools to support students and their educational outcomes, staff, families and the wider school community' (Victorian State Government, Education and Training, 2016c). In an ABC radio interview (Life Matters, 2014), Natasha Mitchell interviewed Peter James, CEO of Scripture Union (SU), and David Stokes of the Australian Psychological Society (APS) to discuss why the NSCP employs only chaplains of a religious faith and not counsellors. Stokes affirmed that chaplains could play a complementary role to counsellors but stated that they should not cross boundaries in regards to psychological services offered, particularly pertaining to issues of mental health. James (CEO of SU) said that chaplains play a multi faceted role but that the primary distinguishing factor was that chaplains were able to respond to issues of a spiritual nature that counsellors could not. As James and Steve Forward, (2014, p. 4) have stated in a report for the National School Chaplaincy Association:

> School chaplains engage around questions of beliefs, values and ethics; help students explore spiritual identity; provide a spiritual/religious perspective on relevant issues; liaise with local spiritual and religious groups; and support students and the school community in times of grief and loss when some of the big questions of life arise for them. Chaplains ensure that spirituality is not forgotten as an essential part of people's overall wellbeing.

James therefore believes that chaplains have additional skills to offer when it comes to dealing with matters that relate to spirituality in young people. Like Stokes, he sees the role of chaplain as complementary to counsellors, and says that chaplains can play a preventative role in early identification and prevention of mental health issues by referring young people to experts if and when they identify them as needing specialised assistance (Life Matters, 2014).

Drawing on the experience of chaplaincy in Irish schools O'Higgins Norman (2014a), argues that when and if students begin to search for purpose and ask the deeper questions of life (responding to existential questions) 'the contribution of the Chaplain is obvious' (pp. 15–16) as they will have been specifically trained in theology and spirituality and will have the skills to accompany students in their search for purpose and meaning. O'Higgins Norman, (2014b), Aine Moran (2014) and John Murray (2014) all note the distinctive elements of chaplains and counsellors but they also acknowledge that they share commonalities, such as building resilience and positive life skills in students, which when the services are used together can work for the benefit of the wellbeing of students.

Furthermore, Ciaran Dalton (2009, p. 977) examines the implications of including spirituality as a dimension when counselling young people. Dalton (2009) cites Brian Thorne (1990) who argues that 'in order to help a young person make sense of this search [for meaning], the therapist needs to be aware of more than traditional psychological and therapeutic values' (Thorne, 1990 in Dalton, 2009, p. 984). Dalton also cites Pat Collins's (1999) research, who states that

> many of these apparent psychological problems presented by young people and their families to counsellors are in fact spiritual in nature and that he or she may be in need of some form of spiritual awakening if recovery is to be fully achieved.
>
> (Collins, 1999, p. 156 in Dalton, 2009, p. 984)

Dalton argues that a counsellor who 'remains detached' from spirituality (inner core) would find it almost impossible to engage with a young person on that level and that if schools are to offer an authentic 'holistic' education then spiritual care cannot be ignored. While these arguments may be problematic to educators, parents and counsellors who may not see themselves as spiritual and/or religious, this chapter argues that they may ring true with many educators, parents and chaplains, who perceive that some of life's problems are spiritual in nature and thereby requiring spiritual attention and solutions. In a society such as Australia, which is increasingly religiously and spiritually diverse, the benefits and dangers of such an approach need to be considered, alongside psychological approaches for managing student's emotional and mental health. Following this argument, chaplains then who deal with matters of spirituality may have a role to play in *complementing* the services offered by counsellors in schools, while not *replacing* them.

As discussed earlier in this chapter Maddox (2014) argued that the NSCP was fraught with complaints and controversy. Dr Phillip Hughes and Professor Margaret Sims (2009), however, in a study on *The Effectiveness of Chaplaincy as Provided by the National School Chaplaincy Association to Government Schools in Australia* surveyed principals, staff, students and parents and reported that:

> . . . Chaplains had also provided support for students in exploring their spirituality and had provided guidance on religious values, and ethical matters although the extent to which this occurred varied . . .
>
> (Hughes & Sims, 2009, p. 6)

Hughes and Sims (2009) also reported that according to school principals, 97 per cent of chaplains had been effective in providing pastoral care services as per the NSCP guidelines and that chaplains assist with student issues such as: development of self; sense of purpose; self-esteem; involvement in the community; social inclusion; 'big picture' and spiritual issues such as developing compassion, behaviour management and social relationships for example, anger, loneliness.

Doctoral studies (Salecich, 2002; Pohlmann, 2005) exploring and measuring the effectiveness of chaplaincy in state schools were also undertaken in Queensland in 2002 and 2005. Overall the data from these early studies showed consensus as to the value that chaplains bring to schools in the area of pastoral care and wellbeing services for students for example, helping students who may feel alienated gain a sense of connectedness, cultivating harmonious relationships and supporting students overcome cynicism and despair by offering hope and meaning for life (Pohlmann, 2005).

In 2009 ACCESS Ministries commissioned the social research group, Social Compass to conduct an independent evaluation of the value of chaplains in Victorian schools. Social Compass surveyed students and parents in 25 Victorian schools. While this study may have the limitation of possible bias as ACCESS Ministries is a NSCP provider themselves, the results confirmed those of previous studies cited above that chaplains 'value added' to schools through the pastoral care services they contributed. The research showed that chaplains supported students in areas of: social connectedness (i.e. building positive relationships), assisting with family problems and making responsible choices when faced with issues such as drugs and alcohol (ACCESS Ministries, 2009, p. 5).

Furthermore, James and Forward (2014) cite research studies conducted by the Research Centre for Vulnerable Children and Families, University of Western Australia (2012) led by Associate Professor Maria Harries and Edith Cowan University (2009) led by Hughes and Sims. They argue that these studies illustrate that the issues that chaplains deal with relate to personal aspects of students' development, are not religious in nature nor undermining of secularism. While the studies were commissioned by chaplaincy providers, they were conducted by independent researchers. The 2012 study involving a range of stakeholders from school leaders and staff, to professionals such as psychologists, revealed that 96 per cent of respondents supported the work of school chaplains in providing social and emotional support to students (James & Forward, 2014, p. 5). The specific work of chaplains in a school context may also cover 'sense of belonging, positive school climate, required responsibility and helpfulness, school norms against violence etc. which are valuable contributions for Australian secular schooling' (p. 6).

Hughes and Sims' (2009) study into the effectiveness of chaplaincy in Australian government schools also documented a similar response to chaplaincy services. The study revealed that the average score across Principals surveyed, using a scale of 1–10 with 10 being excellent, showed that Principals scored chaplains 8 out of 10 for making a major contribution to school morale (p. 5), and 75 per cent of students felt their chaplain was highly important to the school scoring their importance as '8 or more out of 10' (p. 6).

These studies reveal the strong support that the NSCP program has in schools and that chaplains provide a distinctive service to schools in caring for the spiritual needs of their students, while counsellors are able to provide psychological and emotional support, and that the two can complement one another.

## Chaplains in schools and spiritual wellbeing

Drawing on the research findings above, this chapter contends that chaplains have particular expertise relating to making meaning and developing purpose and strength in people to draw upon in difficult times. By applying the Existential Spirituality idea of 'becoming', chaplains may create learning spaces where students can explore religious and spiritual domains and dimensions between the 'finite' (temporal) and the 'infinite' (eternal) in times of crisis, accepting and engaging in new challenges and thus developing a sense of agency or self-efficacy. Chaplains could also nurture spiritual wellbeing in their students and provide them with spiritual tools to respond to questions of an existential nature, tools which counsellors are not necessarily trained or qualified to deliver and as (Dalton, 2009) argues, counsellors could also employ a referral system for matters relating to clients' spiritual health (p. 985). As chaplains support students in 'problem-solving skills, internal locus of control, social competence, social skills. good coping style, optimism, moral beliefs etc.' (James & Forward, 2014, p. 6) they are well positioned to equip students to make responsible choices. Chaplains can also foster the aspects of purposefulness, connectedness and belonging by being sensitive to the needs of others, building on the cultural experiences, religious and spiritual experience and/ or spiritual heritage of students and their respective communities. A key task for chaplains is creating environments where students feel a sense of belonging and where friendships can be formed within a caring community. Chaplains may also promote meaning and connectedness in schools for example through special programs and activities they may run such as lunchtime clubs, grandparents day, cultural days, mentoring programs and other liturgical practices such as prayer and worship. Guidance officers and school counsellors may be limited in their capacities to offer these spiritual opportunities.

Through the application of a framework of existential spirituality, this chapter argues that chaplains could nurture the spiritual wellbeing of their students by recognising that they are in a process of 'becoming' an authentic self and support students in developing a sense of agency, self-efficacy and connectedness in the following ways, by:

- Actively listening with empathy and creating safe, trusting and respectful environments for students to engage in honest dialogue including in the exploration of spiritual domains and religious perspectives, through an enquiry-based approach (Webster, 2009).
- Affirming students' sense of personal identity as something formative and in a constant state of growth as they journey through their adolescent years by

building and extending upon ideas, spiritual perspectives and possibly religious beliefs.

- Encouraging students to think critically especially through decision-making processes leading towards making responsible decisions when faced with moral dilemmas.
- Inspiring students to be constantly reflective, as opposed to being narrow-minded or closed-minded when making decisions.
- Supporting students in implementing their spiritual or religious reflective practices (e.g. prayer and meditation) when responding to events which challenge the meaning and purpose of their life (e.g. loss and grief, life and death) to instil hope for the future.
- Assisting with the development of resilience and courage through providing a safe, caring and supportive environment in which targeted programs on areas such as self-esteem, and promoting spiritual thinking, can be introduced. A proactive and early intervention approach can influence students towards resilient behaviours so that when they are faced with emotional challenges such as depression, lack of motivation, anxiety and fear, they would have potentially acquired the skills to successfully navigate their way through such issues.
- Creating a sense of belonging and connectedness by engendering environments that bring teachers, parents and students together and that foster friendships between students.
- Leading whole school communities through times of crisis through pastoral and spiritual care services such as liturgical practices and rituals inclusive of all religious and non-religious beliefs for example, prayer, meditation, memorial services and reflection.
- In times of crisis, assisting with grief and loss, and possibly suicidal thoughts. Chaplains can provide spiritual and religious perspectives (spiritual care which counsellors may not be able to provide) which create an awareness about the 'finite' (temporal) and the 'infinite' (eternal) worlds, guiding them towards a hopeful future with meaning and purpose in life.
- Referring students to other professionals such as counsellors if required.
- Promoting and celebrating cultural and religious diversity and diverse spiritual heritages to foster more inclusive societies, as part of their unique role as spiritual facilitators.

Therefore this chapter proposes that the NSCP provides a unique and important way for enabling schools to respond to the specific goal of the Melbourne Declaration (2008) to promote and nurture spiritual wellbeing in the context of a secular, multifaith democratic context.

## Conclusion

This chapter has explored how spiritual wellbeing could be understood, applied and provided for through the NSCP using a framework that has been influenced by Kierkegaard's philosophical approach of existential spirituality. It has identified the role and work of chaplains in schools and discussed the effectiveness of current chaplaincy programs in addressing the spiritual wellbeing of students. It has also examined some of the resistance towards the NSCP program. Finally, it provides sound reasons as to why Chaplaincy programs should continue in school settings.

The NSCP offers Australian schools an avenue to respond to the Melbourne Declaration (2008) to nurture spiritual wellbeing in young Australians. The value of nurturing spiritual wellbeing in students allows them to develop a set of tools to navigate their way through the existential questions of life which all are faced with. Furthermore fostering spiritual wellbeing helps students to discover purpose and meaning in life, and a sense of connectedness with their peers and broader society. This chapter has provided empirical evidence that demonstrates that chaplains have particular skill sets essential in nurturing spiritual wellbeing in students. Given the lack of explicit guidelines on how to nurture spiritual wellbeing within the Australian Curriculum, the NSCP is one of the only available avenues to address this Melbourne Declaration goal. Furthermore as we live in an increasingly multifaith and secular society, chaplains, ideally of many religions and denominations, can assist schools with not only enhancing spiritual wellbeing, but also with building resilience and providing pastoral care to their students. At the same time, there also needs to be state support provided for counsellors in government schools such as the Student Support Officers program funded by the Department of Education NSW to meet the wellbeing needs of students and parents who do not wish to be supported by chaplains, or who may not equate wellbeing with spirituality. By doing so chaplains and counsellors could work together to provide complementary wellbeing services, enabling a more socially inclusive environment, which will make schools a welcoming place for all students. This chapter therefore concludes with the strong contention that the NSCP should continue to be endorsed by the Australian government beyond 2018.

## Note

1   This chapter is focused on spiritual wellbeing and the NSCP. There is considerable debate surrounding religion and spirituality in education in Australia which are beyond its scope, see Maddox (2014), Byrne (2014) and Halafoff (2015).

## References

ACCESS Ministries (2009). *The value of chaplains in Victorian schools.* Retrieved 4 April 2015 from https://accessministries.org.au/sitebuilder/chaplains/knowledge/asset/files/4/social compassresearchreportthevalueofchaplainsinvictorianschools.pdf

Ammerman, N. (2013). Spiritual but not religious? Beyond binary choices in the study of religion. *Journal for the Scientific Study of Religion, 52*(2), 258–278.

Asher, A. (2011). *Administration of the national chaplaincy program.* Canberra: Commonwealth Ombudsman.

Australian Government, Department of Education and Training (2016). *National Schools Chaplaincy Program*, Retrieved July 2016 from https://education.gov.au/national-school-chaplaincy-programme

Australian Teacher Magazine (July 2014). *The divine divide, the role of religious chaplains in our state schools, 10*(6).

Bouma, G. (2006). *Australian soul: Religion and spirituality in the twenty-first century.* Melbourne: Cambridge University Press.

Byrne, C. (2014). *Religion in secular education: What in heaven's name are we teaching our children?* Leiden: Brill.

Carlisle, C. (2005). *Kierkegaard's philosophy of becoming: Movements and positions.* Albany: State University of New York Press.

Dalton, C. (2009). Spirituality, meaning and counselling young people. In M. de Souza, L. J. Francis, J. O'Higgins Norman & D. G. Scott (eds), *The international handbook of education for spirituality care and well-being* (pp. 977–989). Dordrecht: Springer.

Davenport, J. (2013). Selfhood and spirit. In J. Lippitt & G. Pattison (eds), *The Oxford handbook of Kierkegaard*, (p. 1). New York: Oxford University Press.

de Souza, M. (2009). The spiritual dimension in educational programs and environments to promote holistic learning and wellbeing: An introduction. In M.de Souza, L. J. Francis, J. O'Higgins Norman & D. G Scott (eds), *The international handbook of education for spirituality care and well-being* (pp. 525–532). Dordrecht: Springer.

de Souza, M. (2010). Meaning and connectedness: Contemporary perspectives of education and spirituality in Australia – an introduction. In M. de Souza & J. Rimes (eds), *Meaning and connectedness: Australian perspectives on education and spirituality* (p. 3). Mawson ACT: Australian College of Educators.

de Souza, M., Francis, L., O'Higgins Norman, J., & Scott, D. G. (2009). General Introduction. In M. de Souza, L. J. Francis, J. O'Higgins Norman & D. G. Scott (eds), *The international handbook of education for spirituality care and well-being* (p. 2, 3 & 677). Dordrecht: Springer.

Department of Education Science and Training. (2007). *National Schools Chaplaincy Programme guidelines.* Retrieved June 24, 2014 from: http://www.genr8ministries.org/system/apps/chaplains/employment/ChaplaincyGuidelines30Jan07.pdf

Donnelly, K. and Wiltshire, K. (2014). *Review of the Australian Curriculum – Final report*, Canberra: Australian Government Department of Education.

Halafoff, A. (2015*).* Education about diverse religions and worldviews, social inclusion and countering extremism: Lessons for the Australian Curriculum. *Journal of Intercultural Studies, 36*(3), 362–379.

Holm, A. (2013). Kierkegaard and the church. In J. Lippitt & G. Pattison (eds), *The Oxford handbook of Kierkegaard.* New York: Oxford University Press.

Hughes, P. (2009). Spiritual confidence and its contribution to wellbeing: Implications for education. In M. de Souza, L. J. Francis, J. O'Higgins Norman, & D. G. Scott (eds), *The international handbook of education for spirituality care and well-being* (pp. 907–920). Dordrecht: Springer.

Hughes, P., & Sims, M. (2009). *The effectiveness of chaplaincy as provided by the National School Chaplaincy Association to government schools in Australia.* Armidale: University of New England.

James, P., & Forward, D. (2014). *School chaplaincy: Dispelling myths and answering questions.* Retrieved 7 February, 2015 from http://schoolchaplaincy.org.au/files/2014/06/school-chaplaincy-myths-questions.pdf

Life Matters (2014). *School chaplains or counsellors?* ABC Radio Interview, 19 May 2014. Retrieved 7 February, 2015 from http://abc.net.au/radionational/programs/lifematters/school-chaplains-or-counsellors3f/5461234

Maddox, M. (2014). *Taking god to school: The end of Australia's egalitarian education?* Crows Nest: Allen and Unwin.

Moran, A. (2014). Chaplains in schools: Constitutional, legislative and policy perspectives. In J. O'Higgins Norman (ed.), *Education matters readings in pastoral care for school chaplains, guidance counsellors and teachers* (pp. 259–271). Dublin: Veritas Publications.

Murray, J. (2014). Chaplain and guidance counsellor as professional: Some theological reflections. In J. O'Higgins Norman (ed.), *Education matters readings in pastoral care for school chaplains, guidance counsellors and teachers* (pp. 282–298). Dublin: Veritas Publications.

Ministerial Council on Education, Employment, Training and Youth Affairs (MCEETYA). (2008). *Melbourne declaration on educational goals for young Australians.* Melbourne: Ministerial Council on Education, Employment, Training and Youth Affairs. Retrieved August 8, 2014 from MCEETYA Website: www.curriculum.edu.au/verve/_resources/National_Declaration_on_the_Educational_Goals_for_Young_Australians.pdf

O'Higgins Norman, J. (2014a). Pastoral care in schools. In J. O'Higgins Norman (ed.), *Education matters readings in pastoral care for school chaplains, guidance counsellors and teachers* (pp. 13–18). Dublin: Veritas Publications.

O'Higgins Norman, J. (2014b). The evolving role and identity of chaplains in schools. In J. O'Higgins Norman (ed.), *Education matters readings in pastoral care for school chaplains, guidance counsellors and teachers* (pp. 272–281). Dublin: Veritas Publications.

Pohlmann, D. (2005). *Measuring the effectiveness of chaplaincy services In Queensland state schools.* Unpublished doctoral thesis, Griffith University.

Salecich, J. A. (2002). *Chaplaincy in Queensland state schools: an investigation: North Rockhampton,* Unpublished doctoral thesis, University of Queensland.

Singleton, A. (2014). *Religion, culture and society: A global approach.* Los Angeles, CA: SAGE.

Sontag, F. (1979). *A Kierkegaard handbook.* Louisville: John Knox Press.

Taylor, C. (2007). *A secular age.* Cambridge: Harvard University Press.

Victorian Curriculum and Assessment Authority (VCAA). (2015a). About the Humanities, www.victoriancurriculum.vcaa.vic.edu.au/the-humanities/introduction/about-the-humanities

Victorian Curriculum and Assessment Authority (VCAA), (2015b). Learning in Ethical Capability, www.victoriancurriculum.vcaa.vic.edu.au/ethical-capability/introduction/learning-in-ethical-capability

Victorian Curriculum and Assessment Authority (VCAA). (2015c). Learning about World Views and Religions, www.victoriancurriculum.vcaa.vic.edu.au/static/docs/Learning about World Views and Religions.pdf

Victorian State Government, Education and Training (2016a). *National schools chaplaincy program code of conduct.* Retrieved July 2016 from http://education.vic.gov.au/school/principals/health/Pages/nscpchaplaincy.aspx#link4

Victorian State Government, Education and Training (2016b). *National schools chaplaincy program funding, reporting and accountability.* Retrieved July 2016 from http://education.vic.gov.au/school/principals/health/Pages/nscpchaplaincy.aspx#link62

Victorian State Government, Education and Training (2016c). *National schools chaplaincy program.* Retrieved July 2016 from http://education.vic.gov.au/school/principals/health/Pages/nscpchaplaincy.aspx#link48

Webster, R. S. (2004). An existential framework of spirituality. *International Journal of Children's Spirituality, 9*(1), 1–19.

Webster, S. (2009). *Educating for meaningful lives: Through existential spirituality.* Boston: Sense.

# 16

# FOSTERING A SENSE OF BELONGING AND IDENTITY THROUGH SOUND AND SPIRITUALITY

*Dawn Joseph*

> Bach gave us God's word, Beethoven gave us God's fire, Mozart gave us God's laughter, God gave us music so that we may pray without words.
> (Anonymous. Written on the wall of a German Opera house)

## Introduction

Music plays an important role in the social, political, economic, religious and cultural fabric of many societies around the globe. People in multicultural societies may find through music they have a sense of belonging and identity as they connect with like-minded people in secular and sacred settings. Also, music engagement has been shown to benefit wellbeing (Lamont, 2011; Creech et al., 2014; Weinberg & Joseph, 2016).

Music has the power to connect people from all walks of life. In a country like Australia, with approximately 24 million people from 200 different countries who speak over 300 languages and belong to more than 100 different religious groups (Australian Bureau of Statistics, [ABS] 2016), music is an effective platform to celebrate diversity in sacred and educational settings. In this chapter, the word music encompasses singing, playing, listening, accompanying and composition.

Music contributes to people's growth and development (Hallam, 2010) and this chapter examines music in sacred Christian settings (churches and choirs) where learning occurs in situated and social contexts (Lave & Wenger, 1990). The teaching and learning about religion, faith and spirituality occurs when people engage 'in shared patterns of practice in concrete settings' as 'communities of practice' (Smith & Smith, 2011, p. 12). Religious sites, like schools, are 'communities of practice' where members are committed to a shared domain of interest, interacting and engaging in activities (Wenger, 1998). Within this space, clerics, lay people[1] and musicians build relationships that provide opportunities to learn from each other as they share music and faith. This shared interaction, like that in school settings, is developed over time where individuals participate as a social community (Wenger, 1998). Music is valued as a community of practice in sacred settings where parishioners learn how 'the power of music [can] transform the heart, soul, mind and spirit of the individual' (Victorian Curriculum, 2016).

This chapter situates itself within my wider ongoing study on *Spirituality and Wellbeing: Music in the community*.[2] It builds on my research into perceptions and understanding of music in schools and in the wider community. The data collection took place in Christian churches and choir settings in Victoria (2013–2015). This small sample is a limitation in itself where generalisations will not be made to other musicians, community settings or faith organisations in Australia. The findings are informative and confirm the strong connection music has to spirituality, God and the human person. Through music, people connect with Christians from around the globe even if they don't know them; they form an identity and sense of belonging through singing similar and familiar songs. The Parliament of Victoria Inquiry (2013) recognised the myriad benefits of music education in schools and the wider community. In a similar way, music in non-Christian communities can positively engender wellbeing and a sense of belonging as music transcends cultural, linguistic and faith barriers, thereby, fostering spiritual growth.

## Spirituality and music

The notion of spirituality can be experienced individually or collectively with a Supreme Being who is 'sometimes referred to as God, or by various names and in different forms in different faith traditions' (de Souza, 2014, p. 1). Spirituality may be part of a religion or may lie in a space that is outside of religion but which may involve some form of belief. Being spiritual is sometimes perceived as helping people to be godly (Akers, 2014) while religion is about a relationship with God. Religion closely aligns doctrine to 'scripture, rituals, myths, beliefs, practices, moral codes, communities, social institutions and so forth that is, the outward and objectified element of a tradition', whereas spirituality is 'more elusive and varying in its meaning' (Roof, 2005, p. 138). Often the terms religion and spirituality have been intertwined and used together and interchangeably (Fisher, 2000).

In this chapter I concur with Charles Seifert (2011) that musical involvement is fundamentally interwoven with spiritual experiences in a personal or ecclesiastical way which Philip Sheldrake (1991, p. 37) refers to as 'life in the Spirit'. Since biblical times, music has formed an essential part of Christian worship, it may be seen as a way to approach God through sound, whereby the expression and experience of God's presence through song brings the act of worship to life, thereby transforming the feel and mood of worship.

Traditional hymns and psalms were usually sung with organ or piano/keyboard accompaniment. In Charismatic/Pentecostal places of worship, a contemporary style of music using a range of instruments and orchestration is favoured, focusing on praise and worship (Williams, 2005). In both traditional and non-traditional

Christian settings, singing and/or playing assists in retaining a memory of the words and tunes long after the sermon (Linman, 2010). According to Birgitta Johnson:

> the inclusion of a praise and worship period by churches has attracted many Christians seeking a deeper spiritual connection as well as those who want to exercise a more expressive worship lifestyle that does not end when Sunday service is over.
>
> (2008, p. 265)

As a tertiary music educator and church musician, I have found music can connect people from all walks of life; it traverses age, ethnicity, language and culture and offers people a sense of belonging that contributes to their wellbeing.

## Wellbeing and belonging

This section cannot do justice to the plethora of research undertaken in areas of the behavioural, social and health sciences regarding wellbeing, belonging and identity. Activities that lend themselves to individual or group participation and commitment lie strongly in the domain of music-making and sharing, where elements of wellbeing including that of 'positive emotion, engagement, relation-ships, meaning, and accomplishment' are explored (Seligman, 2011, p. 24). Some of these traits will be evident in the findings of this study.

Writing specifically about active ageing with music, Creech et al. (2014, p. 17) found 'group identity, collaborative learning, friendship, (and) social support' are important factors that hold a choir together. In a similar way, intergenerational groups exploring, experiencing and engaging in choir membership, worship ensembles and congregational singing also feel a sense of belonging where indi-viduals and groups are valued. This connection impacts on their sense of wellbeing in relation to 'personal growth, mental health, caring, compassion . . . and respon-siveness to common good' (Prilleltensky & Prilleltensky, 2006, p. 235).

Studies undertaken in Australia show that musical engagement such as singing has a wide range of social, psychological, emotional, health, cultural and linguistic benefits (Bailey & Davidson, 2005; Hays, 2005; Lally, 2009; Joseph, 2009; Southcott & Joseph, 2013). Being part of a choir, congregation or a music worship group creates a strong sense of social and communal belonging (Jacob et al., 2009). Through this connection, members seek social support and companionship. Singing in a choir, be it at a school or in a church setting, 'is not only an enjoyable special interest activity but can also be beneficial for the health and wellbeing of individuals and communities' (Gridley et al., 2011, p. 6). Research has shown that music can positively impact on improving health and wellbeing (Davidson, 2008; MacDonald et al., 2012; Clift, 2012). In addition, it may improve physical health and emotional wellbeing (Khalifa, et al., 2003, Weinberg & Joseph, 2016). As well, there is a connection between physical and mental health in relation to religious or spiritual

practices which promote wellbeing (George et al., 2000, Lippe, 2002). As a practising musician playing organ and piano positively contributes to my wellbeing as
I provide listeners with enjoyment that momentarily improves their wellbeing
(Croom, 2012). In church settings I form a strong sense of identity and belonging
with the congregation through worship (Joseph & Petersen, 2015).

## Methodology

Having gained ethical approval through the university, the Plain Language
Statement (PLS) was emailed to six churches (these included Anglican, Uniting
church, Assemblies of God and Pentecostal) and seven choir groups, inviting them
to be participants in the project. The PLS explained the aims of the project and
the process of collecting information. It included consent forms for organisations
and participants. Once approval was gained, questionnaires were emailed to clergy,
musicians and choir members to gain an understanding of their perceptions, beliefs
and attitudes. The open questions allowed participants to express their opinion and
share their understandings (Bird, 2009) of the importance of their involvement
with music in the church and whether music played a role in their spiritual journey
and/or wellbeing.

Some participants volunteered to be interviewed (individual and small focus
groups ranging between two and twenty people). The interviews were semi-
structured and conversational exploring perceptions and understandings of how
music affects spirituality, belonging and wellbeing.

## Discussion

This chapter presents the findings from the analysis of qualitative data, collected
between 2013–2015, from observations, questionnaire and a focus group interview. There were six church musicians (identified as M1–M6). Four of these were
conductors (identified as C1–C4), six clergy (identified as P1–P6) and seven choirs
(identified as CM1–CM7). I used Interpretative Phenomenological Analysis (IPA)
to analyse and code the data (Smith & Osborn, 2003; Fade, 2004). As IPA is
phenomenology, it explores participants' perceptions from their own perspectives
(Malcolm, 2013) and uncovers meanings that the researcher then interprets and
processes. Through reading and re-reading the questionnaire and interview data,
initial themes were identified and grouped into two overarching themes (Biggerstaff
& Thompson, 2008): 'Spiritual and Musical connections to God' and 'Social and
Wellbeing connections'.

### *Spiritual and musical connections to God*

In general, church musicians and choir members felt their playing/singing was a
gift and an offering to God. This was reflected in the following response from

a keyboard player: 'Playing is expressing that love for God and to God, in a way it is a very personal thing and private thing as well as being a corporate thing' (M3) and a brass player (M5), found that through music, he made a spiritual connection to God as a way of 'serving, by being a part of the team'.

For many of the musicians the music deepened their understanding and spiritual connection to God. One organist (M2) found 'it just kind of takes us to another place' and another (M1) claimed 'it caused me to reflect, to think of my own walk with God'. Though musicians play a crucial role in worship, a pastor (P1) pointed out performing or playing in church is not for self-fulfilment or self-enjoyment. Rather, he argues 'you're doing it because you're trying to honour God in what you do'. He firmly believed 'all the glory goes to God' so that using one's gifts and talents to pamper one's own ego is something musicians should guard against or they could become egotistical.

Overall, for many of the choir members who participated in the study, connecting to spirituality was connecting to God. C1 felt 'music and church seem to go together'. Another choir leader (C4) admitted 'I'm not a religious person in a formal sense' and strongly felt that spirituality was something he felt 'in nature' rather 'the presence of a gaiety'. CM1 found that 'for most of us, the singing of the hymns is the active part of worship', and CM2, commented, 'I find particularly valuable the way I tend to remember things musically [through song] . . . bible passages that you remember. Finally, remembering and sharing in God's word through song was echoed by choir participants and is summed up in the following excerpt:

> Spirituality is a connection between and God, a personal relationship. Even coming here worshipping, singing songs, suddenly you connect to God through those words, to what you are singing so it gives you peace in your heart, even the troubles, the day to day things, it just goes away and you have that inner peace in your heart.
>
> (CM7)

A similar sentiment was echoed by CM1:

> I would go in a bad mood to church sometimes and the music would start and my negativity sort of melts away and it [the music] always reaches me somewhere that I can't explain.

The clerics, P1–6, all felt spirituality and music go hand-in-hand in terms of making connections to God, his Word and to the people. This is reflected in the following:

> It is connectedness to other people in community and connectedness with God (P5, who is also a musician).

> Spirituality is just being aware of God and having a relationship with God through Christ that brings you to a spiritual awareness that's likely to be beyond yourself, where you're not the boss or the creator of your own world, but there's a God that cares and loves you and having that relationship with Him opens the door to wholesome spirituality (P1).

> If you could take the great command of love God, love your neighbours . . . then you're connected to God, yourself, to other people, and nature, so spirituality is about connectivity (P3).

This sense of connectivity is something profound in the notion of community so that P4 claimed:

> Those of us who are attracted to the person of Jesus, the sayings of Jesus, he teaches a lot about the spirit of life, the creative spirit, and spirituality. We find ourselves gathering together into communities of people who want to think about his words, want to pray, celebrate his life in our midst.

P6 asserted that 'music has the ability to be a vehicle for the carriage of the Gospel, whether sung or instrumental' and P2 stated that:

> Music in a Christian context of worship of God draws you closer to God. I think it opens up your spirit more towards him and it's just a powerful medium to convey what you feel or what you sense, or what you're trying to tell him.

Finally, such thinking requires the choice of repertoire to be prayerfully selected which was affirmed by P1: 'Worship leaders spend a lot of time in prayer, they don't just pull it out from a hat you know!'

## Social and wellbeing connections

All participants in the study agreed that music-making and sharing has strong social connections. The act of coming together is 'about fellowship . . . Looking forward to getting together with like-minded people' (C7). Though people sing in a choir or play as a church musician for a variety of reasons, for these people the music space was 'special', as guitarist M6 described 'there's a bonding that has taken place among us, something a bit more special than how we relate perhaps to others in the congregation'. This unique sense of place and space forms a strong cohesion with members as the focus is about God. CM3 found 'the singing component connects you more with the church as a whole'.

The energy of connection formed a wider social connection beyond the musicians to the wider congregation and ultimately to God. Some choir participants commented that music has an impact on people's social interaction with self and with others:

I like the company and I love to sing (CM3).

I love the spiritual feeling and other stuff, I enjoy it, it's like a connection (CM2).

My church life was my social life (CM7).

I got closer connections with the people in the choir than with the other people . . . doing something together, you come every week (to make music and share friendship) (CM5).

In other words, there was a shared purpose and intent, which secured the bonding experience. Thus, the engagement with music is not only encountered through 'the Word', but as P2 found, 'you can draw people in more quickly to form unity, to form a oneness through the music'. She further expressed the social connection for young people in worship is 'to be there for them, to show compassion and to love them, and always steer them to God'. P2 also felt it important to 'always make them aware that God is there for them because even though they're young they have pressures and different problems and anxieties because we live in a world now where they see things, they experience things'.

Taking an interest in young people was an essential part of connecting them to God, to each other and to the church community. Hence, music has an important role in engendering spiritual connections in the life of the church.

An aspect of social connection beyond the walls of the church was Outreach. P1 talked about developing a 'youth drop-in centre where music is a big part of that . . . going down the streets, just sharing the love of God'. In this way he felt the word of God could be communicated beyond the walls of the church where a community of worshippers can start to grow and be socially connected, 'just listen to them and see if we can pray for people. It's not bible bashing'. Rather, he saw it as sharing the word of God in a socially relaxed context:

There is a lot of church music that actually binds people together who are not church goers . . . if you went down the local pub and you got up and you started to sing Amazing Grace, they'll sing with you. And they don't go to church but they've heard it (P1).

As music has positively impacted on people's livelihood in various ways, P2 pointed out that the importance of words in music can either 'build you up, or it can tear you down':

Some music has been the cause of influencing teenagers to commit suicide. To do drugs . . . do the bad things . . . so I think there has to be a caution . . . I'm just concerned about some of the rap music. Like a lot of them are so angry you know, also violent (P2).

One of the choir conductors, P5, felt 'music in the choir is a vision and hope, it will have an influence beyond just the people that are in the choir'. He believed 'it can create some change' and make people think in different ways about 'social justice, sustainability and the environment'.

The endorphins associated with what makes you happy or joyful is often connected to music-making, such as singing which, overall, was a 'feel good' experience for musicians and choir members. Members across the choirs expressed that music strongly impacted on their sense of wellbeing.

> When you sing with the choir . . . you get an uplifting feeling . . . it raises your mood (CM3).
> I come here and may be feeling a bit flat and I go home afterwards feeling better in a way that I can't explain why I'm feeling better but I do, for me it's a connectedness. You're with other people and you feel that you belong. You're part of this person here and that person there that enriches you. It fills a gap within you (CM2).
> It is uplifting, the words grip you and it does something for you (CM7).

For clerics, music contributed to their personal wellbeing as P2 said 'maybe we had a bad week but music just uplifts the spirit . . . who cannot but melt under that beautiful worship music'. The outpouring of praise and worship songs and hymns brings joy and peace and affirms faith. As well, P1 commented that 'people have had different things happen during the week so we use worship (singing) to lift them from where they are at to where they need to be'. In this way he found people can have a place and space to 'just relax, so that itself brings healing, brings solace, and brings wellbeing to our lives, just letting go of the week . . . by singing, worshipping and playing different instruments, it enhances, it lifts your spirit'. P5 added 'I go home from choir feeling really uplifted. I find it a spiritual and nurturing experience'.

## Concluding comments

In general, participants in the study found music in sacred settings made strong connections to their spirituality, to God, to others and it nurtured their wellbeing. It fostered a sense of identity through sharing sound with like-minded people and provided hope, purpose and meaning to their lives. This reflects Morgan Scott Peck's (2016) contention that through the experience and engagement of music for Christians, people may feel spiritually 'satisfied and quenched' (p. 8). It was evident that music within and beyond the walls of the church offered a sense of hope to those in pain and suffering from loneliness and social isolation. It also raised awareness of social justice issues (see Joseph, 2014, 2015a & 2015b). The act of singing and or playing in church helped people forget their troubles and worries and connected them to something else, something ineffable, intangible and ethereal.

The findings indicate the importance of thinking about the role and place of music in spirituality and how it may impact and contribute to the individual's sense of belonging, identity and wellbeing. They add to the body of knowledge that shows how music may be used to transcend difference in society and unite people (to God and to others). These findings also have the potential to inform learning and teaching in music education. Schools have the capacity to foster cultural understandings through music education where difference and respect can be celebrated, practised and acknowledged. In the multicultural settings of Australian schools, music is a unique art form that has the 'capacity to engage, inspire and enrich all students' (Victorian Curriculum, 2016). Through music, students have the capacity to develop 'respect for music and music practices across global communities, cultures and musical traditions' (Victorian Curriculum, 2016).

Through the teaching and learning of songs from diverse cultures in schools, students may gain a better understanding of themselves and that of others by singing multicultural songs (Ilari et al., 2013). Through singing you can learn about others and include a repertoire from around the world to learn more about other people, their music and culture.

The findings in this study also demonstrate how adults in non-school settings make connections to each other and the wider community either as cleric or musician (conductor, choir member or instrumentalist). In schools, therefore, music can be used to help students connect with each other as a team/ensemble when rehearsing and performing. In music performance in a church setting it is the whole that matters as a performer and not the individual's ego that counts. In a similar way, in school performances it is not the individual but the ensemble as a whole that counts.

The findings also suggest that music students in school settings may develop a strong sense of social and emotional bonding. Lin Marsh (2015) found that, through singing, 'children learn to express ideas with confidence, empathise with others from different cultures and backgrounds, and feel at home in their own skin'. In this way, the act of singing or playing together is a form of learning together that is more than just a 'feel good' buzz word, it has implications for us as humans as we communicate and express our sense of self, culture and identity. Students' access to music (singing) in schools may positively engender their self-identity and their sense of social inclusion, which will eventually be beneficial to the wider society (Welch, 2011).

Though there are myriad social, emotional, psychological benefits of music education (see Parliament of Victoria, 2013), music in school settings, like that in religious settings, brings much joy and happiness to all involved. The exploration, engagement and experience of music in sacred and secular settings in a multicultural nation like Australia has the ability to foster a sense of belonging and identity, where diversity, respect and difference is recognised and celebrated (Australian Government, 2016). Through music, 'a community of practice' may be formed where music can make a strong connection to body, soul and mind thereby nurturing spirituality. Some of the findings in this study regarding the engagement with sacred music on a person's spirituality and wellbeing may resonant with faith-based schools where sacred music may be part of the curriculum.

In the end, this study has shown that music has the power to foster an enhanced sense of personal growth, and that music sharing and music-making nurtures a sense of personal and communal identity and wellbeing.

## Notes

1  Lay people refers to any person in the congregation who is not an ordained cleric.
2  The wider ongoing project Spirituality and Wellbeing: Music in the community began in 2013. It aimed to explore music in formal community settings (churches and choir groups) and in informal community settings (festivals, concerts and social organisations). The project is still in progress. Some of the data for this chapter has been part of the case studies within the wider project (see Joseph, 2014, 2015a, 2015b; Joseph & Petersen, 2015).

## References

Akers, M. (2014). *Morning and evening meditations from the word of god: Education, challenge, inspiration, and encouragement.* Bloomington: WestBow Press.

Australian Bureau of Statistics (2016). *Population clock.* Retrieved from http://abs.gov.au/ausstats/abs%40.nsf/94713ad445ff1425ca25682000192af2/1647509ef7e25faaca2568a900154b63?OpenDocument

Australian Government (2016). Our society. Retrieved from http://livingsafetogether.gov.au/informationadvice/Pages/our-society.aspx

Bailey, B. A., & Davidson, J. W. (2005). Effects of group singing and performance for marginalized and middle-class singers. *Psychology of Music, 33*(2), 269–303.

Biggerstaff, D. L., & Thompson, A. R. (2008). Interpretative Phenomenological Analysis (IPA): A qualitative methodology of choice in healthcare research. *Qualitative Research in Psychology, 5*(3), 173–183.

Bird, D. K. (2009). The use of questionnaires for acquiring information on public perception of natural hazards and risk mitigation– A review of current knowledge and practice. *Natural Hazards and Earth Systems Science, 9*, 1307–1325.

Clift, S. (2012). Singing, wellbeing, and health. In R. MacDonald, G. Kreutz & L. Mitchell (eds), *Music health and wellbeing* (pp. 113–124). Oxford: Oxford University Press.

Creech, A., Hallam, S., Varvarigou, M., & McQueen, H. (2014). *Active ageing with music.* London: Institute of Education Press.

Croom, A. M. (2012). Music, neuroscience, and the psychology of well-being: A précis. *Frontiers in Psychology, 2*(1), 1–15. Retrieved from http://journal.frontiersin.org/article/10.3389/fpsyg.2011.00393/full

Davidson, J. W. (2008). Singing for self-healing, health and wellbeing. *Music Forum, 14*(2), 29–32.

de Souza, M. (2014): The empathetic mind: The essence of human spirituality. *International Journal of Children's Spirituality, 19*(1), 45–54.

Fade, S. (2004). Using interpretative phenomenological analysis for public health nutrition and dietetic research: A practical guide. *Proceedings of the Nutrition Society, 63*, 647–653. Retrieved from http://columbia.edu/~mvp19/RMC/M5/QualPhen.pdf

Fisher, J. W. (2000). Being human, becoming whole: Understanding spiritual health and well-being. *Journal of Christian Education, 43*(3), 37–52.

George, L. K., Larson, D. B., Koenig, H. G., & McCullough, M. E. (2000). Spirituality and health: What we know, what we need to know. *Journal of Social & Clinical Psychology, 19*, 102–116.

Gibson, R., & Ewing, R. (2011). *Transforming the curriculum through the arts*. Malaysia: Palgrave Macmillan.

Gridley, H., Astbury, J., Sharples, J., & Aguirre, C. (2011), *Benefits of group singing for community mental health and wellbeing. Survey and literature review*. Carlton, Victoria, Australia: Victorian Health Promotion Foundation (VicHealth).

Hallam, S. (2010). The power of music: Its impact on the intellectual, social and personal development of children and young people. *International Journal of Music Education, 28*(3), 269–289.

Hays, T. (2005). Well-being in later life through music. *Australasian Journal of Ageing, 24*, 28–32.

Ilari, B., Chen-Hafteck, L., & Crawford, L. (2013). Singing and cultural understanding: A music education perspective. *International Journal of Music Education, 31*(2), 202–216.

Jacob, C., Guptill, G., & Sumsion, T. (2009). Motivation for continuing involvement in a leisure-based choir: The lived experiences of university choir members. *Journal of Occupational Science, 16(3)*, 187–193.

Johnson, B. J. (2008). Music and worship in African American megachurches of Los Angeles, California. A dissertation submitted in partial satisfaction of the requirements for the degree Doctor of Philosophy in Ethnomusicology, University of California, Los Angeles. Retrieved from https://books.google.com.au/books?id=h2CRnIcbGjsC&printsec=front cover#v=onepage&q&f=false

Joseph, D. (2009). Music for all ages: Sharing music and culture through singing in Australia. *International Journal of Community Music, 2*(2&3), 169–181.

Joseph, D. (2014). Spirituality, music and wellbeing: Sharing insights from an Australian setting. *International Journal of Health, Wellness and Society, 4*(1), 1–14.

Joseph, D. (2015a). Spiritual connections through music making: Sharing faith and music in Australian settings. *International Journal of Social, Political, and Community Agendas in the Arts, 10*(1), 29–42.

Joseph, D. (2015b). Using voice to make musical and social connections. *Journal of Local Development, 8*(1), 35–66.

Joseph, D., & Petersen, A. (2015). Experiencing God and expressing his love through words and sounds. *Musiekleier, 35*(1), 56–67.

Khalifa, S., Bella, S. D., Roy, M., Peretz, I., & Lupien, S. J. (2003). Effects of relaxing music on salivary cortisol level after psychological stress. *Annals of the New York Academy of Sciences, 999*(1), 374–376.

Lally, E. (2009). 'The power to heal us with a smile and a song': Senior well-being, music-based participatory arts and the value of qualitative evidence. *Journal of Arts & Communities, 1*(1), 25–44.

Lamont, A. (2011). University students' strong experiences of music: Pleasure, engagement, and meaning. *Musicae Scientiae, 15*(2), 229–249.

Lave, J., & Wenger, E. (1990). *Situated learning: Legitimate peripheral participation*. Cambridge, UK: Cambridge University Press.

Linman, J. (2010). *Holy conversation: Spirituality for worship*. Minneapolis: Fortress Press.

Lippe, A. (2002). Beyond therapy: Music, spirituality, and health in human experience: A review of literature. *Journal of Music Therapy, XXXIX*(3), 209–240.

MacDonald, R., Kreutz, G., & Mitchell, L. (2012). *Music, health, and wellbeing*. Oxford: Oxford University Press.

Malcolm, C. (2013). *The social work dissertation: Using small-scale qualitative methodology*. Berkshire, England: Open University Press, McGraw-Hill.

Marsh, L. (2015). *Why song and dance are essential for children's development*. Retrieved from https://britishcouncil.org/voices-magazine/why-song-and-dance-are-essential-childrens-development

Parliament of Victoria (2013). *Inquiry into the extent, benefits and potential of music education in Victorian schools.* Retrieved from www.parliament.vic.gov.au/images/stories/committees/ etc/Music_Ed_Inquiry/Music_Education_Final_041113.pdf

Prilleltensky, I., & Prilleltensky, O. (2006). *Promoting well-being: Linking personal, organizational and community change.* New Jersey: Wiley & Sons.

Roof, W. C. (2005). Religion and spirituality: Towards an integrated analysis. In M. Dillon (ed.), *Handbook of the Sociology of Religion* (pp. 137–150). Cambridge: Cambridge University Press.

Scott Peck, A. (2016). *What is Christian Spirituality?* Retrieved from http://spirituality-for-life.org/pdf-

Seifert, C. E. (2011). Reflections on music and spirituality. *Epiphany International, 17*(1), 19–28.

Seligman, M. E. P. (2011). *Flourish: A visionary new understanding of happiness and well-being.* New York: Free Press.

Sheldrake, P. (1991). *Spirituality and history: Questions of interpretation and method.* London: SPCK.

Smith, D. I., & Smith, J. K. A. (2011). *Teaching and christian practices: Reshaping faith and learning.* Grand Rapids, MI: WM.B Eerdmans Publishing Co.

Smith, J. A., & Osborn, M. (2003). Interpretive phenomenological analysis. In J.A. Smith (ed.), *Qualitative psychology: A practical guide to research methods* (pp. 51–80). London, UK: SAGE.

Southcott, J., & Joseph, D. (2013). Community, commitment, and the ten commandments: Singing in the Coro Furlan. *International Journal of Community Music, 6*(1), 79–92.

Victorian Curriculum in Australia (2016). *Music.* Retrieved from http://victoriancurriculum. vcaa.vic.edu.au/the-arts/music/introduction/rationale-and-aims

Weinberg, M., & Joseph, D. (2016). If you're happy and you know it: Music engagement and subjective wellbeing. *Psychology of Music,* first published online 29 July, 2016, doi:10.1177/0305735616659552

Welch, G. F. (2011). Psychological aspects of singing development in children. Invited lecture, Goldsmiths College, London (Music, Mind and Brain), February 2011. Retrieved from https://musicmindandbrain.wordpress.com/2011/05/07/psychological-aspects-of-singing-development-in-children/

Wenger, E. (1998). *Communities of practice: Learning, meaning, and identity.* Cambridge, UK: Cambridge University Press.

Williams, D. (2005). Music and the spirit. *Evangel, 23*(1), 10–17.

# 17

# NURTURING THE SPIRITUAL CHILD

Recognising, addressing and nurturing spirituality in early years' classrooms through a dispositional framework

*Brendan Hyde*

## The context

Until recently, Australia has made little provision in legislation for the inclusion of the spiritual in education. The Education Act of 1872 made clear that state education was to be free, compulsory and secular. Terence Lovat (2010) argues that documents which followed the Education Act in the 1880s and 1890s made reference to religion (and, by implication, spirituality because of its then close association with religion), permitting volunteers from church denominations to provide, with parental permission, religious instruction to students. However, most state school students received little in the way of religious or spiritual education. The free, compulsory and secular tenets of education in Australia have remained virtually intact to the present day, with relatively little provision in legislation for the inclusion of religion or spirituality within the formal curriculum.[1]

However, a number of recent documents have been published which, for the first time, and at the policy-making level, make explicit reference to the importance of developing the spiritual dimension of children's lives. For instance, the *Melbourne Declaration on Educational Goals for Young Australians* (MCEETYA, 2008) states that 'schools play a vital role in promoting the intellectual, physical, social, emotional, moral, spiritual and aesthetic development and wellbeing of young Australians' (p. 4). Similarly, Australia's national statement on the education of young children between birth and five years of age, *Belonging, Being and Becoming: The Early Years Learning Framework for Australia* (DEEWR, 2009) states that children's learning includes: 'Physical, social, emotional, spiritual, creative, cognitive and linguistics aspects of learning [which] are all intricately interwoven and interrelated' (p. 9).

In the light of these documents, this chapter presents a framework for nurturing the spiritual development and wellbeing of students in early years' classrooms. Originally emanating from the author's broader research into the dispositions young learners bring to the curriculum area of religious education in Catholic schools (Hyde, 2010, 2012; Hyde & Leening, 2012), it was discovered that these very orientations are in fact the same dispositions through which spirituality may be nurtured (Hyde, 2014). The dispositional framework utilised, the notion of learning stories, and the voice-centred relational method used to analyse early years' teachers' interview transcripts are described below. Some findings from the original research, including a new spiritual disposition emanating from the analysis of some early years' teachers' interview transcripts, are also presented. The chapter concludes with some recommendations for practice indicating how early years' educators might recognise, address and nurture the spirituality of their students.

## Describing spirituality

The author's understanding of the word *spirituality* is not synonymous with religion. Spirituality is more primal than institutional religion (Tacey, 2000) although religious traditions may enable people to give expression to their spirituality. Spirituality concerns an individual's sense of connectedness with Self, Other, the cosmos and the transcendent, which, in the Christian tradition, is named as God (Hay with Nye, 2006). In some instances, this sense of connectedness of Self with Other may be described as a movement towards Ultimate Unity, which, for some, has the potential to lead to deepest and widest levels of connectedness whereby an individual experiences becoming one with other (de Souza, 2006; Hyde, 2008).

Spirituality is ontological. It belongs to each person's being (O'Murchu, 2012; Hay & Socha, 2005) and continually seeks expression in human living. As a natural human predisposition, spirituality is developed and expressed through social interactions by people of all ages, including children (Adams et al., 2008). It is important, therefore, that educators are able to recognise, address and help to nurture the spirituality of their students in educational contexts.

## Learning dispositions

The concept of a disposition comes from developmental psychology. It is a quality possessed by a person, often used to signal temperament, for example 'she has a cheerful disposition'. Such attributes have been variously termed dispositions (Katz, 1988; Perkins et al., 1993), orientations (Dweck, 1999) and habits of mind (Costa, 2000). Margaret Carr (2001) notes that when motivation is considered, learning dispositions comprise a set of participation repertoires from which learners recognise, select, edit, respond to, resist, search for and construct learning opportunities. Guy Claxton and Margaret Carr (2004) argue that when learning dispositions form the basis of an educational approach, attention is given to the long-term trajectories, rather than to the accumulation of particular bodies of knowledge and skills. The focus includes the habits and orientations towards learning in general which are strengthened (or perhaps weakened) in the learning process. It is concerned with *how* students learn – the *process* – rather than with content, since these processes can be applied across disciplines. Claxton (2007) argues that when educators think only in terms of teaching skills, or problem-solving competencies, while neglecting the need to cultivate dispositions, they often find that any apparent gains in acquiring skills and competencies are relatively short-lived.

Brendan Hyde (2010) refined Carr's (2001) domains of learning dispositions for use with early years' students in religious education. Table 17.1 presents a summary of these learning dispositions with a series of descriptions to indicate their possible

**TABLE 17.1** Learning dispositions in religious education

| *Description of cues* | |
|---|---|
| Curiosity | A sense of wonder and awe |
| | Capturing interest |
| | Being drawn towards story, liturgical action, symbol, sign, gesture, ritual |
| | Recognising the familiar, enjoying the unfamiliar |
| Being dialogical | Dialogue as play |
| | Dialogue partners in a game |
| | Engaging in dialogue with Self and Other |
| | Being playful with others and/or materials |
| | Deep listening |
| | Engaging in dialogue with story, liturgical action, sign, symbol, gesture, ritual |
| | Trusting others |
| Persisting/living with uncertainty | Paying attention for a sustained period |
| | Sitting with ambiguity |
| | Deep questioning and wondering about |
| | Problem-solving |
| | Lateral thinking |
| Meaning-making | Being moved to express (verbal and kinesthetic) |
| | Verbal and non-verbal communication |
| | Immersed in 'deep play' |
| | Intuitive response beyond words |
| | Discovering/unpacking |
| | Co-creator/constructor of the Tradition |
| | Communication of meaning – making meaning visible |
| Taking responsibility | Taking action that matters |
| | Thinking the learning through into action |
| | Owning the learning |
| | Empower/commitment to a sense of justice |
| | Making a difference for the good |

Source: Hyde (2010).

manifestation among learners. For a more detailed discussion of these learning dispositions, as well as the literature which informed the development of them, see Hyde (2010, 2014). These very orientations are in fact the same dispositions through which spirituality may be recognised, addressed and nurtured (Hyde, 2014).

The means by which to determine the domains of dispositions which students bring to the act of learning, and the means by which to recognise and ascertain the spirituality of students, is the learning story.

## The learning story: a tool for recognising and addressing students' spirituality

The capability of stories to highlight critical incidences of children's learning are well attested to in the literature (e.g. Dunn, 1993; Gettinger & Stoiber, 1998; Lyle, 2000; Walker, 2007; Karlsdottir & Gardarsdottir, 2010). Carr (2001) maintains that learning stories, over time, 'provide a cumulative series of qualitative "snap-shots" or written vignettes of individual children' (p. 96) displaying one or more of the domains of learning dispositions. Learning stories are process-oriented. They attempt to describe *how* the child is disposed to learn or to act in a particular way.

Learning stories are not intended to be lengthy. They comprise short, 'snap-shot-like' descriptions of the observation. Key words and phrases are recorded which capture the kernel of the incident being observed. They may be accompanied (with the child's permission) by a photograph or sample of work exemplifying the disposition(s) displayed in the observation. It is not intended that one learning story be completed for each child every week. Rather, they are compiled over time. Two learning stories for each child each semester is a more realistic undertaking. This renders the use of the learning story tool practical in situations where class sizes are large. Table 17.2 below presents an example of a completed learning story.

As a documented series of anecdotes, learning stories provide a valid and reliable record of children's learning. By indicating what children can do via the dispositions they bring to the act of learning, learning stories apply a credit rather than a deficit approach to assessment (Hatherley & Sands, 2008).

Some contemporary literature is critical of learning stories. For instance Ken Blaiklock (2008, 2010) argues that their situational specificity may limit their value for planning to extend children's learning in different contexts. Notwithstanding, the learning story was utilised in the author's original research since it was deemed an appropriate tool emanating from early childhood practice and literature (see Carr, 2001; Hatherley & Sands, 2008; Karlsdottir & Gardarsdottir, 2010). The theoretical basis which informs learning stories was therefore deemed reliable and rigorous.

## Voice-centred relational method of analysis

The early years' teachers involved in the author's original research were interviewed twice a year using a semi-structured interview guide. The interviews were audio-

**TABLE 17.2** An example of a completed learning story in religious education

|  | *A learning story* |
| --- | --- |
| Curiosity | *Daniel was drawn towards the Parable of the Good Shepherd materials. These materials captured his interest for the fourth time over the past two weeks.* |
| Being dialogical | *He was playful with the materials, placing each one of the sheep, one at a time, onto the shepherd's shoulders, and carrying each individually through the sheepfold.* |
| Persisting/living with uncertainty | *Daniel returned to this same activity on three occasions during the one response time. He seemed to be wondering about these materials, and has returned to them* |
| Meaning-making | *again to make meaning from them – there is something significant about this presentation which requires further unpacking. He was immersed in deep play, and was trying* |
| Taking responsibility | *to make the meaning visible.* |

| *Short-term review* | *What next?* |
| --- | --- |
| Question: What learning did I think went on here (i.e. the main point(s) of the learning story)? | Questions: How might we encourage this interest, ability, strategy, disposition, story to<br>• Be more complex? |
| Through **persisting**, Daniel was making and internalising the meaning of the GS parable, discovering the relevance for him personally. | • Appear in different areas or activities in the program. How might we encourage the next 'step' in the learning story framework?<br><br>How can I encourage the disposition of Taking Responsibility in Daniel in relation to the GS parable? In relation to other stories? |

taped and transcribed. A voice-centred relational method of analysis (Gilligan et al., 2006) was used to ascertain participants' perceptions and experiences in using the learning story. Originally this was with a view to tracking their students' learning. However, it has been discovered through close analysis of the transcripts that in many instances, teachers were able to recognise spirituality being expressed by their students, and as a result, plan to address and help to nurture their students' spiritual development.

The voice-centred relational method of analysis follows the lead of the person being interviewed to discover the associated logic of the psyche and the construction of the mind. It brings the researcher 'into relationship with a person's distinct and multilayered voice by tuning in or listening to distinct aspects of a person's expression with her or his experience' (Gilligan et al., 2006, p. 225) in relation to, in this instance, the use of the learning story and the dispositional framework which underpins it.

The method comprises a series of sequential listenings, each of which requires the researcher to engage with the subjectivity of the research participant. The transcribed interviews are read through multiple times, with each listening tuning into a particular aspect. Each reading or 'listening' is not merely an analysis of the text, but rather a guide for the researcher in tuning into the participant's story being told on various levels. Four listenings typically comprise the analysis.

## Step 1: Listening for the plot

The first listening comprises two parts – listening for the plot and the listener's response to the interview. The transcript is read with the researcher attending to the story being told. The researcher also attends to her or his own response to the narrative, bringing her or his own subjectivities into the process of interpretation, since in qualitative research, a researcher can never be a neutral or objective observer (Denzin & Lincoln, 2008; Morawski, 2001).

## Step 2: I poems

The second listening focuses on the use of the first-person pronouns in the transcript, and from these, constructing 'I poems' (Gilligan et al., 2006, p. 259), enabling the researcher to listen to the participant's first-person voice, and how this voice speaks about her or himself. The researcher colour-codes each first-person 'I' within the text, as well as the accompanying words which seem important. Each of these 'I' phrases is extracted, keeping them in the order that they appear in the text, and placed on a separate line, so that they appear as lines in a poem. This 'picks up on an associative stream of consciousness carried by a first-person voice, cutting across or running through a narrative rather than being contained by the structure of full sentences' (p. 260), enabling the subjectivity of the participant to be foregrounded.

## Step 3: Listening for contrapuntal voices

This step offers a way of developing an understanding of the different layers of the participant's expressed experience in relation to the research question. The rationality is drawn from the musical notion of counterpoint, which consists of the combination of two or more melodic lines. In a musical score each melodic line has its own particular rhythm. Listening for contrapuntal voices in each participant's transcript enables the researcher to listen for the counterpoint in the texts – the multiple facets of the story being told.

## Step 4: Composing an analysis

In the final step of the process, the researcher brings together what has been learnt from each of the listenings. An interpretation of the interviews or transcripts is developed that synthesises what has been discovered.

## Findings

Below are presented some of the author's findings in relation to how the use of learning stories was effective in enabling these early years' teachers to describe the learning that was occurring in religious education and to recognise and nurture the spirituality and spiritual development of their students. As well, a new spiritual disposition emanating from the analysis of some early years' teachers' interview transcripts – connecting to life – is explained and analysed.

A number of the participants were immediately enthused by the notions of learning stories and were able to incorporate them into their teaching practice without too much difficulty. This was particularly evident, for instance, in the examination of Tony's I poem:

> I can go back in and read . . .
> I've actually gone to and purposefully tried to look a little bit more deeply
> . . .
> I've looked and discovered a lot of evidence around being dialogical and
>    curiosity
> I found I was doing a lot of observation and recording
> I can see
> I want to start working from . . .
> I think it gives a snap-shot
> I'm finding it easy
> I just sat and watched

What is interesting in this I poem is Tony's recognition of the dispositions of being dialogical and curiosity as indicators of students' spirituality (Hyde, 2010, 2014), and his ability to find evidence of his students displaying these dispositions in the learning stories he had composed.

Similarly, another participant, Allison, also indicated that she had found the learning story a useful tool for recognising, addressing and nurturing the spirituality of her students:

> I think it's brilliant – I saw how the kids went off into different tasks and made choices . . . I saw how this particular boy was able to make meaning by playing with the materials and by innovating on the story[2] . . . [learning stories] help me to forward plan . . . they help me to see where I can plan activities that will give them a chance to look for meaning . . . to make meaning for themselves from stories and different events.

Allison's explicit reference to meaning-making from Hyde's (2010) framework indicates the dispositional framework used provided her with the necessary cues and descriptions to recognise this orientation being displayed by her students.

Another participant Laura, when asked, 'how do learning stories help you to nurture the spirituality of your students?' responded:

... particularly with one of the children that I followed – he's a very quiet student, he is a deep thinker ... So being able to watch this particular student and how he was processing, um, and document that was fantastic. I could see and record how he seemed to be questioning and wondering – how he was persisting with uncertainty.

What is interesting in Laura's response is the recognition of the dispositions of curiosity (wondering) and persisting/living with uncertainty, as being indicators of students' spirituality (Hyde, 2010, 2014), and her ability to find evidence of this student displaying these dispositions in the learning stories she had composed.

These observations are significant as they suggest that the author's dispositional framework provided these teachers with the necessary cues and descriptions that enabled them to recognise these orientations being displayed by their students. This dispositional framework may then be helpful in enabling spiritual dispositions to be identified and possibly nurtured by teachers.

## Connecting to life

A close analysis of the interview transcripts of some early years' teachers indicated the emergence of new disposition not part of Hyde's (2010) original framework. This disposition has been termed 'connecting to life'. It refers to the students' predisposed ability to relate particular concepts, content and ideas directly back to their own lived experiences. It is important to note that while none of the interviewed teachers explicitly stated that they had encountered a new disposition, a close analysis of the transcripts of these teachers suggested the emergence of this particular disposition in this study. For instance, Tony, whose I-poem is presented above, had maintained that his students were:

... thinking about the message of the story and linking it back to their own lives even at such a young age ... one child created a story that linked the meaning of the parable about the Good Shepherd looking after his sheep to the concept of a caregiver looking after him and his siblings.

Similarly, another early years' teacher, Amelia, also recognised the emergence of this orientation among the students she was observing:

They are actually connecting their learning back to themselves, how they would feel and putting themselves in their [another's] shoes ... they were actually thinking of a situation that was similar, that they'd had in their lives.

Siobhan, another of the interviewed early years' teachers, summarised the effect of this emerging disposition on her as follows:

. . . a big thing for me is whether they can relate the Christian story to their own life . . . when you ask them [the students] what it [an element from the Christian story] means to them and they tell you *their* story it's just really special.

## An initial analysis of *connecting to life*

While further research is necessary to determine the existence of this disposition, connecting to life, from the short excerpts of the transcripts above, there appear to be four particular elements of this emerging disposition – (1) making connections between stories and lived experiences; (2) discovering the significance of stories for one's own life; (3) placing one's self in the shoes of the Other; and (4) considering one's own story within a Universal Story.

The first and second of these elements – the ability of students to be able to make connections between stories and their own lived experience, and to discover the significance of story for their own lives – are related. The nature of lived experience, at its most basic level, involves the immediate, pre-reflective consciousness of life (van Manen, 1990). That is, lived experience constitutes awareness unaware of itself. Because it is experienced in the present moment it is not reflected upon. However, lived experience may be understood to have a temporal structure. While it cannot be grasped in its immediacy, it can be grasped reflectively as past presence. Through the act of reflection upon a lived experience, an individual can discern its particular 'structural nexus' (Dilthey, 1985, p. 227) – its pattern or unit of meaning, which may then become part of a system of contextually related experiences that are reflected upon. In this way, lived experiences then gather significance as they are reflected upon and an individual gives memory to them.

The excerpts from the transcripts above suggest that this is precisely what the participants perceived their students to be doing. In thinking about the story or content of the lesson, students were able to recognise experiences from their own lives, the patterns (or units of meaning) of which reflected in some ways critical elements of the content and story being explored. While the significance of their lived experiences may not have been grasped in their immediacy, the act of reflection, provided by the early years' teachers, enabled students to discern significance, and to connect these with the content and stories being presented by the teacher, even, as Tony noted, at such a young age. Through conversations, learning stimuli, inspirations and other interpretive acts, the students were able to assign meaning to the phenomena of lived life.

The third element, placing one's self in the shoes of the Other, suggests that the predisposed ability of the students to reflect upon lived experience can result in empathy. The literature affirms that empathy has long been recognised as a spiritual trait of children (e.g. Champagne, 2003; Hart, 2003; Hay with Nye, 2006; Hyde, 2008). Children do feel an engagement with the wider world and events which occur both within their own lives and the wider world can provoke feelings of empathy in them (Adams et al., 2008). They are capable of having a sense of connection to various others, including those with whom they have no direct contact.

The excerpt from Amelia's transcript above suggests that she perceived her students to have developed a sense of empathy. Through the process of reflection they were able to place themselves in the shoes of another to display compassion and understanding in relation to the Other's lived experience, that is, empathy. With this knowledge, Amelia is now in a position to plan other activities and experiences within her classroom program to enable students to further develop and nurture this spiritual disposition. Such deliberate planning is essential, for as Marian de Souza (2006) notes, as children grow older, their capacity for empathy can be suppressed or, in extreme cases, lacking altogether. It is critical then, that early years' teachers like Amelia are able to plan learning experiences that assist students to develop and nurture their sense of empathy.

The fourth element is considering one's own story within a Universal Story. For faith schools with a Christian orientation, this equates to the Christian Story and vision of life. Charlotte Linde (2009) maintains that there is a relationship between institutional stories, such as the Christian story, and the ways in which members tell their own stories within this field of prior texts (Scripture, Tradition, doctrine and the like), and how their stories are shaped in relation to these prior texts. Thus, an individual's story is not only personal, but is rather shaped as a response to earlier stories, and the appropriate values and actions which those stories teach.

Similarly, Michael Jensen (2015) argues that the telling of stories is a theological exercise. Narrating a story, including one's own story, is to engage theology – the storyteller is invoking a realm in which there are certain principles or forces which give meaning and significance, and even direction, to events (see also Berryman, 2009). For the Christian, God constitutes the force at work which gives particular meaning and significance to the events of everyday life.

The brief excerpt from Siobhan's transcript above suggests that she recognised her students connecting their personal stories to, and telling them within, the field of prior texts from the Christian tradition. To various degrees, the students' stories have been shaped by the prior texts of the Christian tradition, which provide an interpretive schema against which they can give meaning to their experiences. In doing so, they were engaged in theology, placing a reflection upon their own lived experiences – their stories – within the framework of the Christian story. Through the process of reflection upon their lived experiences, they were able to make connections between their own individual stories and the Christian story and vision.

Each of the four elements of the disposition, connecting to life, are presented in Table 17.3.

## Some recommendations for practice

As has been shown, the framework above provides a way for educators to recognise, address and nurture the spirituality of their students. It also positions them to intentionally plan experiences that enable the development of these dispositions

**TABLE 17.3** Description of cues for connecting to life

|  | Description of cues |
| --- | --- |
| Connecting to life | Making connections between stories and lived experience |
|  | Discovering the significance of stories for one's own life |
|  | Placing one's self in the shoes of the Other |
|  | One's own story within a Universal Story |

through the curriculum. It should also be noted that Hyde's (2010) framework is not intended to be fixed and rigid, as exemplified by the possible emergence of a new disposition, in this case connecting to life. With further research, additional dispositions may also be identified and incorporated into the framework.

In conclusion, some recommendations for practice are offered below. These are not intended to be exhaustive, but rather starting points for educators who wish to identify and nurture the spiritual development and wellbeing of their students in the classroom context using a dispositional framework.

- As learning stories provide qualitative snap-shots of students, it would be valuable for teachers to collect four or five learning stories over the course of the year that, when reviewed collectively, indicate an emerging story about a student's learning or spiritual disposition.
- Having collected and developed learning stories about particular students, teachers can utilise these stories to plan activities and experiences that enable the spirituality of students to be nurtured through the various subjects areas that comprise the curriculum.
- Continued opportunities for professional learning about the dispositional framework and the possibilities presented by learning stories need to be provided so educators might become empowered to draw upon this tool in their pedagogical practice.

As discussed above, learning stories, and the dispositional framework that underpins them, can be an effective way of discerning not only the ways in which students are predisposed to learn, but also the ways in which they might express their spirituality and, as a result, the way in which their spiritual wellbeing may be nurtured within the context of their curricula.

## Notes

1  While opportunities now exist to teach about diverse religions in the new Australian Curriculum and Victorian Curriculum, few guidelines and resources have been developed to facilitate this, and the treatment of spirituality within these new curricula remains unclear.
2  The student was being observed during the responding time of a classroom adaptation of the Godly Play process. For a comprehensive outline of this process, see Berryman (2009).

## References

Adams, K., Hyde, B., & Woolley, R. (2008). *The spiritual dimension of childhood*. London: Jessica Kingsley Publishers.

Baiklock, K. (2008). A critique of the use of learning stories to assess the learning dispositions of young children. *New Zealand Research in Early Childhood Education, 11*, 77–87.

Baiklock, K. (2010). Te Whariki, the New Zealand early childhood curriculum: Is it effective? *International Journal of Early Years Education, 18*(3), 201–212.

Berryman, J. W. (2009). *Teaching Godly play: How to mentor the spiritual development of children*. Denver, CO: Morehouse Education Resources.

Carr, M. (2001). *Assessment in early childhood settings: Learning stories*. London: Sage.

Champagne, E. (2003). Being a child, a spiritual child. *International Journal of Children's Spirituality, 8*(1), 43–53.

Claxton, G. (2007). Expanding young people's capacity to learn. *British Journal of Educational Studies, 55*(2), 1–20.

Claxton, G., & Carr, M. (2004). A framework for teaching learning: The dynamics of disposition. *Early Years, 24*(1), 87–97.

Costa, A. L. (2000). Describing the habits of mind. In A. L. Costa & B. Kallick (eds), *Habits of mind: Discovering and exploring* (pp. 21–40). Alexandria, VA: Association for Supervision and Curriculum Development.

Department of Employment Education and Workplace Relations (DEEWR). (2009). *Belonging, being and becoming: An early years' learning framework for Australia*. Barton, ACT: Commonwealth of Australia.

Denzin, N.K., & Lincoln, Y.S. (2008). The discipline and practice of qualitative research. In N. Denzin & Y. Lincoln (eds), *Collecting and interpreting qualitative materials* (3rd edn) (pp. 1–43). Thousand Oaks, CA: Sage.

de Souza, M. (2006). Rediscovering the spiritual dimension in education: Promoting a sense of self and place, meaning and purpose in learning. In M. de Souza, K. Engebretson, G. Durka, R. Jackson, & A. McGrady (eds), *International handbook of the religious, moral and spiritual dimensions in education* (pp. 1127–1139). Dordrecht, The Netherlands: Springer.

Dilthey, W. (1985). *Poetry and experience*. Selected works. Vol V. Princeton, NJ: Princeton University Press.

Dunn, J. (1993). *Young children's close relationships*. London: Sage.

Dweck, C. S. (1999). *Self theories: Their role in motivation, personality and development*. Philadelphia, PA: Psychology Press.

Gettinger, M., & Stoiber, K. C. (1998). Critical incident recording: A procedure for monitoring children's performance and maximising progress in inclusive settings. *Early Childhood Education Journal, 26*(1), 39–46.

Gilligan, C., Spencer, R., Weinberg, K., & Bertsch, T. (2006). On the listening guide: A voice-centred relational method. In S. N. Hesse-Biber & P. Leavey (eds), *Emergent methods in social research* (pp. 253–271). Thousand Oaks, CA: Sage.

Hart, T. (2003). *The secret spiritual world of children*. Maui, HI: Inner Ocean.

Hatherley, A., & Sands, L. (2008). So what's different about learning stories? *The First Years Nga Tau Tuatahi: New Zealand Journal of Infant and Toddler Education, 4*(1), 8–12.

Hay, D., with Nye, R. (2006). *The spirit of the child* (revised edition). London: Jessica Kingsley Publishers.

Hay, D., & Socha, P. M. (2005). Spirituality as a natural phenomenon: Bringing biological and psychological perspectives together. *Zygon, 40*(1), 589–612.

Hyde, B. (2008). *Children and spirituality: Searching for meaning and connectedness*. London: Jessica Kingsley Publishers.

Hyde, B. (2010). A dispositional framework in religious education: Learning dispositions and early years' religious education in Catholic schools. *Journal of Beliefs and Values, 31*(3), 261–269.

Hyde, B. (2012). Learning stories and dispositional frameworks in early years' religious education. *Journal of Religious Education, 60*(1), 4–14.

Hyde, B., & Leening, L. (2012). Teachers' perceptions and experiences in using a dispositional framework in Catholic school early years' religious education to track student's learning. *Journal of Catholic School Studies, 84*(1), 56–67.

Hyde, B. (2014). Nurturing spirituality through a dispositional framework in early years' contexts. In J. Watson, M. de Souza & A. Trousdale (eds), *Global Perspectives on Spirituality and Education* (pp. 128–139). London: Routledge.

Jensen, M. (2015). Stories we live by: Fiction, faith and the fragments of human life. *ABC Religion and Ethics*. Retrieved 31 October from http://abc.net.au/religion/articles/2015/11/05/4346010.htm

Karlsdotti, K., & Gardarsdotti, B. (2010). Exploring children's learning stories as an assessment method for research and practice. *Early Years, 30*(3), 255–266.

Katz, L. G. (1988). What should young children be doing? *American Educator* (Summer), 29–45.

Linde, C. (2009). *Working the past: Narrative and institutional memory.* Oxford, UK: Oxford Scholarship Online.

Lovat, T. (2010). Spirituality and the public school. In M. de Souza & J. Rimes (eds), *Meaning and connectedness: Australian perspectives on education and spirituality* (pp. 19–30). Canberra, ACT: Australian College of Educators.

Lyle, S. (2000). Understanding narrative: Developing a theoretical context for understanding how children make meaning in classroom settings. *Journal of Curriculum Studies, 32*(1), 45–63.

Ministerial Council on Education Employment Training and Youth Affairs (MCEETYA). (2008). Melbourne declaration on educational goals for young Australians. Retrieved March 30, 2013 from www.mceetya.edu.au/verve/-resources/National_Declaration_on_the_Educational_Goals_for_Young_Australians.pdf

Morawski, J. (2001). *Feminist research methods: Bringing culture to science.* In D. Tolman & M. Brydon-Miller (eds), Feminist dilemmas in qualitative research: Public knowledge and private lives (pp. 119–146). Newbury Park, CA: Sage.

O'Murchu, D. (2012). *In the beginning was spirit: Science, religion and indigenous spirituality.* Maryknoll, NY: Orbis Books.

Perkins, D. N., Jay, E., & Tishman, S. (1993). Beyond abilities: A dispositional theory of thinking. *Merrill-Palmer Quarterly, 39*, 1–21.

Tacey, D. (2000). *ReEnchantment: The new Australian spirituality.* Sydney, Australia: HarperCollins.

van Manen, M. (1990). *Researching lived experience: Human science for an action sensitive pedagogy.* London, Ontario: State University of New York Press.

Walker, K. (2007). *Play matters.* Melbourne, VIC: Australian Council for Educational Research.

# INDEX

# Taylor & Francis eBooks

## Helping you to choose the right eBooks for your Library

Add Routledge titles to your library's digital collection today. Taylor and Francis ebooks contains over 50,000 titles in the Humanities, Social Sciences, Behavioural Sciences, Built Environment and Law.

**Choose from a range of subject packages or create your own!**

**Benefits for you**

» Free MARC records
» COUNTER-compliant usage statistics
» Flexible purchase and pricing options
» All titles DRM-free.

**REQUEST YOUR FREE INSTITUTIONAL TRIAL TODAY** | **Free Trials Available** We offer free trials to qualifying academic, corporate and government customers.

**Benefits for your user**

» Off-site, anytime access via Athens or referring URL
» Print or copy pages or chapters
» Full content search
» Bookmark, highlight and annotate text
» Access to thousands of pages of quality research at the click of a button.

## eCollections – Choose from over 30 subject eCollections, including:

| | |
|---|---|
| Archaeology | Language Learning |
| Architecture | Law |
| Asian Studies | Literature |
| Business & Management | Media & Communication |
| Classical Studies | Middle East Studies |
| Construction | Music |
| Creative & Media Arts | Philosophy |
| Criminology & Criminal Justice | Planning |
| Economics | Politics |
| Education | Psychology & Mental Health |
| Energy | Religion |
| Engineering | Security |
| English Language & Linguistics | Social Work |
| Environment & Sustainability | Sociology |
| Geography | Sport |
| Health Studies | Theatre & Performance |
| History | Tourism, Hospitality & Events |

For more information, pricing enquiries or to order a free trial, please contact your local sales team: **www.tandfebooks.com/page/sales**

 Routledge
Taylor & Francis Group | The home of Routledge books | **www.tandfebooks.com**

# DATE DUE

| | | | |
|---|---|---|---|
| | | | |
| | | | |
| | | | |
| | | | |
| | | | |
| | | | |
| | | | |
| | | | |
| | | | |
| | | | |
| | | | |
| | | | |
| | | | |
| | | | |
| | | | |
| | | | |
| | | | |
| | | | |
| | | | |
| | | | PRINTED IN U.S.A. |
| | | | |